Lecture Notes in Computer Science 5770

Commenced Publication in 1973
Founding and Former Series Editors:
Gerhard Goos, Juris Hartmanis, and Jan van Leeuwen

James Noble   Ralph Johnson (Eds.)

Transactions on Pattern Languages of Programming I

 Springer

Editors-in-Chief

James Noble
Victoria University of Wellington
School of Engineering and Computer Science
Wellington 6140, New Zealand
E-mail: kjx@ecs.vuw.ac.nz

Ralph Johnson
Siebel Center for Computer Science
201 North Goodwin Avenue, Urbana, IL 61801, USA
E-mail: rjohnson@illinois.edu

Managing Editors

Uwe Zdun
Vienna University of Technology, Information Systems Institute
Argentinierstrasse 8/184-1, 1040 Wien, Austria
E-mail: zdun@infosys.tuwien.ac.at

Eugene Wallingford
University of Northern Iowa, Department of Computer Science
Cedar Falls, IA 50613, USA
E-mail: wallingf@cs.uni.edu

Library of Congress Control Number: 2009942032

CR Subject Classification (1998): D.2, D.3, D.1, K.6, K.6.3

ISSN   0302-9743 (Lecture Notes in Computer Science)
ISSN   1869-6015 (Transactions on Pattern Languages of Programming)
ISBN-10   3-642-10831-8 Springer Berlin Heidelberg New York
ISBN-13   978-3-642-10831-0 Springer Berlin Heidelberg New York

springer.com

© Springer-Verlag Berlin Heidelberg 2009
Printed in Germany

Typesetting: Camera-ready by author, data conversion by Scientific Publishing Services, Chennai, India
Printed on acid-free paper   SPIN: 12804610   06/3180   5 4 3 2 1 0

Preface

From conception to birth is traditionally nine months. The first emails regarding the volume you now hold in your hands—or the bits you have downloaded onto your screen—are dated 11 June 2005. From conception to birth has taken over four years.

Springer's LNCS Transactions on Pattern Languages of Programming is dedicated, first and foremost, to promoting, promulgating, presenting, describing, critiquing, interrogating, and evaluating all aspects of the use of patterns in programming. In the 15 years or so since Gamma, Helm, Johnson, Vlissides's Design Patterns became widely available, software patterns have become a highly effective means of improving the quality of programming, software engineering, system design, and development. Patterns capture the best practices of software design, making them available to everyone participating in the production of software.

A key goal of the Transactions Series is to present material that is validated. Every contributed paper that appears in this volume has been reviewed by both patterns experts and domain experts, by researchers and practitioners. This reviewing process begins long before the paper is even submitted to Transactions. Every paper in the Series is first presented and critiqued at one of the Pattern Languages of Programming (PLoP) conferences held annually around the world. Prior to the conference, each submitted paper is assigned a shepherd who works with the authors to improve the paper. Based on several rounds of feedback, a paper may proceed to a writers' workshop at the conference itself. In a writers' workshop, pattern authors are given concentrated feedback on their papers in a focused discussion that considers all aspects of the papers, from the most abstract ideas down to the use of whitespace. The papers are revised once again, before being collected in a patterns conference proceedings, often six months after the conference.

Finally, after all these stages of editing, often going back to conferences more than once, the paper may be ready for submission to the *Transactions on Pattern Languages of Programming*. At this stage, every paper receives at least three final reviews before publication. Our reviewers include both experts in patterns and experts from the domains of the patterns, ranging across all the disciplines of software. Only when these reviewers are satisfied that the paper is as good as it can be—perhaps after several further review cycles—are the papers ready for publication. To avoid conflicts of interest, Editors-in-Chief may not submit papers to regular issues of the journal, and similarly Guest Editors of special issues may not submit papers to volumes that they edit. Submissions by associate editors, or by close colleagues of Editors-in-Chief or Guest Editors, are assigned to an editor without conflicts, and the results of the editorial process are only reported back when it is complete. For the record, this first volume was handled primarily by James Noble as Editor-in-Chief, and Uwe Zdun as Associate Editor.

The eight papers in this volume are the first to have emerged from this highly selective reviewing process. In the first paper, Andrew Black and Daniel Vainsencher present a substantial pattern language for constructing an important part of an integrated development environment: the underlying representation of the program. With a careful analysis of the underlying forces, Andrew and Daniel describe how models can be made extensible, while also performing efficiently and correctly.

The second and third papers are primarily concerned with larger scale systems. Francisco J. Ballesteros, Fabio Kon, Marta Patiño, Ricardo Jiménez, Sergio Arévalo, and Roy H. Campbell describe how systems can be made both more efficient, and more flexible, by batching individual requests between clients and servers, and Titos Saridakis describes how systems can be made more reliable via Graceful Degradation.

While many of the papers in this volume are relatively large, we have also aimed to publish short, focused patterns that address a single problem. In the next paper, Michael J. Pont, Susan Kurian, and Ricardo Bautista-Quintero show how Sandwich Delays can ensure real-time code that always takes exactly the same time to execute.

The last two patterns papers in this volume address service-oriented architectures. Carsten Hentrich presents a small pattern language for synchronization, and then he is joined by Uwe Zdun to describe a second pattern language for process integration and macro/micro workflow design.

Our last two papers do not present new patterns themselves. Rather, they show how patterns can be combined into systems, and then used to document those systems' designs. Mark Mahoney and Tzilla Elrad describe how the State, Interceptor, and Factory Method pattern can be used to model complex state transition systems, and James Siddle shows how the documentation of a complex system can be structured around the patterns in that system's design.

We believe the papers in this volume represent some of the best work that has been carried out in design patterns and pattern languages of programming over the last few years. We thank all the authors for taking the effort to prepare their papers for publication, and our indefatigable reviewers for their many suggestions for improvement. As with any birth, we are justly proud of the result: and we hope that you will enjoy the fruits of our labors!

August 2009

James Noble
Ralph Johnon
Uwe Zdun
Eugene Wallingford

Organization

Editorial Board

Table of Contents

A Pattern Language for Extensible Program Representation[*]

Daniel Vainsencher[1] and Andrew P. Black[2]

[1] The Technion
danielv@techunix.technion.ac.il
[2] Portland State University
black@cs.pdx.edu

Abstract. For the last 15 years, implementors of multiple view programming environments have sought a single code model that would form a suitable basis for all of the program analyses and tools that might be applied to the code. They have been unsuccessful. The consequences are a tendency to build monolithic, single-purpose tools, each of which implements its own specialized analyses and optimized representation. This restricts the availability of the analyses, and also limits the reusability of the representation by other tools. Unintegrated tools also produce inconsistent views, which reduce the value of multiple views.

This article describes a set of architectural patterns that allow a single, minimal representation of program code to be extended as required to support new tools and program analyses, while still maintaining a simple and uniform interface to program properties. The patterns address efficiency, correctness and the integration of multiple analyses and tools in a modular fashion.

1 Introduction

Our view of programs is that they are not linear text but complex, multi-dimensional structures [5]. Our view of programming environments is that they are tools to reveal and elucidate this structure. As programs become more complex, it is thus not surprising that integrated program development environments (IDEs) are growing in importance and sophistication.

This view of programs and environments is not new, but in recent years it has become more widely accepted. The agile development community, for example, emphasizes the importance of incremental design, which implies frequent refactoring of the code base. Refactoring tools require deep knowledge of the structure of the program, and to be maximally effective they also require ways of displaying that structure to their users [32]. In short, the agile revolution could not have happened without supportive tools.

---

[*] A preliminary version of this article was workshopped at Pattern Languages of Programming (PLoP) 21st–23rd October 2006, Portland, OR, USA.

J. Noble and R. Johnson (Eds.): TPLOP I, LNCS 5770, pp. 1–47, 2009.
© Springer-Verlag Berlin Heidelberg 2009

1.1   IDEs Are Ecosystems

Integrated development environments (IDEs) are ecosystems in which three different "species" — communities of contributors — meet and interact. Two of these species are easy to identify: the *architects* of the development environment itself, and the *toolsmiths*, who build plugins and components to support some user task. The third species comprises the program *analysts*: the people who write the code that builds the parse trees, ASTs, dependency graphs, and other structures that the toolsmiths need to do their job.

The biological metaphor is imperfect because the same contributor may belong to more than one of these species, but it useful to distinguish them, because the contributions require different expertise. Nevertheless, powerful forces urge these three species to cooperate. Their works are synergistic: a widely used IDE provides the analysts with a platform; the availability of the analyses makes it simpler for the toolsmiths to build more sophisticated tools; the availability of more tools makes the IDE more attractive to programmers, and having more programmers use the IDE is the goal of the architects. All three species therefore collaborate to design the interfaces through which the tools, analyses and the architectural framework interact.

Getting these interfaces "right" — or at least right enough — is not easy. We believe that merely recognizing that there are three inter-dependent communities helps in the process, because the vital role of the analyst has not always been recognized. Traditionally, some basic analyses were built into the architectural framework; if a particular tool needed a deeper analysis, or just a different one, the toolsmith would incorporate this analysis into the tool itself. In effect, the analyst was excluded from the ecosystem.

We became involved in this work because we were building *Multiview* programming environments — IDEs in which *multiple* tools provide different views on the *same* program elements. This was easy to do when the architect had provided a shared code model that exposed all the information needed by the views. However, as our views started to expose latent properties of the program — properties whose calculation required significant analysis — we were faced with the problem of where to put the analysis code. Putting the analysis into the tool would not work: the results of the analysis had to be shared by several tools. It seemed clear that the right place for the analysis was in the code model itself: all we had to do was invent a "universal" shared code model that was general enough to provide the data for all views. Such a shared model would need to make available not only all of the information present in the code directly, but also all of the information that could be inferred from it, just in case some tool might need it. This may be difficult, but has the important advantage of ensuring that all of the views are consistent.

This article advocates such a shared code model. We are by no means the first to do so; as long ago as 1991 Scott Meyers wrote: "many problems ... would be solved if all the tools in a development environment shared a single representation ... Unfortunately, no representation has yet been devised that is suitable for all possible tools" [28].

In three years of work, we also failed to devise a general, abstract and efficient shared code model suitable for all possible tools. With the benefit of hindsight, we believe that the task is impossible: generality and efficiency are almost always at odds with each other. It now seems obvious that what we need instead is an *extensible* code model, so that generality can be added when it is found to be needed, but not before. Moreover, by focussing the computationally expensive analyses on those parts of the code base that the programmer actually finds interesting, we can avoid wasting cycles computing information that will never be used.

Instead of searching for a "silver bullet" code model for each programming language — a model that will satisfy all of the possible needs of toolsmiths, analysts and architects — we need an architecture and a common language that allows them to build on each others' work in mutual co-dependence. It is the beginnings of such an architecture and language that we seek to provide in this article.

1.2 The Pattern Language

The main contribution of this article is a pattern language for an abstract, extensible and efficient shared code model. The patterns are presented in four groups. The first group, described in Section 3.1, answers the primary question posed above: how should the responsibilities of a multi-view programming environment be divided among the code model and the tools that maintain the views? The second group (Section 3.2) presents some common categories of information that are strong candidates for integration into the code model. The third group is devoted to performance considerations, and how these affect the proposed design (Section 3.3). One unfortunate consequence of performance work is that it may add difficult-to-find bugs; the fourth group of patterns (Section 3.4) is about removing them.

List of patterns	
Building the Code Model	
Shared Code Model	9
Model Extension	12
Generic Tools	17
What to Model?	
Alternative Representation	19
Inverse Mapping	21
Layered Extension	23
Performance	
Explicit Interest	27
Life-long Interest	29
Minimal Calculation	31
Eager Update	32
Lazy Update	33
Batch Calculation	35
Correctness	
Canonical Implementation	37
Formal Definition	39

The essence of the pattern language is to apply the model-view architecture to program development environments. The code — *and all of the interesting analyses on it* — becomes the model; the various tools in the environment become views that do nothing more than ask the model for the data that they need and present it on the screen, using *Observer* to ensure that they are notified of changes. This architecture hides the distinction between those attributes of the code that are stored explicitly in the model (or can be computed from it immediately), and those attributes that must be derived from a code analysis, perhaps at considerable computational cost. The key to accommodating all of these analyses in the model — including the ones that we haven't yet realized are interesting — is to make the model extensible. Some of these analyses will be complex, and will expose global properties of the code. And yet: each model extension must be able to answer, at any moment, any sequence of questions about the code that a tool might ask. Moreover, it must do so quickly, so that the view can respond in real-time as the code is modified.

The benefits of this architecture to the toolsmith should be obvious: the toolsmith no longer has to know which attributes are part of the model and which are calculated by analyses, and if multiple tools need to use similar analyses, the results are easily shared.

In the Eclipse code model, in contrast, clients must be aware of this distinction between stored and computed attributes. For example, the interface org.eclipse.jdt.core.IType, representing a Java Class or Interface, has methods getSuperclassName() and getSuperInterfaceNames(), but it does not have methods to return the type's subclasses or subinterfaces. The toolsmith who needs that information must build an ITypeHierarchy object and invoke its getAllSubtypes(IType) method. The ITypeHierarchy is not automatically updated when the model is changed; that too is the client's responsibility. The toolsmith is also warned that "once a type hierarchy has been created, it is more efficient to query the hierarchy for superinterfaces than to query a type recursively. Querying an element performs a dynamic resolution, whereas the hierarchy returns a pre-computed result"[12]. Thus, for optimal efficiency, the client needs to keep track of whether an appropriate ITypeHierarchy object has been computed (in which case it should be used), or not (in which case the IType must be queried directly).

We hypothesize that the reason that the Eclipse JDT expects its clients to be aware of all of these details is that hiding them was deemed to be too expensive. Of course it would have been possible to build all of the functionality of an ITypeHierarchy into the base model, and to refresh it every time that the model changed. But the computational cost would be high, particularly as programs become large. Moreover, much of the information thus computed would never be used: making programmers using the IDE wait at the keyboard for information that they do not want to see is a bad idea.

For this reason, our patterns pay particular attention to performance. Without a way to reduce the cost of computing derived information, the architecture proposed here would be nothing more than a hollow shell, attractive in the abstract, but completely infeasible in practice.

In the next section (Section 2) we introduce a particular code model extension, which we have implemented in the Squeak environment for Smalltalk. We use this example throughout the article to illustrate the issues and how the patterns address them. But first, we offer an apology.

1.3   Patterns or Proto-patterns?

In the introduction to Linda Rising's collection *Design Patterns in Communi-cations Software* [36], Douglas Schmidt writes:

> Patterns represent successful solutions to challenges that arise when building software in particular contexts. When related patterns are woven together, they form a pattern language that helps to (1) define a vocabulary for talking about software development and integration challenges and (2) provide a process for the orderly resolution of these challenges. [36, p. XII].

While there is no one definition of the term "design pattern", a useful rule of thumb, as Schmidt indicates, is that a pattern presents a solution to a problem in a context. Another criterion is that a pattern should not seem startlingly new to practitioners: on the contrary, the expected response to a pattern is: "how elegant; I might have thought of that myself, if I had been faced with that problem" or "right; I have done that before in other contexts, and I see that it might be useful here too". The purpose of presenting design ideas in pattern form is to define a language for architecture in a specified domain, and to open a dialog in and around it. The language that we present here does not pretend to deal with all possible problems in the space of program representation, but we believe that it is self-contained, in that it does provide the terminology needed to talk about its own pattern, their consequences, and the concomitant solutions.

By all of these criteria, the pattern form is appropriate for this work. However, there is commonly an expectation that a pattern distills from multiple experiences. For example, Buschmann *et al.* [7] propose finding at least 3 examples of an idea when pattern mining, and Gamma *et al.* [17] offer at least two examples of each pattern. By this criterion, some of the strategies that we propose do not yet qualify as patterns because we cannot offer evidence that they are currently in wide use. However, we feel that these strategies are more than proto-patterns: we have applied them to a difficult programming problem, and found that things suddenly became easier. Our implementation was in the context of the Smalltalk programming environment, but the patterns are certainly not language-specific. We have found some (but not all) of them adopted in other environments, for example, the Eclipse environment for Java. We feel that reporting on our experience and presenting these patterns now will enable more development environments to build on this architecture in the future, and in the process extend and evolve our contribution into a pattern language that covers an ever-increasing part of the problem space. In this spirit, we particularly welcome additional examples for, or counterexamples to, our putative patterns.

Having raised this issue, for conciseness we will nevertheless refer to a specific proposed solution as a pattern in the remainder of this article.

2   A Running Example

Our implementation of these patterns has so far taken place in Squeak Smalltalk, where we have been working on tools to support traits [6,40]. Although Smalltalk has no explicit syntactic marker that identifies an abstract class, abstract classes are widely used in practice. They can be identified because they are missing critical methods. An example is the class Collection, which is the abstract superclass of many of the concrete kinds of collection, such as Sets, Bags and Dictionaries. Collection is abstract because it does not provide implementations for add:, remove:ifAbsent:, and do:; it is the responsibility of its subclasses to provide these methods. This is indicated by the existence of explicit *marker methods* on these messages, *i.e.,* methods with the body self subclassResponsibility. (Such a method will raise an error if it is ever invoked.) Collection *does* provide concrete methods for addAll:, remove:, collect:, select:, *etc.*, which are all ultimately implemented in terms of the abstract methods.

However, not all abstract methods are indicated by marker methods like subclassResponsibility. An examination of the methods provided by class Collection also reveals that a message with selector atRandom: is sent to self in another method, even though there is no maker method indicating that atRandom: is abstract: atRandom: is an *implicit* abstract method. Thus we see that an analysis of the whole of the class Collection can reveal that the class is abstract, and can also infer the names of the four abstract methods that must be provided by subclasses. However, this analysis can be computationally intensive for a large class or a deep inheritance hierarchy.

While programming in Smalltalk, we have found it very useful to show, in real time, which *classes* are abstract. When viewing a particular class, it is also useful to show a list of the abstract *methods* — which we call the *required methods* of the class, or simply its *requirements* [39]. Inferring the required methods supports "programming by intention," a style of programming in which methods are used before they are written [24]. The constant display of the required methods acts as a "to-do list" for the programmer, reminding her of the methods that she has yet to write. In Figure 1 the Smalltalk browser is showing the required methods of Collection. We call this the "requires view"; it is an example of a view that reflects the result of an extensive non-local analysis of the code base.

In seeking to implement the requires view, we started out with Schärli's efficient algorithm for determining if a particular method is required by a specific class and its subclasses [37,39]. Our problem, then, was to construct from this algorithm a practical browser that would indicate which classes in a possibly long list of classes were abstract, and which methods were required by a particular class.

It turns out that when programmers use browsers they frequently change the display of the list of classes. The naïve approach of running Schärli's algorithm on every defined selector on every class in a long list was far too slow: the results were not available within the 100 ms time box that is the norm for interactive response. Our problem was how to efficiently reify the information needed for the *requirements* calculation in the code model so that this information could be shared amongst various tools, without repeatedly recalculating it.

By "reify the information" we mean "make the information concrete". In a sense, the implicit information is there in the code model all the time, but a lot of computation is required to extract it. Reified information, in contrast,

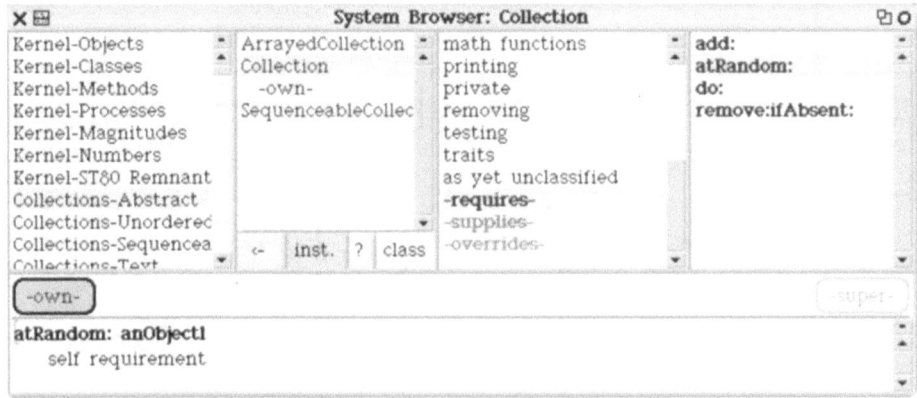

Fig. 1. The Smalltalk browser showing abstract classes and required methods. In the method list pane (at the top, on the far right), all four of the required methods of class Collection are listed. In the class pane (at the top, second pane from the left), abstract classes are highlighted in blue. The list of required methods and the fact that a class is abstract are both deduced by code analysis.

is directly available through an appropriate method with little computational overhead. An additional problem was that Schärli's algorithm itself required walking the inheritance hierarchy, and obtained part of its efficiency from the careful use of caches to avoid recalculating on behalf of a subclass the same results that had already been calculated for its superclass. We hoped to be able to reuse these caches in a more general setting, so that the cached information would become available to other tools as part of the model, rather than being the exclusive property of one algorithm.

3   The Patterns

As we mentioned in Section 1.2, we have arranged our description of the patterns into four groups. The first group (Section 3.1) describes the division of responsibilities between the code model and the tools that use it; the second group (Section 3.2) addresses the content of the extended model; the third group (Section 3.3) provides guidance on making the extensible model fast enough, and the fourth and final group (Section 3.4) addresses correctness. Figure 2 shows the relationships between the patterns and the problems that they address. When we use the names of these patterns in the body of this article, we will set them in a *slanted sans-serif font*.

3.1   A Code Model Supporting Multiple Tools

Underlying any development environment is a representation of the code of the program under development. A very common scheme for this representation is code files in directories, possibly with additional files for metadata about

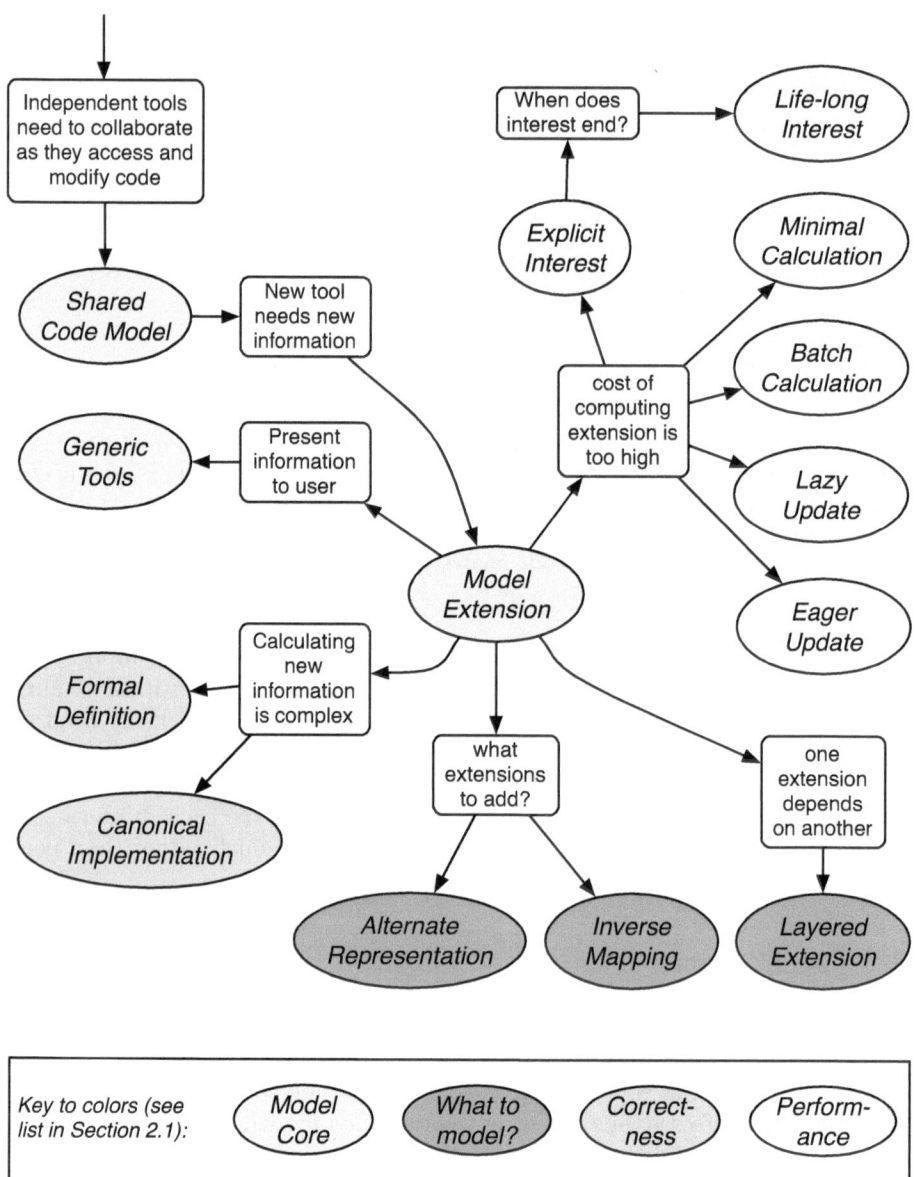

Fig. 2. Text in rounded rectangles summarizes a problem. Shaded ellipses name patterns discussed in the body of the article; they are colored by group. Arrows show how problems are addressed by the patterns, and how the use of the patterns gives rise to new problems.

the project. In contrast, Squeak Smalltalk [23], on which we implemented the requirements browser, uses a rather different code model, although it is one that is commonly used for Smalltalk. Our first pattern describes the structure of this code model and some of the features that contribute to its extensibility. The existence of these features in Smalltalk systems is not coincidental: there has been a long tradition in the Smalltalk community of programmers augmenting the set of available programming tools. *Shared Code Model*, described below, provides the foundation for programming tools that display information that is available explicitly in the model.

Shared Code Model

Context. You are designing, refactoring or extending a program development environment that contains several independent tools giving different views on the same code.

Problem. How can you ensure that each tool is up-to-date regarding all of the changes made in every other tool, and that the tools are consistent with one another in their interpretation of the code?

Forces. The following forces are in play.

- The tools may be written by different developers.
- Multiple representations of the code increase maintenance costs, and lead to inconsistencies between the tools.
- The model needs to be *complete* enough so that all tools can be based on it.
- The whole development environment needs to be responsive to common actions, so requests on the model should be sufficiently cheap.
- The size of the screen and the capacity of the user's brain are limited, so the user will most often be examining and changing only a small number of program elements at any one time.
- Many tools may need access to the coarse structure of the whole program, for example, the type hierarchy.
- The tools may live in separate address spaces, in which case communication between the tools and the model will be costly.
- When one tool changes the model, other tools viewing the model need to be able to reflect the change promptly.

Solution. Maintain a single direct representation of the high-level syntax of the program as a graph of objects, organized to permit efficient browsing and searching. Lower levels of syntax need not be built as object structures; instead they can be kept as text.

Keep the shared code model *minimal* to avoid redundancy, and the complexity and inconsistencies that result from it. This means that information that can be calculated from the model quickly should not be cached in the model. Some other reasons for minimality are that specialized information is likely to be useless to most of the tools, and that a minimal model is simple to understand.

In order to keep the tools and other clients up to date, the code model must implement a notification mechanism, such as an *Observer* [18]. The notification events should include enough information for a tool to update the relevant parts of its output efficiently. In Squeak this information includes the identity of the code model element (*e.g.,* the method or class) that changed, and the nature of the change (addition, removal, or modification).

Consequences. This solution has the following consequences.

- The *shared* nature of the code model and the use of *Observer* to notify clients of changes together allow multiple tools to remain synchronized and yet oblivious of each other.
- The representation of the high levels of code as objects makes common navigation tasks easy. For example, it is easy to access the superclass of a class, or to enumerate the methods of a class.
- Detailed, structured representations of small parts of the program can either be stored as part of the *Shared Code Model*, or can be computed on demand from a textual representation.
- Repeatedly computing an alternative representation on demand may be too slow. Rather than forcing clients to cache this information themselves, cache it in the shared code model as an *Alternative Representation* (p. 19).
- The *Shared Code Model* may turn out not to be complete: new tools may require information about the program that you did not anticipate. In this case, implement a *Model Extension* (p. 12).

Implementation. One of the decisions that must be made when applying *Shared Code Model* is which parts of the code to represent as structured objects and which parts as linear text. A second decision is what to put in main memory, and what to leave on the disk. Along with the choice of representation, this will obviously dictate the memory footprint of the model, and thus the scalability of the environment.

The two decisions are not entirely independent, because the operation of following an object reference on the disk is roughly 10 000 times slower than following a reference in main memory, and so disk storage is much more suitable for sequential representations, and main memory for linked ones. In Squeak, the class hierarchy and compiled methods are stored as an object graph in main memory, whereas method bodies are represented by pointers to text on the disk. An environment for the manipulation of very large programs might be forced to keep more information on disk; in this case various kinds of database index structure could be used to improve access times.

Known Uses. Possibly the first development environment to use a structured code model was the Cornell Program Synthesizer [41], which represented programs as threaded "executable derivation trees". This model was "shared" by the editor and the interpreter. The Synthesizer was targeted at beginning PL/I programmers; it seems unlikely that it could handle commercial-size programs.

The Smalltalk-80 development environment [21] implemented a *Shared Code Model*, and this model is alive and well in its decedents, such as Squeak. However, it is not as complete and straightforward as might be expected, principally due to the limited memory on the early Smalltalk-80 systems. For example, the navigation from a class to its methods and back again is rather convoluted, reflecting some implementation decisions that ought to have been better hidden.

The Cadillac programming environment [14], developed at Lucid for C++ and later named Energize, also had as its goals easy extension by the builders of the environment, and tight integration of the tools as perceived by the user. It achieved these goals by defining tool protocol interfaces that could be used to access a shared code model of persistent objects that were stored either in ISAM files or in an object-oriented data base.

The most well-known contemporary example of a *Shared Code Model* is in the Eclipse Java Development Toolkit (JDT), which is designed to be extensible [16,34]. The JDT includes a model of Java code in which objects (implementing the interface IJavaElement and its subtypes) represent elements of the program under development. It provides a way to examine the code, and includes a change notification mechanism. The Java model is computed from the source code on demand, and then cached in subinstances of class JavaElementInfo. One consequence is that programmers must be aware of this caching; Gamma and Beck warn that "finding a method by traversing the Java model starting at the root and then drilling down to methods is expensive. It will fully populate the element info caches." [16, p. 315]. However, when used as intended, at least one commercial IDE developer reports that performance is satisfactory even for queries that require traversing the code of a whole project.[1]

The Eclipse JDT Java model thus fits many aspects of the *Shared Code Model* pattern. However, we cannot say that the Eclipse JDT follows the intent of this pattern, because it also contains at least two other code models: the AST model (ASTNode and its subtypes), which represents the syntax of a single compilation unit, and the bindings model (IBinding and its subtypes), which represents the network of connections reachable from a compilation unit. The intent of *Shared Code Model* is that there be a *single* model on which all tools can rely.

According to some of our reviewers, the C++ language component of Eclipse called CDT also does not have a single shared code model. It instead uses several separate representations of the code, making it difficult to decide which to use for particular purposes.

Related patterns and variants. Riehle *et al.* [35] present the Tools and Materials metaphor, which motivates the distinction between the application (a tool) and the model on which it operates (the materials), and defines particular interfaces between them. In terms of this metaphor, our pattern language aims to make the code model a better material, by moving the boundary between it and the tools. While both approaches are intended to make the environment more extensible, they address different aspects of the problem, and make different assumptions. For example, we strive for the ability to add properties to a fixed set of code

---

[1] Brian Wilkerson, Instantiations, Inc. Personal communication.

elements, while they consider the set of properties fixed and make the system extensible with new kinds of materials that enjoy those properties.

Other patterns such as MVC [7] also make the distinction between the model and the tools that allow the user to operate on it.

We have already mentioned the role of the *Observer* pattern [17] in connecting the code model to the tools that operate on it, and the use of *Alternative Representation*, described on page 19, when it is necessary to make available two different representations of the same program element.

———————————————— □ ————————————————

It was our goal to implement a tool that uses some information that the Squeak code model does *not* provide explicitly: the *requirements* of a class. We wanted to access the requirements in at least two places: first, to annotate a class as being abstract when its name appears in the browser's list of classes, and second, to display the requirements of a class when the programmer browses that class. In addition, because there were other kinds of code browser that might be extended to use the *requirements* property, we wanted to make it very easy to access this property — as easy as it is to access the base properties of the code model. For example, getting the names of the instance variables of the class Morph in Smalltalk is very simple, because instance variables are explicit in the base model: the programmer merely issues the query Morph instVarNames. Our goal was to provide access to the requirements of a class using an equally simple query: Morph requiredSelectors.

However, our starting point was quite different: Schärli's algorithm, for good performance reasons, was implemented to update a global cache of requirements. So, getting up-to-date values required first updating the cache for the class in question, and only then accessing it. So, if we were interested in the requirements of class Morph, the code that we had to write was

```
Morph updateRequiredSelectors.
requirements := Morph requiredSelectors.
```

Thus, clients had the responsibility of ensuring that the cache was up to date: this was both inconvenient and error-prone. We felt that this was the wrong trade-off, and that simplicity of interface was more important than simplicity of implementation [13]. The next pattern, *Model Extension*, shows how to retain both.

Model Extension

Context. A development environment uses a *Shared Code Model* to represent the code and includes several tools that operate on it.

Problem. How do tools access properties that are not stored in the code model, but are calculated from it? How can such properties be shared by multiple tools?

Forces. The following forces are in play.

- Many of the tools in an IDE exist to access properties and structures that are *implicit* in the code, and therefore not present in a minimal shared code model. Nevertheless, users of the code model would like to be able to interrogate these properties and structures through a simple and concise interface.
- Despite the fact that several tools may wish to access the same properties and structure, the same calculations should not be repeated.
- Analysis algorithms should not be implemented multiple times; the same implementation should be available to multiple tools.
- One of the ways in which a new analysis can add value is by defining new properties or making visible a new level of structure, so these parts of the code model should be open to extension.
- The implementation of an analysis may be complex; it should be encapsulated and separated from the core of the model.

Solution. Express each new property as an extension to the interface of an appropriate class in the *Shared Code Model*. Implement the calculation of this property as a *Model Extension*, that is, place it outside the *Shared Code Model* itself, but place an interface to it inside the code model.

In our running example, the interface that we desire is that the class model understand the additional message requiredMethods. This will make the set of required methods accessible in the same simple and direct way as other properties of the code model: by sending a message to the appropriate object in the model.

Figure 3 shows diagrammatically three alternative organizations for the code necessary to support this new property of Class. In Fig. 3(a), Class is part of the shared code model, shaded buff. The algorithm to compute the required methods has been added in a separate class, shaded blue. This means that the user of the extension must be aware that it *is* an extension, and must learn a special-purpose interface for accessing the information that it represents. The user may also need to be concerned with initializing and finalizing the classes that implement it.

In (b), the whole of the implementation of the extension has been placed in the existing model class. This makes it possible to present a uniform interface, but fails to encapsulate the new algorithm, and makes it hard to provide (potentially more efficient) alternative interfaces. It also requires that the implementation language support a very complete form of class extension.

Alternative (c) illustrates *Model Extension* (p. 12): the *interface* to the extension is in the appropriate model class, but the *implementation* is encapsulated in its own class. Only the most modest class extension mechanism is required.

To the tool writer, extensions like requiredMethods add richness to the otherwise minimal *Shared Code Model*, making it a more useful representation of the code. By accessing *all* aspects of the code through the code model, the implementations of the various tools become simpler, and the interfaces to the output

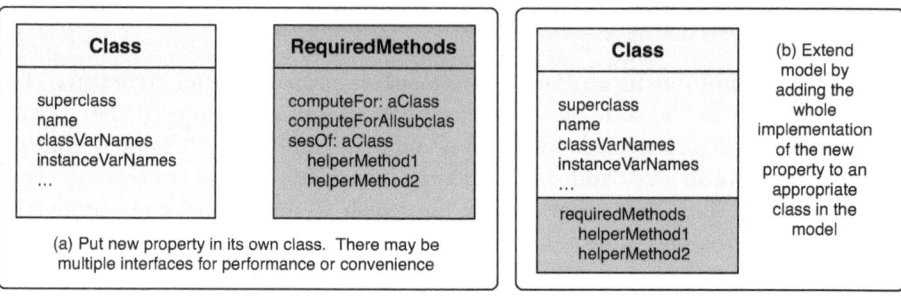

(a) Put new property in its own class. There may be multiple interfaces for performance or convenience

(b) Extend model by adding the whole implementation of the new property to an appropriate class in the model

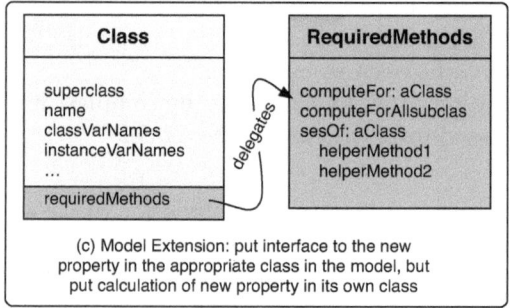

(c) Model Extension: put interface to the new property in the appropriate class in the model, but put calculation of new property in its own class

Fig. 3. Here we show three alternatives for enriching a *Shared Code Model*. In (a), the algorithm to extend the model (shaded buff) been added in a separate class (shaded blue). In (b), the whole of the implementation of the extension has been placed inside the model class. Alternative (c) exploits *Model Extension*: the *interface* to the extension is in the appropriate model class, but the *implementation* is encapsulated in its own class. See *Model Extension* (p. 12) for more details.

of the tools become more uniform. This makes it easier to use, understand and maintain the various tools.

Although Figure 3(c) shows the implementation of the extension as a single class, more complex properties might require many classes. The intent of the pattern is to separate the implementation of the extension from the interface in whatever way is most appropriate, allowing authors of model extensions to address the complexities of correct and efficient computation of each property without increasing the complexity of the *Shared Code Model* itself.

The extensions to the interface of the code model demanded by this pattern should be *class extension* methods if the implementation language supports open classes [8,9], or Extension Objects [15] it it does not.

Consequences. This pattern says that the derivation of properties by interpretation of the *Shared Code Model* should be an extension to the code model itself rather than a part of the tool that needs to use the properties. The consequence is that these derived properties are made available to other tools. This synergy between tools enables a rich suite of tools to be developed more quickly and with less effort. At the same time, the *Shared Code Model* itself remains simple, and the interfaces to direct and derived properties can be consistent.

Implementation. Many programming languages do not recognize the importance of *open classes* [8]; they make it hard to *extend* classes that have already been written by another programmer or obtained from an outside organization. In Java and C++, for example, any extension to the interface of a standard class library requires *editing* (rather than augmenting) its implementation; this may be impossible unless the implementation is under the control of the extender. Some Java variants such as MultiJava [8] and AspectJ [25] recognize the value of open classes and do provide for class extension; programmers using ordinary Java can fall back on the *Extension Object* pattern [15].

Smalltalk supports open classes: the Smalltalk programmer can extend the interface of the code model by adding new methods in a separate package that contains what is known as a class extension. However, Squeak's class extension mechanism does not allow an extension package to modify the *representation* of an existing class, that is, an extension package can add a method, but cannot add an instance variable.

This pattern places all of the logic of the *Model Extension* in new classes. Thus, the only extension facility that it requires is the ability to add a new stateless method to an existing class. This mitigates the effect of any deficiency of the chosen implementation language.

Known Uses. In addition to our use of *Model Extension* to support the *required method* property, this pattern is also used in the Eclipse JDT to add higher-level functionality to primitive objects. However, because Java does not allow class extensions, an implementation of this pattern in Java is somewhat inconvenient.

To see how this pattern is used in Eclipse, consider the interface org.eclipse-.core.resources.IFile, which represents raw data and support methods like get-Contents() that make it possible to read that data. If the data represents a Java class, some tools may prefer to deal with a structured representation in which one can examine individual fields, the set of defined methods, and so on. This more structured interface is called IType.

Eclipse uses the Extension Object pattern to effectively add IType's methods to IFile. IFile implements the IAdaptable interface, which means that it provides the method getAdaptor(Class). Asking an IFile for an adaptor to IType answers an object that represents the same file, but which has type IType, and which will be able to respond to questions about the structure of the code in the file.

In addition to the non-uniform interface and the extra lines of code, Extension Object has a further disadvantage: its use must be anticipated. There is no way to proceed if the need arises to extend a class that does not implement IAdaptable, and thus does not support the getAdaptor(Class) method. For example, while IType implements IAdaptable, ITypeHierarchy does not.

Related patterns and variants. This pattern specifies the mechanism of interface extension, and the separation of interface from implementation, but says nothing about the form of the implementation itself. However, implementation is critical: although the architecture that we have specified so far is functionally complete,it is insufficient to allow implementations to obtain reasonable performance on code models of any significant size. Later we will describe the performance issues, and some patterns that help resolve them. The most important of these is *Explicit Interest*, described on page 27, which describes a simple interface addition that allows various implementation strategies, including the well known *Caching* [26].

———————————————— □ ————————————————

Using the patterns that we have described, we implemented a *requirements browser* for Squeak, which flags classes that are abstract and displays their requirements. In the process we also implemented a reusable *Model Extension*, which is thus available to existing Smalltalk browsers — if they are extended to use it. However, implementing a simple interface that answers a useful question can be more rewarding than this: it should be possible to make use of a model extension even without requiring that a tool developer write new tools or modify old ones. From the perspective of the user, discovering the existence and usefulness of a code analysis of which he had not previously been aware should not require him to learn to use a new tool. We can lower the costs of using model extensions to both tool developers and users by providing *Generic Tools* that are easily adapted to make use of new model extensions.

What do we mean by a "generic tool" and how could one have helped us with the *requirements* analysis? To answer this question, consider a generalization of the requirements browser. Our requirements browser displays in blue the names of classes that respond positively to the message isAbstract. It could easily be modified to use some other predicate to decide which classes to color. With a little more work, the browser could be made to show users a list of all of the predicates on classes, and allow them to decide *which* predicate will determine class coloring. Every new model extension that is a predicate would be added to this list automatically, making the extension immediately usable, even before a tool tailored to take advantage of the extension has been written. Even after tailored tools have been developed, any programmer opening the configuration dialog of the generic tool will see all the predicates defined on classes, and can choose to explore their usefulness without having to learn to use the more specialized tools.

Of course, the idea of *Generic Tools* is not limited to model extensions that are predicates. Ducasse and Lanza [10] describe a tool that allows for the *ad hoc* definition of code visualizations based on code metrics. In their tool, a code element is represented by a rectangle, and the values of different metrics determine its height, width and color. These metrics can be implemented as model extensions whose values are numeric.

Thus, we see that a new code analysis, if given a sufficiently abstract interface, provides us not just with one new tool or view, but with a new kind of information that can be used from many existing and familiar views and the tools that implement them. We capture this idea in the pattern *Generic Tools*.

Generic Tools

Context. A development environment exists, various *Model Extension*s are implemented, and specialized tools use them.

Problem. How can you make the views of the program corresponding to these model extensions accessible without requiring tool-builders to write new tools, and application programers to learn to use them?

Forces. The following forces are in play.

- Many useful code analyses have been devised by experts on static analysis and published in the literature.
- These analyses are understood by few practitioners and used by even fewer — even though tools exist to apply them.
- The problem is that activating a specialized tool just to access an analysis takes time; this makes the analysis less valuable. Even more importantly, activating a specialized tool disrupts the programmer's workflow, forcing the programmer to divert her attention from the task at hand. Finally, the specialized tool will be unfamiliar, and the programmer must learn how to use it.
- For the developer of a code analysis, being forced to also create a tool that displays the results of that analysis raises the barrier to entry.
- While some code analyses result in specialized models of the code, many others result in representations of the code in terms of ordinary data types such as booleans, numbers, collections and graphs. Such data can be visualized and manipulated using general-purpose tools that are not dependent on the meaning of the data.

Solution. Instead of creating tools that are specialized to show a specific model extension to best effect, create generic tools that allow a programmer to make opportunistic use of a variety of model extensions. Such tools should provide a generally useful mechanism for using information about code. Generic tools should be extensible, that is, they should be able to use information from different sources.

Note that the requirement here is extensibility by a programmer, which can be achieved by different means at different levels. A tool framework might be extended to use a new *Model Extension* by coding a simple plugin. In some cases, a configurable tool might be extended without any programming, by merely specifying the name of an extension. The main requirement is that the writer of a *Model Extension* can make it visible from tools with small amounts of effort.

Consequences. A development environment with a suite of *Generic Tools* encourages the writing of reusable code analyses; exposing the outputs of code analyses also encourages the addition of new specialized tools that make use of them.

Note that *Generic Tools* are likely to sacrifice some aspects of usability. This is because they give the programmer a generic user interface rather than one specialized to a particular task. We might deduce that generic tools are more likely to complement than to replace more specialized tools. However, the user can be overwhelmed by a plethora of tools: a small number of more powerful, generic tools might actually be more friendly to the user, who is, after all, a practicing programmer.

Known Uses. We present two more examples of *Generic Tools*. First, we observe that a unit testing framework such as SUnit [2] can be thought of as a generic tool. SUnit allows convenient, reproducible checking of assertions about code. The assertions are usually about code functionality, and are checked by running application code on examples with known results. However, the assertions can also be about structural properties of the code, in which case they can be checked by sending messages to the objects in the *Shared Code Model*. Any new model extension can be used in this way immediately, without writing any new tools.

For example, unless one is building a framework extensible by inheritance, it is reasonable to expect that any abstract classes will have at least one concrete subclass. Leveraging the *requirements* model extensions and SUnit, this assertion can be expressed as follows.

```
(MyPackage allClasses) do: [ :each | self deny:
        (each subclasses isEmpty and: [each isAbstract]) ]
```

A suite of SUnit tests containing assertions like this may be thought of as turning the SUnit test browser into a general tool for maintaining invariants about the structure of the code. Naturally, such structural test suites complement, rather than replace, conventional test suites that check the function of the code.

The second example is the StarBrowser [44], which was designed by Wuyts *et al.* specifically to allow unanticipated integration of new properties. It displays a tree of nodes that can represent different types of objects, including code model elements. The StarBrowser can be made to display a specific set of child nodes, for example the required methods of a class, in an *ad hoc* fashion: one passes it an anonymous function that returns the set of nodes. It can also be customized more systematically, by creating a glue class that defines a new menu item on the appropriate node type. The latter kind of customization can be undertaken by a tool integrator who is the author of neither the StarBrowser nor the model extension. Thus, the working programmer can be exposed to the model extension through the StarBrowser without having to do the integration work.

———————————————————— □ ————————————————————

3.2   Applications of Model Extensions

This section presents two general situations in which application of *Model Extension* (p. 12) can help to resolve a design problem; the patterns discuss the concerns specific to each, and how different *Model Extension*s may be composed. The discussion is heavy with performance concerns, because experience (both personal and vicarious) shows that performance can be quite critical in development environments that expose deep properties of the code in their views. In each pattern we therefore mention the performance problems typical to each kind of model extension, and point towards solutions. However, the reader might prefer to ignore this discussion on the first reading and focus on the effects of applying each pattern, rather than the details of its efficient implementation.

Alternative Representation

Context. The development environment has a specific representation for each kind of element in the shared code model.

Problem. This representation is not the most appropriate for the specific tool that you are implementing. For example, the representation of a method might be textual; if you are implementing parenthesis matching, an syntax tree representation would be more convenient.

Forces. The following forces are in play.

- We cannot change the representation of the shared code model to suit our application.
- Because the *Shared Code Model* is complete, the information that we need is in the model somewhere.
- However, the information that we need is implicit; we would like it to be explicit.

Solution. Define the representation that you prefer as a *Model Extension* (p. 12). Calculate it when required in the conventional way, for example, build an abstract syntax tree by running a parser on the textual representation of the code. Efficiency may require the use of *Caching* [26].

Consequences. There is inevitably a cost in providing an alternative representation: time to compute it when needed, or space if it is to be cached, or possibly code complexity if some more efficient (but elaborate) solution is found. However, some of these costs are inevitable as soon as an IDE needs to expose aspects of the code that are implicit in the primary representation. For example, when implementing parenthesis matching, if we do not introduce the alternative syntax tree representation, we would instead need to do some form of ad-hoc parsing to find the parenthesis. This ad-hoc parsing has an execution cost, may need to be cached, and so on.

As with all *Model Extensions*, an *Alternative Representation* can be shared by multiple tools. Thus, this pattern helps to avoid code duplication, and reduces long-term maintenance costs. For example, the ad-hoc parsing code mentioned above would to some extent duplicate the normal parsing code that exists elsewhere.

Known Uses. The Squeak *Shared Code Model* represents methods as pointers into a text file kept on disk. This preserves all of the documentary structure of the source code [43], and provides access to the code that is fast enough for editing and browsing. However, an *Alternative Representation* is clearly needed for execution: Squeak uses bytecode. When the source code is edited (and when new code is read into the environment), it is immediately compiled to bytecode and the compiled methods are cached as objects. Other Smalltalk implementations, such as VisualWorks, compile directly to machine code. However, in all cases the existence of the cached of executable code is hidden from the user of the environment, who is given the consistent illusion of editing and manipulating source code.

Alternative Representations are commonly used by tools internally, even though they may not be exposed to other toolbuilders and users. For example, in addition to their target language, compilers commonly use a variety of intermediate representations, including control flow graphs, dependency graphs, and single static assignment form. These representations might be useful to programmers seeking to better understand their programs, but they are rarely exposed. Even if the compiler provides a way of exporting these representations, most IDEs do not make them readily visible. Compilers are only one source for potentially useful alternate representations; the program analysis literature has many more. Program slices, for example, can be very useful when debugging and transforming code [4].

———————————————— □ ————————————————

We now move on to another application of *Model Extension*. We note that a common activity when reading code is navigating through chains of references; for example, in a procedural language, a procedure call is linked to the definition of a procedure by the scoping rules of the language. It is common for IDEs to automate this navigation, allowing the programmer to navigate from the call site to the definition with a single click. In an object-oriented language, an IDE may provide a pop-up menu on a message-send that allows the programmer to choose between the several correspondingly-named method bodies. This functionality is not particularly difficult to implement; it is enough to parse the particular method being browsed (this might be an *Alternative Representation*) and keep track of procedure and method definitions in the program.

Our next pattern is motivated by a related feature: the ability to navigate in the other direction, from a procedure to its call sites or from a method to the senders of the corresponding message. Navigating in this direction is useful when attempting to understand how a procedure or method is used, or when considering a refactoring such as adding a parameter. Note that answering the query in the naïve way (by searching for all calls to the procedure) would be expensive even if the parse tree of whole program were available, so an *Alternative Representation* is not the solution. Our proposed solution is captured in the next pattern, *Inverse Mapping*.

Inverse Mapping

Context. The code model contains various natural reference structures. These are accessible via the *Shared Code Model* or by *Alternative Representations*, and used by programmers and tools.

Problem. How can we allow efficient navigation in the opposite direction?

Forces. The following forces are in play.

- Because the shared code model is minimal, many mappings that it supports directly will be one-way. For example, a class might have a direct reference to its superclass, but not to its subclasses.
- Both end-user tools and higher-level *Model Extensions* may wish to use these mappings in the other direction.
- Traversing the code base to search for such references is expensive.

Solution. Provide each *Inverse Mapping* as a *Model Extension*, so that the mapping is available to clients directly, but the implementation details are hidden.

Efficient implementation of inverse mappings can be complex. The basic difficulty is that finding all references to a code model element is a non-local task: references can be anywhere in the code base. This means that traversing the whole code base at each request is expensive. *Caching* the precomputed inverse mapping allows us to avoid multiple traversals of the whole code base for multiple queries. Then the basic difficulty shows up in a different way: to correctly answer queries about arbitrary reference targets this cached inverse mapping has to be of the whole code model, making it space-intensive for references that are common, such as procedure calls or message sends.

Using a cache also means that the cache must be kept up-to-date. Suppose that a procedure definition is modified, and corresponding changes are made to the appropriate part of the code model. To keep the cache current, we have to remove those entries corresponding to references that the procedure *used* to make, and add entries for the references that it *now* makes. The latter is straightforward, but the former poses a potential problem: how do we find the references that the previous version of a procedure used to make?

Sometimes this problem is solved by the change notification mechanism providing access to the *previous* definition of the changed element as well as to the new one. If this is not the case, it may be necessary to keep a separate record of all references in the forward direction, just for the purpose of cache invalidation. In the worst case, it may be necessary to rebuild the cache from scratch by exhaustive search.

Known Uses. Squeak Smalltalk maintains the superclass of each class as an instance variable defined in class Behavior. It also caches the inverse mapping, the set of subclasses, in another instance variable (defined in class Class, a subclass of Behavior). When a class is redefined (possibly changing its superclass) the change notification mechanism provides the model with both the old and the new definitions, so the cache of subclasses can be updated incrementally.

However, Squeak is not always so organized: there are other places where this pattern could be applied, but is not. For example, it is easy to find the set of classes referenced by a class, but harder to find all the classes that reference a particular class. If this pattern were used in a Smalltalk environment, c referencedClasses would answer the set of classes referenced by c; The inverse mapping would be c referringClasses, which would answer all of the classes that refer to c. Whereas referencedClasses can be evaluated locally, by scanning the names referred to by all of c's methods, a naïve implementation of referringClasses would require a global traversal of all of the classes in the environment, searching for classes that refer to c.

At present, Squeak does not put *either* enquiry into the code model; instead the functionality to find all references to a class is implemented in the SystemNavigation tool (using global search). Another tool, the Refactoring Browser, implements the same functionality again. This illustrates the sort of problem that extensible code models will help to avoid.

Consequences. The maintenance of an *Inverse Mapping* might be expensive even with a sophisticated implementation. There is usually a tradeoff between space and time: making an inverse mapping available quickly will usually save time but cost space, because it will necessitate keeping a cache of an inverted index. However, notice that keeping a cache requires that the cache be re-validated when there is a change in any of the information on which it depends. If the re-validation process is very complex, it can also cost time. If maintaining an *Inverse Mapping* costs *both* space *and* time, use of this pattern may not be appropriate.

Related patterns and variants. As we mentioned above, the efficient implementation of an inverse mapping will sometimes require more than just a general cache. *Explicit Interest* makes it possible to maintain a more selective cache, for example, one that contains information only about references to specific code model elements. *Batch Calculation* and *Lazy Update* show us how to take maximal advantage of each non-local scan, particularly when a number of code model elements are updated at one time.

When offering examples of inverse mappings, we assumed a knowledge of the references from a method to other classes and messages. These references might

be found in an *Alternative Representation*, created by analyzing the source code
or by abstract interpretation of the bytecode.

———————————————————— □ ————————————————————

We now return to our motivating example, the task of listing the methods
required by a class. This means that we seek to implement a model extension
required methods. A method m can be required by a class c either because m is
explicitly marked as required, or because m is sent to self in a method of c even
though m is not implemented by c or its superclasses.

How can we find out whether a particular method is required in a class? The
simplest thing that could possibly work would be the following. For every selector
s that may be required, scan every method implementation to see if it self-sends
s. This defines a mapping *self sends* from methods to sets of selectors. This is a
poor implementation technique: it would scan every method in every class many
times. What we need here is the *Inverse Mapping self senders of* which provides,
for each selector, the methods that self-send it. Thus, we find that we have quite
naturally partitioned the complex computation of required methods into three
layers of *Model Extension*, each built on a simpler one. This leads us to our next
pattern: *Layered Extension*, described below.

Layered Extension

Context. You have a definition of an interesting but complex *Model Extension*.

Problem. How do you implement this *Model Extension* efficiently, while at the
same time promoting reusability?

Forces. The following forces are in play.

- Calculating this *Model Extension* requires as input other, expensive to compute information.
- This other information might itself be useful as a code property, available to
  other analyses.
- The calculation of the interesting and complex *Model Extension* can be broken
  down into a series of smaller, loosely coupled definitions.

Solution. Define each complex *Model Extension* on top of simpler ones, in layers. A higher-level property expresses *Explicit Interest* (p. 27) in the lower-level
extensions that it requires. Note that layering model extensions requires us to
be careful in ordering recalculations. For example, we do not want to recalculate the *requirements* property before we have recalculated the *self senders of*
mapping for the methods in the relevant classes. This ordering constraint can
be addressed by *Lazy Update*, described on page 33.

Implementation. When implementing a *Layered Extension*, a number of competing forces come into play. For reusability, it is tempting to break the definition of an extension into small fragments. For performance, one needs to take care that each layer encapsulates a sufficiently expensive calculation to warrant the existence of that layer. For example, we found that in Squeak, caching the information "which superclass of C implements a method on selector s" is useless, because the dictionary lookups required to access the cache were about as expensive as traversing the superclass chain to recalculate the information. While this might be regarded as commentary on a specific dictionary implementation, the larger lesson should be clear: application of these patterns complements, rather than replaces, good engineering and performance-oriented design.

Related patterns and variants. This pattern is a specialization of the *Layers* pattern [7]. When one *Model Extension* depends on another, it is important that they are recalculated in the right order. This is easy if the extensions are truly layered. If the dependencies become more complicated, one way to find an update order that respects the dependencies is to use *Lazy Update*, described on page 33.

------------------------------------ □ ------------------------------------

In our running example, we created a *Model Extension* for the required methods of a class. We expect that as other code analyses are presented this way, more patterns will emerge, enriching this pattern language for discussing the implementation architecture of program analyses.

3.3   Making it Fast Enough

This subsection is devoted to performance, a topic we have mentioned several times, but haven't yet tackled seriously. A very important rule of thumb for optimization, codified in *Lazy Optimization* [1], is to avoid it until it proves necessary. This rule certainly applies here, and we advocate adhering to it.

Why Performance Matters. Why does performance play such a major role in our pattern language? It is our belief that efficiency considerations are an inherent part of this domain. Before we dive into detail, we will use an analogy to explain why performance is a pervasive problem, and how we alleviate it. The analogy is with the model-view architecture for graphical interfaces and the central role that the *Observer* pattern plays in making that architecture feasible.

The key idea in the model-view architecture is to decouple the model from the view. In an ideal world, the model will know nothing at all about the various views: it will just get on with the business of representing its domain. Whenever a view needs to know some aspect of the state of the model, it asks. The problem with this naïve scheme is that the view needs to redraw itself on every display refresh cycle; it would be hopelessly inefficient to poll the model 60 or 80 times per second, usually to find that nothing has changed. The standard solution is to use the *Observer* [17] pattern, which requires the model to notify the views of any changes. The model is no longer oblivious to the existence of views, but it knows little or nothing about them beyond the fact that they exist. No description of model-view can be complete unless it shows how to address the performance challenge that arises from the decoupling of model and view.

The key insight to solving the performance problem of extensible program representations is that only a small part of the program is in view at any one time. Thus, the extensions need complete their analyses for that part alone. But how can the extensions know *which* part?

Explicit Interest, described on page 27, provides a way for a tool to notify the code model that *someone* is interested in a particular part of the code without the model having to care about *who* is interested.

The Demands of Interaction. When and how do issues of performance arise when computing a *Model Extension* (p. 12)? The most naïve implementation of an Extension would simply compute the property whenever it is requested. For properties that can be computed cheaply enough, this is a good choice: if computing the property is not much more expensive than retrieving it from a cache, there is no point in precomputing it. However, as properties start to be used in development environments to give interactive feedback to programmers, the meaning of "cheaply enough" is becoming more exacting. For example, whereas matching parenthesis used to be a by-product of the parsing step of a compiler, performed every few minutes, today most environments match parenthesis as they are typed. Similarly, whereas in the past it might have been thought sufficient to report missing "required" methods at release time, our desire to show this information interactively to support new styles of work [38] requires a much more sophisticated implementation. Thus, the frequency of use of an analysis can change from once every few minutes to multiple times per second.

Caching, and other Patterns from the Literature. The patterns literature contains quite a few performance-related patterns relevant to implementing a *Model Extension*. If some values are very common for a particular property, *Flyweight* [17] might be justified. Beck discusses *Caching*, and observes that the biggest problem with caches is ensuring that they remain valid. To simplify this problem, he suggests reducing the scope and extent of the variable used for the cache. Thus, while it is usually quite easy to keep a caching temporary variable up to date, it is harder to do so for a caching instance variable [3, p. 44–5]. The variation that is most specifically relevant to us is the caching of *Model Extension* values *between client calls*. After all, the fastest way to compute something that hasn't changed since the last time we were asked is probably not to compute it at all, but to cache our last answer.

While a cache is certainly an important performance tool, caches can also be tricky in the best of cases, and costly in many. So let us examine some techniques for managing caches. Throughout, we assume that the implementation of each *Model Extension* keeps a cache of property values.

The third volume of *Pattern Oriented Software Architecture* [26] presents a set of patterns for managing resources efficiently. A cached *Model Extension*, containing as it does computed results, is not exactly the kind of resource assumed in this volume, but some of the patterns are still relevant. *Evictor* is a mechanism for ensuring that the elements of a cache are flushed at the appropriate time; it may be useful to us because we want to minimize the memory consumption of cached model extension data, and also prevent these data from being used when they are stale. However, *Evictor* gives us only the mechanism: how do we find an efficient policy for deciding which *Model Extension* to evict?

One way to avoid performing unnecessary analyses is to give the implementation of a *Model Extension* more information about the intentions of its clients. This is not a new idea, indeed, one of the advantages of monolithic programming tools is that usage information is available to their analysis components. However, once we have separated the tools from the model, we need to provide a way for the tools to pass usage information to the analyses. The pattern *Explicit Interest*, described on the next page, and its specialization *Life-long Interest*, described on page 29, show how to do this.

Performance issues in the Running Example. We use a *Model Extension* to give client tools a simple interface for obtaining the requirements of a class. Unfortunately, this simple interface makes it hard for the implementation to achieve good performance. For example, Schärli's algorithm is efficient when it is used to calculate the requirements of a class *and* its subclasses *at the same time*. What happens when a sequence of separate requests is made of the model? If the first class requested is the superclass of the others, then queries about the subclasses can be answered from the cache. However, if the tool happens to request subclasses before their superclass, the algorithm would repeatedly calculate the same information. A tool might try to work around this problem by applying the algorithm to some parent of the class in which it is really interested; however, this parent might have many subclasses in which the tool will never be interested, in which case this work would be wasted.

The root cause of the inefficiency is that the calculation mechanism does not know beforehand which classes the tool is going to enquire about. This situation is not specific to the required methods example. Consider the task of computing an *Inverse Mapping*: the most efficient procedure is to traverse all of the relevant code exacly once, gathering information about references to just those elements that clients will to ask about. We believe that the need to know in advance what will be interesting will be very common when performing a non-local code analysis.

One way of giving the calculation mechanism this extra information about usage would be to provide an additional "batch" interface. For example, we could provide an additional interface for required methods so that the client tool could ask for the requirements of several classes at once. However, this interface would be inconsistent with the *Model Extension* pattern. Moreover, since the simple interface and the "high performance" interface would be quite different, the existence of the two interfaces would encourage premature optimization. Therefore we feel that it is better to keep the simple interface unchanged, and to add a separate interface by which the tool can explicitly express an interest in specific classes. The pattern *Explicit Interest* on the next page describes this additional interface, while *Batch Calculation* (p. 35) describes how to use it to obtain the same advantages as the additional "batch" interface that we just dismissed. *Minimal Calculation* (p. 31) examines when we can avoid updating the *Model Extension* at all, while *Eager Update* (p. 32), and *Lazy Update* (p. 33) address when to perform the updates that cannot be avoided.

Explicit Interest

Context. You have a model extension that depends on calculations that are significant enough to require optimization.

Problem. How do client tools provide the information necessary to aid the optimizations?

Forces. The following forces are in play.

- Real-time display of the code and its properties requires interactive response times, which means 100 ms or better.
- Property calculations may be expensive and non-local, and the code model may be large.
- Caching all model extensions over the whole code model requires too much space, or re-validating such extensive caches after a change to the model requires too much computation, or both.
- The tools that are the clients of a model extension are focussed on only a small part of the whole code base at any given time.
- Having more information about the usage of a property can mean that we are better able to optimize the process of obtaining it.
- The code model is not completely static, because the programmer will occaisionally type in a change, or modify significant parts of the model by loading a new version of parts of the code.
- Any implementation tricks necessary to make the various model extensions fast enough should be hidden from client tools. The interface to each model extension should be as simple and uniform as possible

Solution. Add an interface to the model that allows clients to explicitly declare and retract their interest in a specific model extension for a specific code element. At any time, the parts of the *Shared Code Model* in which interests are declared are said to be *interesting*.

   This solution is based on the assumption that, although caching the model extensions over the whole model is infeasible, caching them over the interesting parts of the code model is both feasible and cost-effective.

Consequences. Once this pattern has been applied, we may assume that tools will make queries on only the interesting elements of the code model. This assumption provides various opportunities for optimization. For example, caches can be focused on interesting information. This allows the client tools to assume that the space costs of caches are linear in the number of interests that they have registered.

Access to calculated properties of code elements not declared interesting can be either prohibited (useful to ensure that the interest declarations are complete), or merely less efficient (more friendly to tools before they adapt). This choice might also be controlled by a mode switch, to support different stages in the development of tools.

Related patterns and variants. *Explicit Interest* and *Observer* may seem similar because both make a model object aware of its clients. However, there are significant differences in the intent, effect, and consequences of the two patterns. An *Explicit Interest* is an optimization hint given to the provider of information by the consumer. This hint allows the provider more freedom of implementation; if the hint is not needed, it is always correct to ignore it. In contrast, adding an *Observer* creates the responsibility for the information provider to notify the new consumer of changes; this new responsibility can constrain the implementation, and cannot be ignored. For example, a requirement to include information about the new state in the notification message would force the calculation of that information before the message is sent. *Explicit Interest* has little consequence on the architecture of the application: declaring an interest does not affect when or how the consumer requests the value of the property. In contrast, *Observer* affects the control flow by placing initiative with the model, which must call the observer. The final difference is that with *Explicit Interest*, the model is not concerned with *who* expresses an interest, but solely with *which part* of the model is interesting. In contrast, *Observer* does say *who* is interested, but does *not* communicate which part of the model is interesting. In this sense, *Observer* and *Explicit Interest* are duals; they manage separate concerns, and can be used together.

Because the model is unconcerned with how many times an interest has been expressed, interests have some similarity to *reference counts* on the data structures supporting a model extension. As described by Meyers [29, Item 29], reference counting is a pattern used at the application level to ensure that a data structure stays available for as long as it has at least one client. (Murray earlier outlined the same idea, under the name "use counts" [33, §3.2].)

Explicit Interest provides information that could be used by the other implementation patterns mentioned above. For example, *Lazy acquisition* might be applied only to non-interesting elements, and interest information could be used by an *Evictor*.

---- □ ----

In applying *Explicit Interest* (p. 27) we decided that each instance of our code browser will tell the shared code model which classes it is currently displaying. Note that two browsers may display overlapping sets of classes, in which case there will be two registered interests in the requirements of those classes. Maintaining the interest registration requires the browser to declare interests when new classes are first displayed (for example, when a new browser is opened) and remove them later (when a browser is closed, or when the user changes the set of classes being viewed).

As is typical in large software development projects, we did not write this browser from scratch, but instead used an existing framework, the OmniBrowser[2]. The OmniBrowser is highly object-oriented: an OmniBrowser window does not display mere text strings, but model-specific *node* objects, each of which corresponds to (and references) a part of the code model, for example, a class or a method. These node objects have behavior, for example, they can react to mouse-clicks in useful ways.

In our browser, the node object representing a class has a life-span that matches quite precisely the interest of the browser in that class. Whenever a class is displayed, a node object corresponding to the class is created and included in the browser's display list; when the browser is no longer displaying that class, it ceases to reference the node object. We made the creation of a node object register an interest in the corresponding class; we also declare a finalization action, triggered when the node is garbage collected, that de-registers the interest. Thus, the requirements of a class are a *Life-long Interest* of the node that represents that class in our browser; this pattern is described below.

Life-long Interest

Context. You have a tool that derives its extensibility from being an instance of a framework.

Problem. You wish to adapt this tool to present a new property. This property is captured by a *Model Extension*, so to use it efficiently, you need to express *Explicit Interest* in parts of the model being presented. How should you do this in a manner consistent with the tool framework?

Forces. The following forces are in play.

- If the framework pre-dates the publication of these patterns, it is unlikely to support *Explicit Interest* directly.
- To be effective, interests have to be declared before queries are made, and must eventually be retracted, though the timing for retraction is not critical.
- Failing to express an interest will hurt performance, possibly making the tool unusable.
- Extending a framework in a way that its designers did not anticipate is likely to produce code that is fragile and hard to understand.
- A well-designed object-oriented framework is likely to have *objects* representing the model elements that are interesting, and is likely to allow for customization by changing or replacing these objects.

---

[2] http://www.wiresong.ca/OmniBrowser/

Solution. Find the framework objects representing the parts of the model that enjoy the new property, and adapt them to express *Explicit Interest* in the corresponding part of the *Shared Code Model* for the *whole of their lifetime*. This can be achieved by making each of these objects register its interest when it is initialized or constructed, and retract its interest in when it is finalized or destroyed. A life-long interest can also be declared by modifying the factory that creates the representation objects. If we assume that the tool creates the representation objects before using the model extension, the interest declarations will be early enough; the language's object deallocation mechanisms will guarantee that interest is eventually retracted. This gives your objects the desired property, while assuming little about the framework, and making only local and easily understandable adaptations to the code.

Consequences. Life-long Interest is not always applicable: the framework may not have an object with an appropriate lifetime, the object may not be extensible, or its factory may not be available for modification. Using this pattern therefore constrains the implementation freedom of the framework. For example, caching the framework objects, rather than deallocating and reallocating them, will interfere with the use of this pattern.

The exact moment when a declared interest is retracted depends on when the run-time environment runs the garbage collector, and even on the nature of the garbage-colleciton algorithm.

Related patterns and variants. The C++ idiom *Resource Acquisition is Initialization* (RAII) can be used to implement this pattern. The C++ constructor will express an interest, and the destructor will retract it [22]. The immediate retraction that is the hallmark of RAII is not needed to implement *Life-long Interest*, but it does no harm.

———————————————— □ ————————————————

So far we have discussed how to design an *interface* that encapsulates a code analyis as a model extension, while providing it with information about client intentions. We now resume the discussion of *implementing* a code analysis efficiently in the context created by these patterns.

Returning to our running example, it is clear that the naïve approach of recalculating the requirements of every class on every request is far too expensive. In order to make calculations efficient, we look more closely at *what* to calculate, and *how* and *when* to do so. These three questions are not completely separable; we present patterns to address each, but they interact and the boundaries between them are not always clear.

Minimal Calculation, described on the next page, is about limiting what we calculate. *Eager Update*, described on page 32, and *Lazy Update*, described on page 33, are about when to perform the calculation; each has its advantages and disadvantages. *Batch Calculation*, described on page 35, tells us when and how to perform the calculation of a non-local property that benefits from economies of scale: not as eagerly as *Eager Update*, not as lazily as *Lazy Update*, and all at once.

Minimal Calculation

Context. You have a *Model Extension*, and an interface through which clients express *Explicit Interest*. You are maintaining a cache to avoid re-calculating the extension.

Problem. When the *Shared Code Model* changes, how do you avoid unnecessary re-computation of the cached properties in the *Model Extension*?

Forces. The following forces are in play.

- The code model is large, and ordinary editing operations change only a small part of it.
- However, this is not the case when changes to the code model are mechanized, as happens when a new package is loaded into the development environment, or a global refactoring (such as re-organizing the class hierarchy) is performed. In these situations, many parts of the model can change at the same time.
- At any particular time, only a small part of the code model affects the user's display.

Solution. Update only those model extensions that are both interesting *and* affected by changes in the code. The first criterion is applied by consulting the *Explicit Interests*. The latter is calculated using notification of changes to the code model and a knowledge of the dependencies of the property represented by the *Model Extension*.

Consequences. Implicit in the use of this pattern is that queries about *uninteresting* elements of the *Model Extension* can be answered slowly (or rejected outright). This should not be a problem, because these elements should not be queried often: that is the purpose of requiring a declaration of *Explicit Interest*. However, correctness requires that a *Model Extension* employing this pattern must invalidate cached information that is no longer interesting, rather than letting it go stale. (The invalidation might be lazy, that is, it could be done when the cache is queried).

If computing the update is not too expensive, and the frequency of calculations have been sufficiently reduced by the the use of this pattern, then it may be perfectly satisfactory to use *Eager Update*, described on the next page, to actually perform the computation as as soon as a change is notified. This will often be the case when the first force applies.

When the second force applies, this pattern can help to avoid slowing down the important work (the package load or the refactoring) by not wasting computation on updates to the code model that will not affect the tools that are currently in use.

Related patterns and variants. Even after employing this pattern, the amount of computation required to recalculate a global property may still be great enough that using *Eager Update*, described below, slows down the important work. Moreover, it does so needlessly, because it repeatedly recalculates properties that will soon be invalidated. In these situations, consider using *Lazy Update* on the next page. If the computation exhibits economies of scale, also consider *Batch Calculation* on page 35.

———————————————————— □ ————————————————————

When we have to recalculate the value of an interesting *Model Extension*, we can choose to do the work as soon as possible, or we can try to defer it as long as possible. *Eager Update*, described below, characterizes the first situation, and *Lazy Update*, described on the facing page, characterizes the second. Which is the better choice depends on the forces that apply and their relative strengths.

Eager Update

Context. You have defined a *Model Extension* (p. 12) or a *Layered Extension* (p. 23) on top of a *Shared Code Model* (p. 9).

Problem. When should the properties that are captured by the *Model Extension* be recalculated?

Forces. The following forces are in play.

- The *Model Extension* is an *Observer* of parts of the *Shared Code Model*, and is notified when the relevant parts of the model change. Alternatively,
- the *Layered Extension* is an *Observer* of a single, lower-layer *Model Extension*.
- Recalculating the property is a fast, local operation.
- Most of the time, the user wants interactive response. However, bulk changes to the code, such as applying a patch that updates 100 classes, should not be interactive because this will needlessly delay the bulk operation.

Solution. Update the *Model Extension* eagerly, that is, as soon as you are notified of the change to the *Shared Code Model* or the lower-layer *Model Extension* on which it depends.

Consequences. Eagerness has several benefits.

1. The code is simple and readable: performing the update calculation is the simplest and most obviously correct response to a change notification.
2. The *Model Extension* will always be up-to-date, and thus client queries can be answered instantly.

3. *Eager Update* supports notification of changes to any tool or *Layered Extension* that depends on your *Model Extension*.

However, this pattern also has some disadvantages.

1. In the case of a bulk change to the code model, this pattern can be inefficient, because bulk changes may trigger many intermediate updates to the *Model Extensions*. These updates may be useless because they are almost immediately overwritten, or because the relevant part of the model becomes uninteresting before the user has the opportunity to query them.
2. A *Layered Extension* must not be recomputed until after the update of the lower-layer *Model Extension* on which it depends. However, if the *Layered Extension* is also dependent on the *Shared Code Model* directly, then it may receive a change notification from the model before this update has completed. This can be a source of subtle and hard to find bugs.

—————————————————————— □ ——————————————————————

Eager Update earns its place in the pattern language not because it is says anything surprising or unexpected, but because it supplies a name for the simplest thing that could possibly work. In particular, it provides a baseline to contrast with *Lazy Update*, described below.

Lazy Update

Context. You have defined a *Model Extension* (p. 12) or a *Layered Extension* (p. 23) on top of a *Shared Code Model* (p. 9). You are maintaining a cache to avoid re-calculating the extension.

Problem. When, and in what order, should the cached properties that are captured by the *Model Extension* be recalculated?

Forces. The forces are similar to those that apply to *Eager Update*.

- The *Model Extension* may depend on other *Model Extensions* as well as on the *Shared Code Model*, and may be an *Observer* of all of them.
- The *Model Extension* will be notified when the relevant parts of the model change. However, the order in which the notifications arrive may be undetermined.
- The interdependencies between properties may be complex. The order in which the various *Model Extensions* are updated should be consistent with the dependencies.
- Recalculating the properties is a fast, local operation.

– Most of the time, the user wants interactive response. However, bulk changes to the code, such as applying a patch that updates 100 classes, should not be interactive because this will needlessly delay the bulk operation.

Solution. The *Model Extension* keeps track of all the relevant changes to the code model, but does not recompute its cached properties. Instead, it simply invalidates its cache. The *Model Extension* is updated lazily, that is, only in response to client queries; the new values are cached at that time.

Consequences. Laziness has several benefits.

– Model extensions that are not needed are not calculated.
– Batched changes will be executed without useless intermediate updates to the model extensions. The eventual update can be made more efficient using *Batch Calculation* (p. 35).
– Assuming that the dependencies between different *Layered Extensions* are not cyclic, their calculation will be performed in an appropriate order. Note that it is perfectly acceptable for the value of a property on one part of the code model to depend on the *same* property on a different part of the code model, even if both are maintained by the same *Model Extension*.

However, this pattern also has some disadvantages.

– The first access to a *Model Extension* after an update will take more time than other accesses. This may be visible to the programmer at the user interface.
– Perhaps the most significant disadvantage, in comparison with *Eager Update*, is that *Lazy Update* does not support change notifications on the model extensions.

Known Uses. In our running example, we used *Lazy Update* to minimize the set of classes for which we recalculate the required methods.

Related patterns and variants. When used in combination with *Batch Calculation*, this pattern is not completely lazy, so specific parts of a *Model Extension* may be calculated in spite of not yet having been requested. However, this is a reasonable tradeoff as long as the interests declared by the tools are sufficiently precise.

The pattern *Lazy Acquisition*, also from *Pattern Oriented Software Architecture — Volume 3* [26], suggests that delaying the moment of requesting a resource may improve performance, because sometimes the resource will not be used after all. *Lazy Update* can been seen as an application of this pattern, under the assumption that the client of the *Model Extension* does not actually request the resource until it is essential.

———————————————— □ ————————————————

We now turn our attention to performing the calculation of a property as efficiently as possible. The required methods property is non-local — for example, a method selector may be self-sent by some superclass, making the corresponding method required; to find such requirements we need to check the code of all superclasses. This is reflected in Schärli's algorithm, which examines a class before its subclasses. These non-local aspects of the requirements calculation make it attractive to update the model extension in a *Batch Calculation*, described below, rather than one class at a time.

Batch Calculation

Context. You have defined a *Model Extension* (p. 12) that depends on non-local aspects of the *Shared Code Model* (p. 9). For example, the value of a property for a class depends on the properties of all of its superclasses. Re-calculating this non-local property will therefore benefit from economies of scale. The interface to the model extension allows clients to express *Explicit Interest* (p. 27) in parts of the model.

Problem. How can you organize the recalculation of the property to take advantage of these economies of scale? In other words, how can you avoid repeated re-calculation of the *Model Extension*?

Forces. The following forces are in play.

- The properties upon which the *Model Extension* depends may change severally and repeatedly before the properties of the model extension itself are requested.
- The client of the *Model Extension* may request the extension's properties for multiple classes in succession.
- On the one hand, deferring updates of the properties until their values are requested, and then naïvely satisfying these requests, would result in multiple traversals of the common parts of the model on which they depend.
- On the other hand, recalculating the properties eagerly means calculating properties that may never be used.

Solution. Each *Model Extension* keeps track of all the relevant changes to the code model, but defers acting on them. When the model extension eventually updates its caches of calculated information, *all* changes are dealt with, and the extension properties are calculated for *all* interesting code elements, all at the same time. This makes it possible to use each traversal optimally.

Consequences. *Batch Calculation* reduces the number of traversals of the common parts of the model. However, it also means that for a period of time, the properties maintained by a *Model Extension* are invalid. Steps must therefore be taken to prevent clients seeing this invalid data.

This pattern tells us to defer acting on updates, but does not tell us when to stop procrastinating and get to work!

Known Uses. We applied this pattern in our implementation of the requirements browser for Squeak. *Batch Calculation* allowed us to use Schärli's algorithm as it was designed to be used: to compute in one pass a batch of requirements for classes that have an inheritance relationship.

Related patterns and variants. The timing and ordering of the deferred re-calculation may be determined by *Lazy Update*, described on page 33. When this pattern is used in combination with *Lazy Update*, the computation of the *Model Extension* will not be completely lazy. Specific parts of the *Model Extension* may be calculated earlier than necessary, that is, before they are actually requested by a client. However, this is a reasonable tradeoff. As long as the interests declared by the tools are sufficiently precise, it is likely that those parts of the *Model Extension* that are calculated earlier than necessary will be requested by a client in the near future. Moreover, the economies of scale that accrue from *Batch Calculation* are likely to outweigh any inefficiency caused by computing a few properties that are never used.

―――――――――――――――――― □ ――――――――――――――――――

The problem of displaying code properties maintained by a *Model Extension* is incremental in two different ways. First, requests for the property values are made incrementally. Second, changes to the code model are often small and spread over time.

Consider the timing of the recalculation of a property. *Eager Update* performs the calculation as early as possible: as soon as the new model elements on which it depends have been established. *Lazy Update* performs the calculation as late as possible: if it were left any later, a client request could not be answered. Between these extremes there may be a significant interval of time: *Batch Calculation* performs the recalculation somewhere in this interval. In its laziest form, it defers a batch of updates until the effects of *one* of them must be considered in order to satisfy a client request; at that time it eagerly processes the whole batch. A more eager alternative might be to wait until the CPU is idle, and then process the whole batch, ahead of the first client request.

When we implemented the requirements browser for Squeak, we used *Lazy Update* to order the updating of the *required methods Layered Extension* with the updating of the *self senders of Model Extension* that it uses. In its turn, the implementation of *self senders of* uses a combination of *Batch Calculation* and *Lazy Update*—the cache for a class is invalidated when the class is modified, and recalculated when it is requested. *Lazy Update* restricts the re-computation of *self senders of* to the specific class requested, rather than all interesting classes. This is sufficient for this particular model extension because the *self senders of* mapping is local to each class.

The complex interactions that result from these optimization patterns should cause you to delay optimization until you know that you need to do it, and then to reflect on the issues of correctness mentioned in the next subsection.

3.4   Correctness Concerns

As performance concerns drive the code implementing a model extension towards greater complexity, the code becomes more difficult to understand, and it becomes harder to avoid inserting bugs during maintenance and revision. How can we remain confident in the correctness of the implementation? Our answer is to test it against a *Canonical Implementation*, described below.

Canonical Implementation

Context. You have implemented a useful model extension. You believe that the definition of the extension will be obvious to programmers familiar with the language supported by your environment, but the simple and obvious implementation based on the definition is not fast enough.

Problem. How do you improve performance while remaining confident of correctness?

Forces. The following forces are in play.

- Programmers normally have a good mental model of their programming language, so definitions rooted in that model are easy for them to understand.
- The calculation of a model extension must be fast enough for interactive use; this often necessitates optimizations that make the code deviate from that mental model, add complexity, and make it harder to verify.
- The model extension must provide correct information if users and tool builders are to trust it.
- Hand-written unit tests check only what their authors thought of testing.

Solution. Before proceeding to complicate the implementation with optimizations, take the simplest possible implementation and encapsulate it as the *Canonical Implementation*. Now you can freely create an *independent* implementation with better performance; this is the implementation that will actually be used by client tools. Write tests that compare the results of the two implementations over large existing code bases to gain confidence in the optimized implementation.

Consequences. Tests comparing the two implementations complement hand-built unit tests, because the data over which the tests run are independent of the assumptions in the efficient implementation.

For this pattern to be useful, the *Canonical Implementation* should be more likely to be correct than the optimized implementation, and should be more likely to *stay* correct. Why should these things be so?

1. Performance is not a concern for the Canonical Implementation, so you can use well-known, high-level libraries instead of hand-tuned code.

2. The Canonical Implementation need not read from or maintain any caches.

3. The Canonical Implementation can make use of data objects that support the semantics of the desired mathematical operations (*e.g.*, sets) rather than efficient ones (*e.g.*, arrays).

4. The *Canonical Implementation* is used only a test oracle for the fast implementation. This puts fewer constraints on its interface, so it can correspond more closely to a *Formal Definition* (p. 39).

5. You might choose to write the canonical implementation in a higher-level or more appropriate programming language than that chosen for the fast implementation.

6. The canonical implementation is not modified to meet performance or other pragmatic requirements, but only to fix bugs or follow changes in the formal definition. Therefore its code will change much more slowly, and bugs will be introduced into it less frequently, than will be the case for the fast implementation.

Implementation. Realistically, the need for this pattern will not become apparent until after some optimizations have already been applied, and the cost of debugging them has started to show. Thus, finding a good canonical implementation might require using version control to retrieve the simplest version that ever existed, and simplifying it a bit further.

Sometimes the course of development provides you with two different implementations, even though neither of them is canonical. This happened to us when collecting the self-sent messages of a method. The obvious implementation was to analyze the source code, which turned out to be so slow that it was necessary to cache the set of self-sent messages for every method in the system, and to rebuild the cache for a method whenever it was re-compiled. This in turn was found to use excessive memory, so the cache was cleverly compressed.

Some time later, one of us realized[3] that it ought to be possible to obtain the self-send information from the compiled byte-code using abstract interpretation. While debugging the abstract interpreter, we ran tests over *every method in the system*, comparing the results from the abstract interpreter to the cached results from the most recent compilation. We eventually arrived at a situation where there was a single method on which the two implementations differed — and concluded that the implementation that parsed the source code was less accurate. For this reason we hesitate to give it the name "canonical implementation."

Related patterns and variants. A canonical implementation can help you maintain confidence in the correctness of the optimized version. Sometimes a *Formal Definition* is also needed, in which case the canonical implementation can act as a bridge between the non-executable, but maximally clear, formal definition, and the efficient implementation used in practice.

—————————————————— □ ——————————————————

---

[3] Following a conversation with John Brant.

While using the *Minimal Calculation* pattern, we came to believe that we could run the *requirements* algorithm less frequently if we took into account which classes had been modified and which classes implemented or self-sent each method selector. However, we found it difficult to be certain of the correctness of this optimization. What we needed was to prove a claim of the form: "if class C requires a method named s, then one of the following statements must be true about the code. . . "

Proving this kind of theorem would be possible only if we had a formal definition of the *requirements* property. Some relevant formal definitions already existed [11] but were not particularly well-suited to our task. We found it useful to create a minimal *Formal Definition* based on just the concepts relevant to the requirements calculation: method lookup, explicit requirements, reachability through self- and super-sends, and required selectors. We used this definition to prove some necessary conditions for a message selector to be a *requirement*. In particular, we proved that if a selector is not defined in a class, not self-sent in the class, and not a requirement of its superclass, then it cannot be a requirement of the class.

These proofs allowed us to run the requirements extraction algorithm only when the necessary conditions hold. Because these conditions are cheap to check, and hold only rarely, performance was improved significantly, because we ran the costly algorithm much less often. This process is captured in the pattern *Formal Definition*, described below.

Formal Definition

Context. You have thought of a property that is useful, but complex.

Problem. How can you be sure that the property is well-defined in all cases? How can you figure out what implementation shortcuts are possible, and convince yourself that they are correct?

Forces. The following forces are in play.

- The programming language that your IDE supports includes baroque features and corner cases that are rarely encountered in ordinary programs, but which are nevertheless represented in the *Shared Code Model* and over which your property must be defined.
- Informal language is often imprecise when defining a property in such corner cases.
- To improve performance, you will want to refrain from examining parts of the program that cannot affect the value of the property. This implies that you need a way to be sure that a part of the program is *always* irrelevant to the property of interest.

– There may already be a formal system describing part of the language, such as a grammar, or a type system, or a formal semantics.

Solution. Use mathematical language — for example, sets, relations, and constraints — to define the property formally, in terms of primitive facts about the programming language and simpler properties. If possible, base your formal definition on an existing formalization of the programming language. When an optimization relies on a non-trivial claim about the property, *prove* the claim from the formal definition.

Consequences. Although it is still possible that the proof is incorrect and the optimization introduces a bug, the probability of this has been reduced. Moreover, unit testing of the optimized algorithm is likely to expose such a bug early, because the formal definition specifies the test result.

Related patterns and variants. The *Formal Definition*, translated into your programming language of choice without regard for efficiency, can become a *Canonical Implementation* (p. 37). For example, the canonical implementation might be written in terms of sets and relations in a functional style that mimics the mathematics.

————————————————— □ —————————————————

4   Pattern Language Summary

We conclude our description of the pattern language with a quick overview of our solution to the problem of building a extensible, modular architecture for representing a program in Squeak Smalltalk.

One important property of the Smalltalk programming environment is that it has a *Shared Code Model* (p. 9) on which we could build. Since the shared code model does not maintain the required methods of a class, we implemented a *Model Extension* (p. 12) that exposes the required methods as if they were part of the code model. We realized that the Squeak shared code model is not minimal, but in fact includes an *Alternative Representation* (p. 19) for methods.

Calculating the required methods for every class in a large application would be prohibitively expensive, and much of the effort would be wasted because programmers are interested in studying only a few classes at a time. The model extension therefore allows tools to express *Explicit Interest* (p. 27) in the properties of a specific class.

In the browser development framework in which we were working, we found that a simple way of adapting the browser to express *Explicit Interest* was *Lifelong Interest* (p. 29), in which a particular object's interest endures until it is garbage collected. Knowledge of the "interesting" classes creates a context in which various optimization strategies are applicable; two optimizations that we consider are *Minimal Calculation* (p. 31) and *Batch Calculation* (p. 35). *Lazy Update* (p. 33) complements them by determining when recalculation of a property should take place after a model change.

To prevent this preoccupation with efficiency from coming at the expense of understandability and correctness, we used a *Formal Definition* (p. 39) and a *Canonical Implementation* (p. 37) as a test oracle. We found that the (rather complicated) requirements property depends on two simpler properties, which led us to *Layered Extension* (p. 23). One of those properties turns out to be useful both as an intermediate layer for a higher-level calculation and also to the end user. It is an *Inverse Mapping* (p. 21), and as such exemplifies a class of properties that are frequently useful to programmers using the IDE, to analysts, to architects building more complex extensions, and to toolsmiths.

These patterns make it easier to write a second tool that uses an existing analysis, and also make it easier to adapt an existing tool to make use of a new analysis. *Generic Tools* (p. 17) represent the limit of this second case — tools designed to make use of any property of the code model exposed by an extension, and thus to lower the barrier to using a new analysis.

5   Review of the Running Example

A pattern language is useful if it leads to an improvement in the architecture, functionality, performance or reusability of software that adopts it. In this section we return to the Requirements Browser example, and consider how the application of this pattern language has improved it as a product.

The original version of the Requirements Browser [39] was implemented as part of an incremental programming environment. One of the principal goals of this environment is to show the programmer in real time the actual state of the code being developed; this includes what methods are still missing, and which classes are incomplete. Meeting this goal demands responsiveness during typical browsing activities, and the constant display of requirements information. These are difficult demands to satisfy, because the requirements calculation is non-local, and potentially quite expensive.

As we mentioned on page 38, in the initial prototype, all of the self-send information for every method in the image was calculated eagerly and cached in a compressed form. The super- and class-send information was also cached, adding to the space cost. This cache was subsequently replaced by a custom abstract interpreter that computed the send information from the bytecode on demand. However, achieving responsiveness still required that the *Inverse Mapping self senders of* be cached. This cache, and a global cache of requirements information for every class in the system, were updated eagerly whenever a method changed. What were the performance and deployment implications of these caches?

Our measurements showed that the total memory footprint of these caches was around 2 MB, for a code model (class objects and bytecoded methods) of 4 MB. The cache was updated at every change of any method. This worked reasonably well for interactive changes to single methods, but negatively affected bulk recompilations, such as those caused by loading a new version of a package. This was true even if the package being loaded had no effect on the requirements being displayed. Building this cache from scratch, as was required to deploy the requirements browser on a Squeak image for the first time, took tens of minutes.

The patterns described in this article made it easier to overcome these problems. By caching information only for those classes in which there was *Explicit Interest*, we reduced the cache size to be proportional to the amount of code being displayed, rather than the amount of code loaded in the system. *Lazy Update* removed any need for long re-computations when installing the system, and speeded up bulk package loads. Some of the optimization required to make the incremental computations efficient were quite complex, but *Canonical Implementation* and *Formal Definition* greatly increased our confidence in their correctness.

The original Requirements Browser prototype added the implementation of the *required methods* property directly to the *Shared Code Model*; the use of a *Model Extension* allowed us to avoid this modification of the core system classes, which had proved to be a packaging and maintenance problem.

Applying the pattern language presented in this article thus made available for reuse a complex code analysis that was originally buried in a particular tool. At the same time, the analysis became more practical from the point of view of performance, and less intrusive in the code model. We note that while the particular example that we chose — abstract classes — is commonly part of the explicit code model in statically typed languages, global analyses and the enhanced models that they require are not specific to latently typed languages.

6   Historical Context

The idea of multiple-view software development environments has been studied at least since 1986 [19], when David Garlan published the work that led to his doctoral thesis [20]. The Field environment constructed at Brown University in the early 1990s by Steve Reiss and his students was a landmark in the development of such systems. A 1992 study by Meyers and Reiss [31] examined novice users of Field and concluded that multiple views, or at least the particular set of views that Field supported, did indeed help programmers to perform maintenance tasks.

However, Field was constructed as a loose collection of separate tools that communicated using what we would now call a publish and subscribe system (Meyers called it "Selective Broadcast" [28]). Although this made it quite easy to write new tools and add them to Field, each tool duplicated the core data of the system, making it hard to maintain consistency, contributing to high latency when attempting to keep simultaneous views up-to-date, and inevitably forcing programmers to introduce redundancy between the tools. The approach to consistency that we are taking in Multiview is close to what Meyers called "Canonical representation", which seemed then to be an unattainable dream.

Since 1991, the amount of core memory available on a typical development workstation has expanded from 16 MB to 2 GB. This has made it possible to keep all or most of the representation of even quite large software systems in core memory, and this permits the use of more flexible data structures than are supported by a database and, perhaps more importantly, allows the parts of these data structures to link to each other directly. Nevertheless, it is still the case that "no representation has yet been devised that is suitable for all possible tools". The idea of an *extensible* architecture for code models and the pattern language described in this article is a response to the (belated) recognition that no such representation will ever be devised *a priori*.

From a review of previous research, Meyers concludes that a Canonical Representation based on abstract syntax trees (ASTs) is insufficient. Marlin [27] presents an architecture (also called MultiView, but written in CamelCase) that takes this approach, and concludes that at least part of the problem is that the AST "shows through" in the form of the syntax-structured editor. The hybrid style of Smalltalk's *Shared Code Model* avoids this difficulty by representing method bodies as text. Experience has shown that textual views have advantages over structured views at the method-level: textual views keep white space and indentation which, while semantically useless, are important documentation [43]. Editing text also makes it easier for the programmer to transform the code by permitting it to pass through syntactically illegal intermediate states.

Meyers and Reiss [30] describe another problem with ASTs: they do a poor job of supporting views that are unrelated to the program's syntax. In their search for a "single canonical representation for software systems", they present their own Semantic Program Graphs (SPGs), which support a range of views directly. Meyers and Reiss themselves note that SPGs do not faithfully represent all aspects of a program; one of their solutions is to allow clients to annotate them.

The architecture that we propose in this article combines the advantages of a Canonical Representation with those of multiple specialized representations connected by message passing. The *Shared Code Model* solves consistency problems by being the unique modifiable representation, but additional representations can be made available (as *Model Extension*s) to help support disparate views. Thus, the research into advanced representations such as SPGs can be leveraged by using these representations as model extensions.

7   Coda

It used to be that conducting research in program development tools required either settling for a mediocre user interface (making it unlikely that the experimental tool would be widely adopted) or creating an environment in which to embed the tool, a larger investment than most research projects could support. Fortunately, extensible development environments, such as Eclipse, are now available: these environments are creating ecosystems in which IDE architects, toolsmiths and program analysts can support each others' work. In such an IDE, the investment required to move from the idea for an analysis to a usable tool is reduced. Because these environments are widely used, tools embedded in them are more likely to be used than standalone tools. The extensibility of these IDEs make it possible for them to include capabilities beyond their architects' initial planning and priorities; if users are likely to find a tool useful, sooner or later the toolsmiths will respond to that demand.

The patterns presented in this article are intended to facilitate this process. A development environment is made extensible by the frameworks it provides and by the idioms it promotes for sharing code between extenders. The patterns that we have described support the use of a *Shared Code Model* to which code analyses can be added systematically. These analyses can then be shared between different extenders of the development environment, so that not only tools but other analyses can build on them.

The early patterns, particularly *Shared Code Model* and *Model Extension*, are known to exist in Squeak, and in some form in Eclipse; we do not know how widespread they are. Some of the later patterns may not have been used other than in our own tools. Thus the architecture that we propose must be considered preliminary, and it seems likely that some of the proposed patterns will change, and possibly more will be added, as more architects, analysts and toolsmiths gain experience with it.

Our confidence that these patterns will be found useful is based on the same reasoning that argues for the usefulness of the object-oriented paradigm itself. Objects facilitate reuse when they represent entities in the real world. As a consequence, different applications that manipulate the same concerns in the real world are likely to be able to reuse the corresponding objects in an object-oriented design. Of course, these objects may need to be extended — but this is also something that the paradigm supports.

In a program development environment, the "real world" that is the meeting place for the various tools and analyses is the program under development. The representation of that program — the *Shared Code Model* — is highly reusable because every tool builder and analyst understands the subject programming language and the properties of its elements. For example, anyone who knows Java would assume that a code-model element that represents a Java class will provide a method or attribute to access its superclass — and they would be right to do so. In contrast, properties that are available only by running an analysis and building a separate result graph, which the client must then worry about keeping up to date, are much less likely to be reused.

We are aware that there are some flaws in this argument. While many analyses do indeed create new properties of existing elements in the *Shared Code Model*, there are code analyses in the literature that create new entities that are not local to any such element. One example is finding cyclicly dependent sets of classes [42]. While the results of this analysis can be mapped back on to the *Shared Code Model*, that is not the "obvious" way of looking at the them. Also, the tradeoff between *Lazy Update* and *Eager Update* is worthy of more study; we advocated *Lazy Update* for performance, but *Eager Update* has the benefit of allowing a element of a *Model Extension* to be *observable*.

In spite of these issues, we feel that we have made enough progress with this architecture to expose it to the scrutiny of the programming environment community. A demonstration of our implementation is available as a Squeak image at `http://www.cs.pdx.edu/~black/goodies/TraitsBeta3.0/TraitsBeta3.02.tgz`. It has begun to solve the very real problem first identified by Meyers in 1991 [28], and has done so in a way that enables us to build useful tools for Squeak. We hope that others will be encouraged to critique and expand on these patterns, and to report their findings.

Acknowledgments

This work was partially supported by the National Science Foundation of the United States under awards CCF-0313401 and CCCF-0520346. We also thank Emerson Murphy-Hill and Philip Quitslund for motivational discussions, John Brant for help in building the abstract interpreter, and Colin Putney for his willingness to adapt the OmniBrowser to our needs.

We are indebted to an anonymous OOPSLA referee for information about the Cadillac system, to our PLOP 2006 shepherd Peter Sommerlad for his extensive advise and useful comments, and to the many members of our PLOP writers workshop, particularly Ademar Aguiar. The anonymous referees for this journal also provided numerous suggestions that have improved the article.

References

1. Auer, K., Beck, K.: Lazy optimization: patterns for efficient smalltalk programming. In: Pattern languages of program design, vol. 2, pp. 19–42. Addison-Wesley Longman Publishing Co., Inc., Boston (1996)
2. Beck, K.: Simple Smalltalk testing: With patterns, http://www.xprogramming.com/testfram.htm
3. Beck, K.: Smalltalk Best Practice Patterns. Prentice-Hall, Englewood Cliffs (1997)
4. Binkley, D.W., Gallagher, K.B.: Program slicing. In: Zelkowitz, M. (ed.) Advances of Computing, vol. 43, pp. 1–50. Academic Press, London (1996)
5. Black, A.P., Jones, M.P.: The case for multiple views. In: Workshop on Directions in Software Engineering Environments, ICSE 2004, May 2004, pp. 96–103 (2004)
6. Black, A.P., Schärli, N.: Traits: Tools and methodology. In: Proceedings ICSE 2004, May 2004, pp. 676–686 (2004)
7. Buschmann, F., Meunier, R., Rohnert, H., Sommerlad, P., Stal, M.: Pattern-Oriented Software Architecture — A System of Patterns. John Wiley & Sons, Inc., New York (1996)
8. Clifton, C., Leavens, G.T., Chambers, C., Millstein, T.: MultiJava: Modular open classes and symmetric multiple dispatch for Java. In: OOPSLA 2000 Conference on Object-Oriented Programming, Systems, Languages, and Applications, pp. 130–145 (2000)
9. Clifton, C., Millstein, T., Leavens, G.T., Chambers, C.: Multijava: Design rationale, compiler implementation, and applications. ACM Trans. Program. Lang. Syst. 28(3), 517–575 (2006)
10. Ducasse, S., Lanza, M.: Towards a methodology for the understanding of object-oriented systems. Technique et science informatiques 20(4), 539–566 (2001)
11. Ducasse, S., Nierstrasz, O., Schärli, N., Wuyts, R., Black, A.: Traits: A mechanism for fine-grained reuse. ACM Transactions on Programming Languages and Systems 28(2), 331–388 (2006)
12. Eclipse Foundation. JavaDoc page for Interface ITypeHierarchy, http://help.eclipse.org/help32/topic/org.eclipse.jdt.doc.isv/reference/api/org/eclipse/jdt/core/ITypeHierarchy.html
13. Gabriel, R.P.: Lisp: Good news, bad news, how to win big. In: First European Conference on the Practical Applications of Lisp. Cambridge University, Cambridge (1990)

14. Gabriel, R.P., Bourbaki, N., Devin, M., Dussud, P., Gray, D.N., Sexton, H.B.: Foundations for a C++ programming environment. In: Proceeding of C++ at Work (September 1990)
15. Gamma, E.: Extension object. In: Pattern languages of program design, vol. 3, pp. 79–88. Addison-Wesley Longman Publishing Co., Inc., Boston (1997)
16. Gamma, E., Beck, K.: Contributing to Eclipse. Addison-Wesley, Reading (2003)
17. Gamma, E., Helm, R., Johnson, R., Vlissides, J.: Design Patterns: Elements of Reusable Object-Oriented Software. Addison-Wesley, Reading (1995)
18. Gamma, E., Helm, R., Vlissides, J., Johnson, R.E.: Design patterns: Abstraction and reuse of object-oriented design. In: Nierstrasz, O. (ed.) ECOOP 1993. LNCS, vol. 707, pp. 406–431. Springer, Heidelberg (1993)
19. Garlan, D.: Views for tools in integrated environments. In: Proceedings of an International Workshop on Advanced Programming Environments, pp. 314–343. Springer, London (1986)
20. Garlan, D.B.: Views for Tools in Integrated Environments. PhD thesis, Carnegie Mellon University, Pittsburgh, PA (January 1988)
21. Goldberg, A., Robson, D.: Smalltalk 80: the Language and its Implementation. Addison Wesley, Reading (1983)
22. Hanna, J.: The RAII programming idiom, http://www.hackcraft.net/raii/ (accessed January 2007)
23. Ingalls, D., Kaehler, T., Maloney, J., Wallace, S., Kay, A.: Back to the future: The story of Squeak, A practical Smalltalk written in itself. In: Proceedings OOPSLA 1997, November 1997. ACM SIGPLAN Notices, pp. 318–326. ACM Press, New York (1997)
24. Jeffries, R., Anderson, A., Hendrickson, C.: Extreme Programming Installed. Addison-Wesley, Reading (2001)
25. Kiczales, G., Hilsdale, E., Hugunin, J., Kersten, M., Palm, J., Griswold, W.G.: An overview of aspectJ. In: Knudsen, J.L. (ed.) ECOOP 2001. LNCS, vol. 2072, pp. 327–353. Springer, Heidelberg (2001)
26. Kircher, M., Jain, P.: Pattern-Oriented Software Architecture – Patterns for Resource Management, vol. 3. John Wiley and Sons, Chichester (2004)
27. Marlin, C.: Multiple views based on unparsing canonical representations — the MultiView architecture. In: Joint proceedings of the second international software architecture workshop (ISAW-2) and international workshop on multiple perspectives in software development (Viewpoints 1996), pp. 222–226. ACM Press, New York (1996)
28. Meyers, S.: Difficulties in integrating multiview development systems. IEEE Softw. 8(1), 49–57 (1991)
29. Meyers, S.: More Effective C++: 35 New Ways to Improve Your Programs and Designs. Addison-Wesley Longman Publishing Co., Inc., Boston (1995)
30. Meyers, S., Reiss, S.P.: A system for multiparadigm development of software systems. In: IWSSD 1991: Proceedings of the 6th international workshop on Software specification and design, pp. 202–209. IEEE Computer Society Press, Los Alamitos (1991)
31. Meyers, S., Reiss, S.P.: An empirical study of multiple-view software development. In: SDE 5: Proceedings of the fifth ACM SIGSOFT symposium on Software development environments, pp. 47–57. ACM Press, New York (1992)
32. Murphy-Hill, E.: Improving refactoring with alternate program views. Technical Report TR-06-05, Portland State University (May 2006), http://multiview.cs.pdx.edu/publications/rpe.pdf

33. Murray, R.B.: C++ strategies and tactics. Addison Wesley Longman Publishing Co., Inc., Redwood City (1993)
34. Eclipse platform technical overview. Object Technology International, Inc. (2003) (White paper)
35. Riehle, D., Züllighoven, H.: A pattern language for tool construction and integration based on the tools and materials metaphor. In: Pattern languages of program design, vol. 1, pp. 9–42. ACM Press/Addison-Wesley Publishing Co, New York (1995)
36. Rising, L. (ed.): Design Patterns in Communications Software. Cambridge University Press, Cambridge (2001)
37. Schärli, N.: Traits — Composing Classes from Behavioral Building Blocks. PhD thesis, University of Berne (February 2005)
38. Schärli, N., Black, A.P.: A browser for incremental programming. Technical Report CSE-03-008, OGI School of Science & Engineering, Beaverton, Oregon, USA (April 2003)
39. Schärli, N., Black, A.P.: A browser for incremental programming. Computer Languages, Systems and Structures 30, 79–95 (2004)
40. Schärli, N., Ducasse, S., Nierstrasz, O., Black, A.: Traits: Composable units of behavior. In: Cardelli, L. (ed.) ECOOP 2003. LNCS, vol. 2743, pp. 248–274. Springer, Heidelberg (2003)
41. Teitelbaum, T., Reps, T.: The Cornell program synthesizer: a syntax-directed programming environment. Commun. ACM 24(9), 563–573 (1981)
42. Vainsencher, D.: Mudpie: layers in the ball of mud. Computer Languages, Systems & Structures 30(1-2), 5–19 (2004)
43. Van De Vanter, M.L.: The documentary structure of source code. Information and Software Technology 44(13), 767–782 (2002)
44. Wuyts, R.: Star Browser, http://homepages.ulb.ac.be/~rowuyts/StarBrowser/index.html (accessed May 2007)

Batching: A Design Pattern for Efficient and Flexible Client/Server Interaction

Francisco J. Ballesteros[1], Fabio Kon[2], Marta Patiño[3], Ricardo Jiménez[3], Sergio Arévalo[1], and Roy H. Campbell[4]

[1] University Rey Juan Carlos
nemo@lsub.org
[2] University of São Paulo
kon@ime.usp.br
[3] Technical University of Madrid
[4] University of Illinois at Urbana-Champaign

Abstract. The BATCHING design pattern consists of a common piece of design and implementation that is shared by a wide variety of well-known techniques in Computing such as gather/scatter for input/output, code downloading for system extension, message batching, mobile agents, and deferred calls for disconnected operation.

All techniques mentioned above are designed for applications running across multiple domains (e.g., multiple processes or multiple nodes in a network). In these techniques, multiple operations are bundled together and then sent to a different domain, where they are executed. In some cases, the objective is to reduce the number of domain-crossings. In other cases, it is to enable dynamic server extension.

In this article, we present the BATCHING pattern, discuss the circumstances in which the pattern should and should not be used, and identify eight classes of existing techniques that instantiate it.

1   Introduction

Applications such as code downloading, message batching, gather/scatter, and mobile agents follow the client/server model of interaction. A closer look reveals that all of them group a set of operations, and submit them to a server for execution. The submission of operations aims at reducing domain-crossings and/or enable dynamic server extension. For instance, code downloading into operating system kernels intends to save domain-crossings and, at the same time, enable system extension. Message batching and mobile agents intend to save domain-crossings.

Consider a program using a file server such as the one in Figure 1. In a typical client/server interaction, the client sends a command (`read` or `write`) to the server, waits for the reply, and then continues.

Suppose that `read` and `write` are handled by the same server and that cross-domain calls (i.e., calls from the client to the server) are much heavier than calls made within the server. In this case, it will be much more efficient to send the entire `while` loop to the file server for execution.

J. Noble and R. Johnson (Eds.): TPLOP I, LNCS 5770, pp. 48–66, 2009.

```
copy (File aFile, File otherFile) {
while (aFile.read (buf))
   write (otherFile.write (buf));
}
```

Fig. 1. File copy code

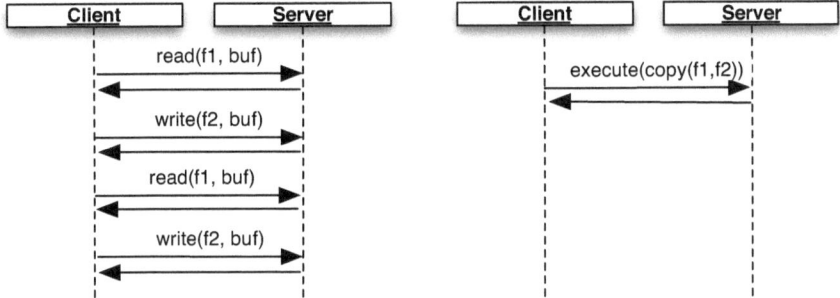

Fig. 2. Interactions corresponding to read/write services and a copy service

Instead of having multiple cross-domain calls, as depicted in the left-hand side of Figure 2, a single call suffices if the client sends the code to the server for execution, as shown in right-hand side of Figure 2. To do so, it is necessary to extend the file server to support the execution of programs submitted by different clients.

2   The Problem

Both cross-domain data traffic and cross-domain call latency have a significant impact on the efficiency of multi-domain applications. Cross-domain calls and cross-domain data transfers also happen on centralized environments. For instance, almost every operating system has a domain boundary between user space and kernel space (both entering and leaving the kernel requires a domain crossing). An application using multiple processes has a domain boundary between every two of its processes. Besides, in a distributed system, the network behaves as a domain boundary.

The line separating two different domains has to be considered while designing the application. There are two main issues causing problems to any application crossing the line: data movement and call latency.

Within a protection domain (e.g., a Unix process), an object can pass data efficiently to any other object. For passing a large amount of data, a reference can be used. However, whenever an object has to pass data to another object in a different domain, data has to be copied. Although some zero-copy networking frameworks avoid data copying within a single node in a network, data still has to be "copied" through the network in distributed applications.

In many domains, such as file systems and databases, data movement can be the major performance bottleneck. Therefore, avoiding unnecessary data transfer operations may be crucial. Under many circumstances, unnecessary data transfers occur just because the object controlling the operation resides far from the data source or sink. That is precisely what happens in the file copy example in the previous section: the client object performing the copy and the file server objects were placed in different domains. Thus, data came to the client just to go back to the server.

Another issue is call latency. A call between two objects residing in different domains takes much more time to complete than a typical method call within a single domain. The reason is simply that a domain boundary has to be crossed; that usually involves either crossing the operating system kernel interface (in a single node), network messaging (in a distributed environment), or both. Therefore, avoiding domain crossing when performing calls is crucial for performance. Any solution reducing the number of domain crossings can make the application run faster.

When designing a solution, it should be taken into account that, under certain circumstances (e.g., when *inexpensive domain crossing* is available and efficiency is the primary objective), the overhead introduced to solve the problem might actually degrade performance. However, even when cheap domain crossing is available, the overhead caused by cross-domain data transfers (e.g., copying data or sending messages over a network) might still cause a performance problem.

Any solution must take into account carefully what is the real penalty caused by data copying and call latency. Also, this solution should be employed only when the overhead it causes is small compared to the penalties it avoids.

3   The Solution

BATCHING, also known as COMPOSITECALL.

By batching separate method calls, i.e., transforming them into a single cross-domain call, one can avoid unnecessary data copying and reduce the number of cross-domain calls. Clients can build a program (a "batch call") and transfer it to the server at once. The program performs multiple operations on that server even though the client had to send it only once.

In our example (see Figure 2, the interactions for copy), if BATCHING is not used, the file content has to travel twice across the network. When a copy program is submitted to the server, however, the file does not leave the server, it is copied locally. It behaves as if we had extended the server functionality dynamically by adding support for a copy operation.

4   Pattern Structure

In the following, we present the general structure of the pattern in its more complete and sophisticated form. Specific instances of the pattern often apply simplified implementations of the pattern. In Section 4.2, we describe the application of the pattern to the file service domain.

4.1 Participants

The class hierarchy corresponding to the BATCHING pattern is shown in Figure 3.

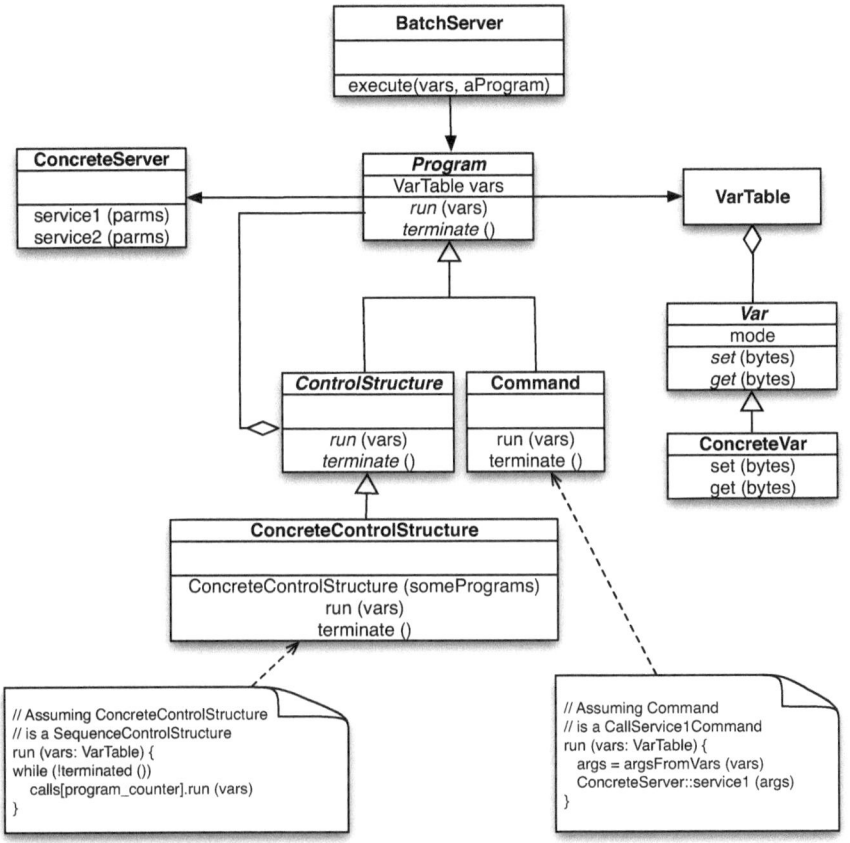

Fig. 3. BATCHING

BatchServer behaves as a FAÇADE [GHJV95] to services provided by the server. An object of this class is located on the server side. It supplies interpretative facilities to service callers, so that clients can send a program to the server side instead of making direct calls to the server. The **execute** method is an entry point to the interpreter [GHJV95], which interprets the "batch" program and returns its results to the client.

ConcreteServer is only present on the server side; it provides the set of entry points that can be called by the client.

Note that the **ConcreteServer** is actually the class (or the set of classes) one has on the server side before instantiating the pattern. It is mentioned here for completeness.

Program is an abstract class that represents the batched calls or program to be interpreted. Clients build **Program** instances and send them to the **Batch-Server** for execution. It is also responsible for maintaining an associated table of variables. The run method of a **Program** class implements the interpreter needed to run it on the server.

The **Program** is also responsible for performing proper program termination when an error occurs. The **terminate** method is provided as an abstract interface for program termination.

An alternate name for BATCHING is COMPOSITECALL since **Program** and the following couple of classes form an instance of the COMPOSITE pattern [GHJV95].

ControlStructure is a construct made of **Programs**. Its purpose is to bundle several **Programs** together according to some control structure (e.g., sequence, iteration, etc.).

ConcreteControlStructures represent structures such as conditionals, **while** constructs, **sequences**, etc. At the server side, this class is responsible for executing the concrete control structure represented by the class. **Concrete-ControlStructure** constructors can be used at the client side to build complex **Programs**.

Command is a **Program** that represents a single operation; it resembles the COMMAND pattern shown in [GHJV95], hence the name. Examples of concrete **Commands** are arithmetic operations, logic operations, or calls to **Concrete-Server** entry points. The only purpose of BATCHING is to bundle several concrete **Commands** together using **ConcreteControlStructures**.

VarTable stores the variables (i.e., the state) of the **Program**. It provides local storage and also holds any input parameter for the program. Output values from the program are also kept within the **VarTable**. The table is built at the client using the set of input parameters for the **Program**. Then, it is used within the server, while the **Program** is interpreted. The table is finally returned back to the user after completion of the **Program**.

There is a variable table per **Program** (pairs of **VarTable** and **Program** are sent together to the **BatchServer**). Thus, all components of a concrete **Program** share a single variable table so that they can share variables.

Var is an abstract class representing a variable of the program sent to the server. It has some associated storage (bytes, in Figure 3). **Var** instances are kept within a **VarTable**. Variables have a *mode*, which can be either **in** (parameter given to the **Program**), **out** (result to be given to the user), **inout** (both), or **local** (local variable). By including the **mode** qualifier, this class can be used for local variables as well as for input/output parameters.

ConcreteVar is a variable of a concrete type (integer, character, etc.). Its constructor is used at the client to declare variables or parameters to be used by the **Program**. At the server side, instances of this class are responsible for handling single, concrete pieces of data used by the program.

Note that in a concrete instance of the pattern, the **Program** (and related classes) may differ from the ones shown. That is, the core of the pattern includes **BatchServer**, **Program**, and **ConcreteServer** classes; but other classes shown here may differ depending on how the pattern is instantiated. The structure shown here is a general form for the pattern and can be directly applied to any particular implementation. However, to solve a concrete problem where the pattern applies, this structure can be modified and a `Program` class might be implemented in quite different ways depending on the particular form for the "program" sent from the client to the server. Doing so would also require changes to `BatchServer` because it must be able to process the program.

For example, all classes used by a client to build a program might be compiled to a bytecode representation of the program, to be sent to the server. In this case the `BatchServer` would be actually a bytecode interpreter. As another example, serialized forms of the program structures shown in this paper could be directly sent to the server, and `BatchServer` would simply use them after unpacking to interpret the program. More radical examples exist, such as making `Program` use a textual representation of the program and `BatchServer`, a compiler or

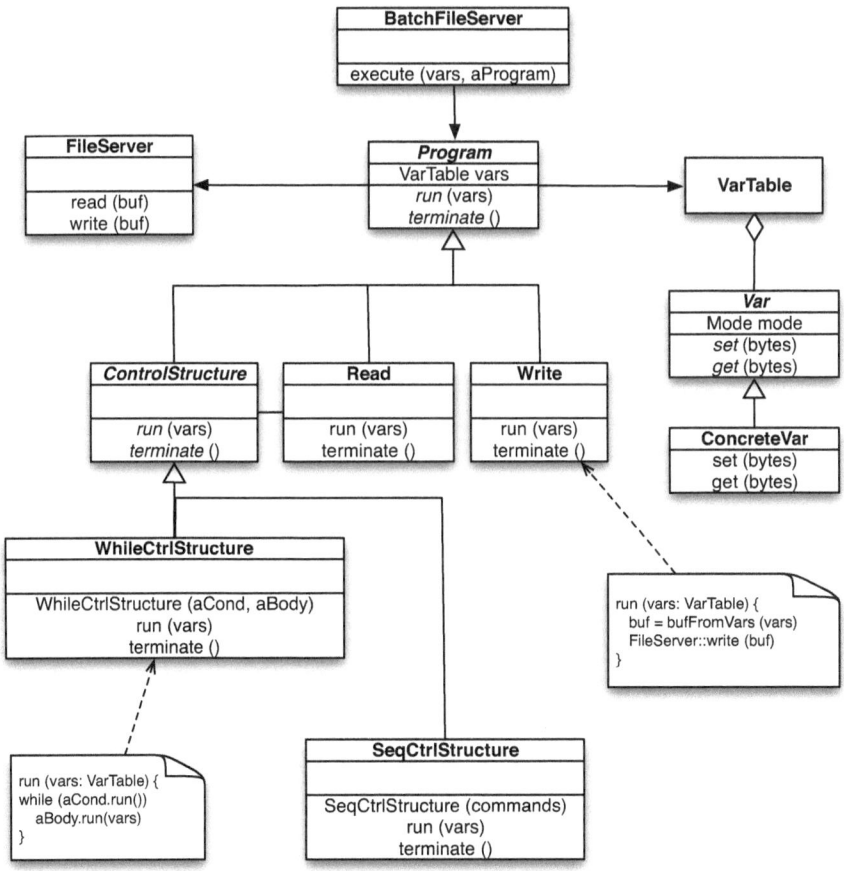

Fig. 4. BATCHING File server

interpreter for such "source"; or yet making `Program` use a binary representation of the program and implementing `BatchServer` simply as a call to the binary code received from the client.

All this said, in general, the structure shown for the pattern suffices and works well to solve the problem addressed by this pattern. In what follows, we use it in all our examples, but one should be aware that there are other useful variants of the pattern that use other forms of programs.

4.2   The Pattern Applied to a File Server

The concrete structure of classes for our file server example is shown in Figure 4. Intuitively, this BATCHING instance simply adds an interpreter (see the INTERPRETER pattern in [GHJV95]) to the file server. That interpreter can execute programs that (1) call `read` and `write` and (2) can use `while` as a control structure.

We took as a starting point the `FileServer` class, which provides both `read` and `write` methods that operate on a file. We simplified the typical interface provided by a file server; a typical file server would contain several `File` objects that would supply `read` and `write` methods. To illustrate the pattern in a simple way, we omitted the file being used[1].

The `BatchFileServer` is co-located with the `FileServer`, providing a new `execute` service that supplies an interpreted version of `FileServer` services. The `BatchFileServer` corresponds to the `BatchServer` in the pattern (see the pattern diagram in Figure 3).

The `BatchFileServer` accepts a `Program`, which is built in terms of `Control-Structures` and `Read` and `Write` commands.

To execute

```
while (read (buf))
    write (buf);
```

the `Program` sent to the `BatchFileServer` must be made of a `WhileCtrlStructure`, using a `Read` as the condition. The body for the `WhileCtrlStructure` must be a sequence made of a single `Write` command.

Here, `WhileCtrlStructure` and `SeqCtrlStructure` correspond to `Concrete-ControlStructures` in the pattern. `Read` and `Write` match `Commands` in the pattern. The buffer used in the read and write operations is handled by a `BufferVar` class instance, corresponding to a `ConcreteVar` in the pattern.

A client can build a program (accessing the file server) by using constructors provided by `WhileCtrlStructure`, `SeqCtrlStructure`, `Read`, and `Write`. The client can later submit this batched call to the `BatchFileServer execute` method.

---

[1] Obtaining a complete implementation is a matter of adding a `File` class and adding `file` parameters to the `read` and `write` methods.

5   Dynamics

The client builds a program (a "script" of commands) and sends it to the server, which interprets it. When the server receives a program, it first deserializes it. The interaction that follows is shown in Figure 5.

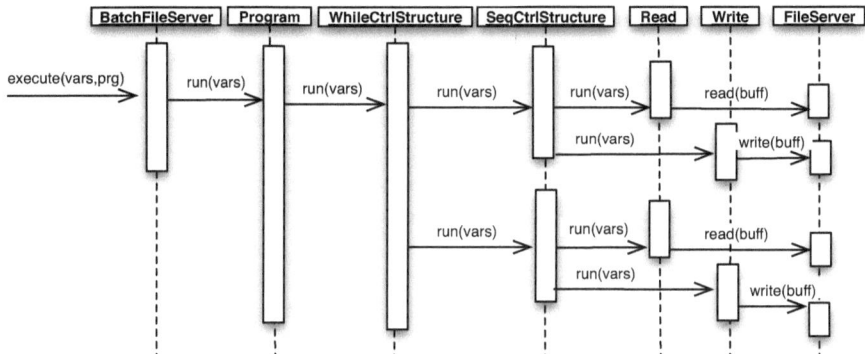

Fig. 5. Interaction diagram for a copy program

A BatchFileServer object at the server side is in charge of interpreting client programs. When its execute method is called, a program and a table of variables must be supplied. The execute method calls the run method of the program providing the table of variables; this method interprets the "batch" program. Once execute finishes, the results are returned.

The actual dynamics resulting from executing the "batch" program depends on the actual form used for the program. In our suggested form, the run method of the Program class implements recursive interpretation. When the program has been interpreted, that is, the run method has finished, the results of the program execution are still in the variable table. As part of the execute method, the table is serialized and sent back to the client.

Figure 5 shows the interaction diagram for our example copy batch program (with calls to Open and Close suppressed for the sake of simplicity). The run method of the Program calls the run method of the ConcreteControlStructure representing the program (the WhileCtrlStructure in the interaction diagram). ControlStructures provide a run method to interpret themselves. That is, a program has built-in its own interpreter, an instance of the INTERPRETER pattern [GHJV95]. So, the While command calls the run method of its inner component (SeqCtrlStructure in the interaction diagram for copy).

6   Implementation Issues

We now discuss two important aspects of using BATCHING: how to build programs for BATCHING and what to do when they fail.

6.1   Composing Programs

How to build a program depends on the structure used for it. As an example, we use in this section the form suggested for programs in the previous description of the pattern. Readers should be aware, however, that other forms of implementing the pattern do exist.

Programs are made of statements and variables. In a BATCHING Program, each statement corresponds to a ConcreteControlStructure or concrete Command. Variables are instances of a ConcreteVar class. To build a program, clients declare an object of the Program class and invoke its constructor method.

Ideally, the client side for an instance of BATCHING would be exactly like the code of a client making direct calls to the server; i.e., like a client not using BATCHING at all. In practice, ConcreteControlStructure constructors (which are functions) are used. Thus, code in the client for a Program looks like the code that the user would write without using the pattern. Command objects are not declared; they are built with functional constructors.

To support the usage of expressions within the Program, subclasses inheriting from an Expr class can be provided (see Figure 6). Expr is a functional service representing an expression, and can be used as a function within expressions.

Program variables are stored in a table. They contain initial values as well as intermediate values and results of the program execution at the server side. To build that table, the programmer of the client must declare an object of the VarTable class. When variable objects are instantiated, they are constructed and stored in that table with an initial value, if any, and their mode, that is, in, out, inout, or local. When a variable table is sent to the server, only values of in and inout variables have to be copied to the server. After the execution of

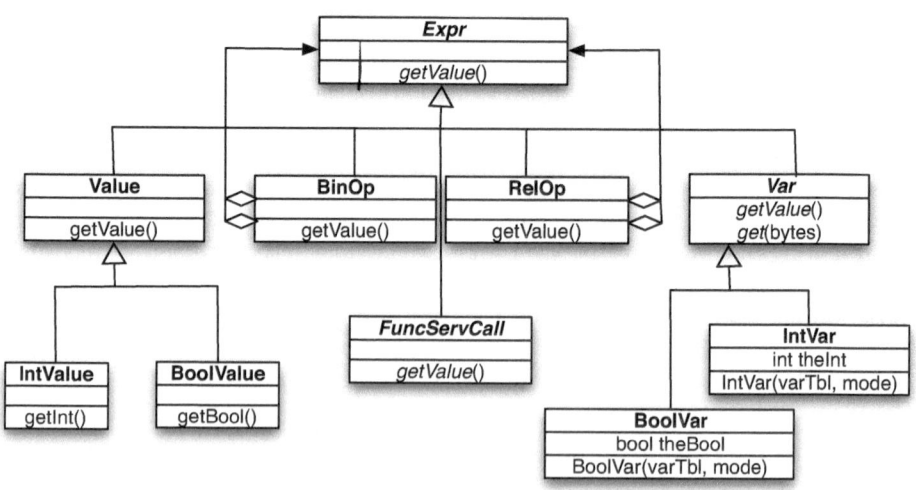

Fig. 6. Expression Hierarchy

the program, out and inout variables are sent back to the client. Variables on the table can be consulted and modified on both sides.

The adequacy of the table implementation depends on the context of the pattern instance. For example, it can be interesting in an operating system to implement the table as a chunk of raw memory, while a remote server could represent it as a heterogeneous list of concrete variables.

This kind of implementation of BATCHING programs has the advantage that most of type-checking is done at compilation time. Note that server calls are type-checked, because the parameters of constructors of server call commands are typed. In a different context, however, a system designer may opt for a different implementation, for example, based on dynamic typing.

Revisiting our example, the code for the copy program is shown in Figure 7. In the figure, constructors are functions that build objects within the program. In this example, SeqCtrlStructure and WhileCtrlStructure are Concrete-ControlStructures of the language. Open, Close, Read, and Write are classes derived from Program. Clients invoke their constructors to let the Program issue calls into the server. Program variables are stored in the vars variable table. In this case, f1, f2 and car are local variables, so their mode is local.

Finally, note that the concrete instruction set used through this section is just an example. Any other one, like a bytecode-based program could be used, too. Instruction sets suggested in the pattern are very simple compared to the ones used in other systems. For instance, μChoices [LTS+96] and Aglets [PPE97] use a Java interpreter. A Modula-3 compiler is used in SPIN [BSP+95], and NetPebbles [MPZ+98] uses a script interpreter.

When implementing the pattern, the design of the instruction set and its interpreter is one of the most important things the designer should keep in mind. The quality of the implementation depends heavily on the instruction set and interpreter being well-balanced and secure.

```
VarTable vars;
Program program;
IntVar f1(vars, local), f2 (vars, local);
CharVar car (vars, local);

program = SeqCtrlStructure ((
        Open (f1, StringLit ("name1")),
        Open (f2, StringLit ("name2")),
        WhileCtrlStructure (Read (f1, car),
            Write (f2, car)),
        Close (f1),
        Close (f2)
        ));
execute (program, vars);
```

Fig. 7. Program for Copy

6.2 Exception Handling

One of the problems of submitting the client code to the server is what happens when a call fails. The server programmer knows when a server call has failed, so he or she can decide to terminate the program in that case. This can be done by calling the **terminate** method of the **Program** class from a **run** method. However, the client could wish to continue the program despite any failures. To support this, we have included two commands in our pattern instances: **AbortOnError** and **DoNotAbortOnError**. They let the user switch between the two modes. When **AbortOnError** has been called, a call to **terminate** causes program termination; otherwise it has no effect. In this way, the client can control the effects of a failed call.

The implementation of **terminate** depends on both the kind of instruction set being implemented and on the implementation language. A bytecode-based program can be stopped very easily as there is a main control loop (in the **run** method), just by setting a **terminated** flag to true. Stopping a structured program (e.g., the one used in our file server example) is a little more complicated. This is due to recursive interpretation: calls to **run** in a **Program** propagate calls to the **run** method of its components. To stop that program, it is necessary to finish all the nested **run** calls. Depending on the implementation language, it can be done in one way or another. In a language with exceptions, such as C++, Java or Python, it suffices to raise and propagate an exception in the **terminate** code, catching it in the **Program run** code. In languages without exceptions, such as C, **setjmp** can be used in the top-level **run** method before calling any other **run**, and **longjmp** can be used, for the same purpose, in the **terminate** body.

7 Consequences

The pattern brings the following **benefits**:

1. *It provides a virtual machine view of the server.* When using BATCHING, clients no longer perceive servers as a separate set of entry points. Servers are now perceived as *virtual machines* [Nai05]. Their instruction set is made of the set of server entry points, together with some general-purpose control language.

   Therefore, it is feasible for users to reuse programs for different BATCHING calls. Programs that interact with the server can be built, and reused later.

2. *It reduces protection-domain crossings*, as the **copy** program did above. If this is the main motivation to use the pattern, domain crossing (client/server invocation) time must be carefully measured. Whenever complex control structures are mixed with calls to the server, or when client computations need to be done between successive calls, the pattern might not pay.

   In any case, the time used to build the program must be lower than the time saved in domain crossing. The latter is approximately the difference between the time to perform a cross-domain call and the time to interpret and dispatch a server call.

3. *It reduces the number of messages* exchanged by clients and servers; provided that the `Program` issues repeated calls to the server and the control structure is simple enough.

   Again, the improvement due to the reduced number of messages can be lower than the overhead due to program construction and interpretation. Therefore, careful measurement must be done prior to pattern adoption.

4. *It decouples client/server interaction from the call mechanism.* BATCHING provides a level of indirection between the client and the server. The client can perform a call by adding commands to a `Program`; while the `Program` can be transmitted to the server by a means unknown to the client.

5. *It decouples client calls from server method invocations.* As said before, a client can perform calls by adding commands to a `Program`. The resulting `Program` can be sent to the server at a different time. Therefore, there is no need for the client and the server to synchronize for the call to be made.

6. *It enables dynamic extension of servers.* Servers can be extended by accepting `Programs` from clients. Those programs could be kept within the server and used as additional entry points into the server. Should it be the main motivation to use the pattern, the concrete command set should be powerful enough.

7. *It makes the communication more secure* because one can encrypt the complete sequence of commands in a single session, with a single signature. Many attack techniques rely on having a large quantity of messages to work with. Having a single message exchanged between the client and the server prevents variants of man-in-the-middle, replay, or other attacks [GSS03] that would operate on individual commands if multiple messages were exchanged within a client/server communication session.

The pattern brings the following **drawbacks**:

1. *Client requests might take arbitrary time* to complete. A batched program might lead to a nonterminating program. If server correctness depends on bounded client requests, it may fail. As an example, a server can use a single thread of control to service all client requests. Should a `Program` not terminate, the entire server would be effectively switched off by a single client.

   In such case, either avoid using BATCHING, or implement `BatchServer` with support for multithreading. That is, arrange for each `Program` to use its own thread. In this case, make sure the instruction set is thread-safe, otherwise programmers will need to rely on locking to protect critical, shared resources.

2. *Server security can be compromised.* The more complex the command set, the more likely the server integrity can be compromised due to bugs in the command interpreter. If *high* security is an issue, either avoid BATCHING or reduce the complexity of the command set to the bare minimum.

   On the other hand, note that the pattern does not add functionality to the server. It simply enables the use of existing functionality in a "batch". Any server must always check its inputs (from clients) and these checks must still be performed when the individual calls come from the pattern interpreter.

3. *It might slow down the application.* When cheap domain crossing is available and efficiency is the primary objective, using BATCHING might slowdown the application if the time saved on domain crossings is not enough to compensate for the overhead introduced by BATCHING.

4. *Clients might become more complex* because they must build the program to be sent, instead of simply issuing the calls to the server when they are needed.

8   Related Patterns

Both `Program` and `ControlStructure` rely on instances of the INTERPRETER pattern [GHJV95]. Indeed, the interpreter of a `Program` is behind its run method.

`Program`, `ControlStructure`, and `Commands` make up an instance of the COMPOSITE pattern [GHJV95]. Composite programs, such as `Sequence` and `Conditional`, are aggregates of `Assignments`, `ServerCalls`, and other primitive commands.

If an instruction set for a BATCHING language is to be compiled, `Program` might include a method to compile itself into a low-level instruction set. Moreover, `Programs` should be serialized (and later deserialized) when transmitted to the server. Once in the server, they can be verified for correctness. All these tasks can be implemented following the VISITOR pattern [GHJV95].

A server call issued within a `Program` might fail or trigger an exception. If that is the case, the entire `Program` can be aborted and program state transmitted back to the client—so that the client could fix the cause of the error and resume `Program` execution. The MEMENTO pattern [GHJV95] can encapsulate the program state while in a "frozen" state. As said before, such program state can be used to resume the execution of a failed program (e.g., after handling an exception). MEMENTOs can also be helpful for (de)serializing the program during transmission to the server.

As a program can lead to an endless client request, single threaded or a-request-at-a-time servers can get into trouble. To accommodate this kind of server so that BATCHING could be used, the ACTIVEOBJECT [LS95] and the RENDEZVOUS [JPPMA99] patterns can be used.

COMPOSITEMESSAGES can be used to transfer the `Program` from the client to the server. The COMPOSITEMESSAGES pattern [SC95] applies when different components must exchange messages to perform a given task. It groups several messages in a structured fashion, doing with messages what BATCHING does with server entry-points. In that way, extra latency due to message delivery can be avoided and components are decoupled from the transmission medium. The main difference is that BATCHING is targeted at the invocation of concrete server-provided services, not at packaging data structures to be exchanged.

COMPOSEDCOMMAND [Tid98] is similar to BATCHING in that it bundles several operations into a single one. However, BATCHING is more generic in spirit.

ADAPTIVE OBJECT-MODELS [YJ02] is an architectural style in which the users' object model is interpreted at runtime and can be changed with immediate effects on the system interpreting it. It is normally seen in advanced commercial systems in which business rules are stored in places such as databases or XML files. Although its implementation might resemble the BATCHING pattern, its major goal is to provide more flexibility and enable runtime reconfiguration of business rules and not to improve the performance.

9   Known Uses

Our experience with BATCHING started when we noticed that a single piece of design had been used to build systems we already knew well. Then we tried to abstract the core of those systems, extracting the pattern. Once we identified the pattern, we tried to find some new systems where it could be applied to obtain some benefit. We did so [BJP+00] and obtained substantial performance improvements.

For us, this pattern has been a process where we first learned some "theory" from existing systems and then applied what we learned back to "practice." In this section, we show how existing systems match the pattern described in the previous sections—certainly, this will lead to a better understanding of the pattern, as happened in our case. We also include a brief overview of the two systems where we applied the pattern ourselves with *a priori* knowledge of the pattern.

Note that the BATCHING design lets a single implementation of the pattern handle the various applications described below. As the activity carried out at the server is specified every time a **Program** runs, the same BATCHING implementation could perfectly handle most of the applications shown below. Nevertheless, existing systems, built without *a priori* knowledge of the pattern, hardly share the common code needed to implement all these applications (e.g., gather/scatter is always implemented separately from message batching facilities, when both are provided.)

Operating System extensions by downloading code into the kernel (as performed in SPIN [BSP+95], μChoices [LTS+96], and Linux [Hen06]) can be considered to be an instance of this pattern. These systems use code downloading as the means to extend system functionality. The mechanism employed is based on defining new programs, which are expressed in terms of existing services.

In this case the **Program** is the extension performed, the set of **Concrete-ControlStructures** depends on the extension language, and the **run** method is implemented either by delegation to the extension interpreter or by the native processor (when binary code is downloaded into the system.)

Agents. An agent is a piece of autonomous code that can be sent to a different domain. Agents may move from one domain to another, carrying its runtime state [BR05]. The aim is to avoid multiple domain crossings (or network messages), improving performance, and support disconnection from the agent home environment.

Programs built using BATCHING are meant to stay at the server until termination, and they possess no **go**[2] statement. However, BATCHING already includes most of the machinery needed to implement an agent system; a **go** statement could be provided by the command language itself. Nevertheless, even within the mobile agent paradigm, a very common situation is to have a single-hop agent that leaves a client, visits a single server and return to the client, as is the case with BATCHING.

Gather/Scatter I/O. In gather/scatter I/O a list of input or output descriptors is sent to an I/O device in a single operation. Each descriptor specifies a piece of data going to (or coming from) the device. Written data is gathered from separate output buffers. Read data is scattered across separate input buffers. Its major goal is to save data copies.

In this case, the program is just the descriptor list, where each descriptor can be supported by a `Command`. The program `run` method iterates through the descriptor (i.e., command) list and performs the requested I/O operations. The services (i.e., commands) are simply `Read` and `Write`.

Note that, by using this pattern, gather/scatter I/O could be generalized so that the I/O device involved would not necessarily be the same for all descriptors sent by the user. Moreover, multiple `Read` and `Write` operations could be bundled into a single one.

Message batching. Grouping a sequence of messages into a single low-level protocol data unit is yet another instance of the pattern. In this case, the `run` method (i.e., the interpreter) is the packet *disassembler*. A program is a bunch of packets bundled together. Each packet, or each packet header, is a command that is interpreted by the packet *disassembler*. This is the BATCHING application that more closely resembles COMPOSEDCOMMAND [Tid98].

Deferred calls. BATCHING can be used to support disconnected operation [MRM06]. Clients build programs while they perform operations on non-reachable servers whenever they are in a disconnected state. Upon reconnection, each program is finally submitted to the target domain for interpretation. Note that *several* clients might add code to a *single* program to be sent to the server later on.

Each operation is a `Command`, the list of operations sent to a server is a `Program`. The interpreter could be either:
1. the piece of code sending each command when the client is reconnected to the server, or
2. an actual `Program` interpreter in the server domain, accepting just a list of commands (a program)—to save network traffic.

Futures or Promises [LS88] can be used by client code to synchronize with server responses.

Improving latency in Operating Systems. Many user programs happen to exhibit very simple system call patterns. This is an opportunity for using

---

[2] The **go** instruction is typical on Agent systems and is meant to trigger the migration of an agent to a different location.

BATCHING to save domain crossings and, therefore, execution time. As a matter of fact, we have done so by instantiating BATCHING for two systems: Linux and *Off*++ [BHK+99]. In both systems, we obtained around 25% speedups for a `copy` program written with BATCHING [BJP+00].

We implemented two new domain-specific languages (i.e., `ControlStructures` and `Command` sets) that let users bundle separate calls into a single one, like in the `copy` example of Section 1. The first language we implemented was based on bytecodes. We included just those commands needed to code loops, conditional branches, and basic arithmetic. This language was used both on Linux and *Off*++. The second language we implemented was a high-level one, designed specifically for *Off*++. It includes just the commands needed to `Repeat` a given operation `n` times and to perform a `Sequence` of operations [BJP+00].

Heterogeneous resource allocation. Most operating systems are structured as a set of resource unit providers. Separate servers provide resource unit allocation for different types of resources. In these systems, users issue multiple requests at a time.

BATCHING can be used to request allocation of multiple heterogeneous resources in a single system call. *Off*++ is an operating system modeled as a set of hardware resource unit providers and it uses BATCHING in this way to improve the performance of its applications [BJP+00].

Transaction processing. A transaction is a set of operations executed atomically in isolation [Gra78]. A given transaction can either terminate normally, by committing, or abnormally, by aborting. Should a transaction abort, its effects must be undone; otherwise (i.e., when it commits), its results should be made permanent.

Commits typically involve multiple disk writes for different data items. Writes must follow a carefully chosen order to preserve the consistency of results, even when failures occur. One of the strategies uses a `redo` algorithm [BHG87]. Such algorithm does not modify the persistent data until the transaction is completed, it works on a volatile copy of the data until the commit is performed. At commit time, a sequence of *redo records* is written into a disk log, followed by a commit record. Redo records contain new values for objects changed by the transaction. Finally, persistent state for objects involved is updated. If the system fails before the write of the commit record, the transaction is aborted and their redo records are ignored. If the system fails after writing the commit record, redo records are replayed.

Another instance of BATCHING is *group commit* [DKO+84], used to avoid the latency of forced disk writes of log records in each commit. In group commit, instead of forcing the log with each commit, a set of consecutive commits are batched. Then, a single forced disk write is performed to write all the log records associated with all the commits, amortizing the latency of forced disk writes across several commits. This results in a substantial improvement in throughput for commits.

BATCHING can be used both to implement commit and for crash recovery. Performance of transactional distributed object systems (e.g., Arjuna [SDP91]) could be improved due to the reduced number of domain crossings.

10   Variant

A widely-used variant of this pattern is the CLIENT-SIDE BATCHING pattern. In this case, instead of the client sending batched code to be executed in the server, it is the server that sends code to be executed in the client.

The CLIENT-SIDE BATCHING pattern is frequently used on the Web where the inter-domain communication latency is normally very large. Known uses include Java applets [Boe02], Javascript functions embedded in Web pages [Fla02], and Macromedia Flash applications [Abe02].

In both BATCHING and CLIENT-SIDE BATCHING, the goal is to improve the response time of the system as perceived by the client and, in both cases, this is achieved by avoiding multiple cross-domain calls. The difference is where the batched program is executed, in the client or in the server.

11   Conclusions

BATCHING unifies several, apparently unrelated, techniques. Most notably, the pattern integrates techniques to (1) reduce domain crossings and (2) avoid unnecessary data copying. Encapsulation of the command language has been a key feature in the integration of existing techniques, decoupling the command set from the submission method.

We showed eight different applications where the BATCHING pattern was previously used and cases where the pattern was applied with *a-priori* knowledge of it. A client-side variant of the pattern is also implemented by different technologies and is widely-used on current Web systems.

Acknowledgments

We are sincerely grateful for the help provided by our shepherd, Frank Buschmann, and for the valuable feedback provided by John Vlissides, who suggested the new name for this pattern (it was previously called COMPOSITECALL). Finally, we are also grateful to the anonymous TPLoP reviewers and to the members of the "Allerton Patterns Project" group of PLoP'99 for their comments and suggestions.

References

[Abe02]   Aberdeen Group: Flash Remoting MX: A Responsive Client-Server Architecture for the Web. Technical report, Macromedia White paper (December 2002)
[BHG87]   Bernstein, P.A., Hadzilacos, V., Goodman, N.: Concurrency Control and Recovery in Database Systems. Addison-Wesley, Reading (1987)

[BHK+99]   Ballesteros, F.J., Hess, C., Kon, F., Arévalo, S., Campbell, R.H.: Object
             Orientation in Off++ - A Distributed Adaptable μKernel. In: Proceed-
             ings of the ECOOP 1999 Workshop on Object Orientation and Operating
             Systems, pp. 49–53 (1999)
[BJP+00]   Ballesteros, F.J., Jimenez, R., Patino, M., Kon, F., Arévalo, S., Campbell,
             R.H.: Using Interpreted CompositeCalls to Improve Operating System
             Services. Software: Practice and Experience 30(6), 589–615 (2000)
[Boe02]   Boese, E.S.: Java Applets: Interactive Programming, 2nd edn. Lulu.com
             (2002)
[BR05]   Braun, P., Rossak, W.: Mobile Agents: Basic Concepts, Mobility Models,
             and the Tracy Toolkit. Elsevier, Amsterdam (2005)
[BSP+95]   Bershad, B.N., Savage, S., Pardyak, P., Sirer, E.G., Fiuczynski, M.,
             Becker, D., Eggers, S., Chambers, C.: Extensibility, safety and perfor-
             mance in the SPIN operating system. In: Proceedings of the Fifteenth
             ACM Symposium on Operating Systems Principles, December 1995,
             ACM, New York (1995)
[DKO+84]   DeWitt, D.J., Katz, R.H., Olken, F., Shapiro, L.D., Stonebraker, M.R.,
             Wood, D.: Implementation techniques for main memory database systems.
             In: Proceedings of the ACM International Conference on Management of
             Data (SIGMOD), pp. 1–8 (1984)
[Fla02]   Flanagan, D.: JavaScript: the definitive guide. O'Reilly, Sebastopol (2002)
[GHJV95]   Gamma, E., Helm, R., Johnson, R., Vlissides, J.: Design Patterns. Ele-
             ments of Object-Oriented Software. Addison-Wesley, Reading (1995)
[Gra78]   Gray, J.: Operating Systems: An Advanced Course. Springer, Heidelberg
             (1978)
[GSS03]   Garfinkel, S., Spafford, G., Schwartz, A.: Practical UNIX and Internet
             Security. O'Reilly, Sebastopol (2003)
[Hen06]   Henderson, B.: Linux Loadable Kernel Module HOWTO. Technical re-
             port, Linux Documentation Project (September 2006)
[JPPMA99]   Jiménez-Peris, R., Patiño-Martínez, M., Arévalo, S.: Multithreaded Ren-
             dezvous: A Design Pattern for Distributed Rendezvous. In: Proc. of ACM
             Symposium on Applied Computing, February 1999, ACM Press, New York
             (1999)
[LS88]   Liskov, B., Shrira, L.: Promises: Linguistic Support for Efficient Asyn-
             chronous Procedure Calls in Distributed Systems. In: Proc. of ACM
             Conf. on Programming Language Design and Implementation, pp. 260–
             267 (1988)
[LS95]   Lavender, R.G., Schmidt, D.C.: Active object – an object behavioral pat-
             tern for concurrent programming. In: Proceedings of the Second Pattern
             Languages of Programs conference (PLoP), Monticello, Illinois (Septem-
             ber 1995)
[LTS+96]   Li, Y., Tan, S.M., Sefika, M., Campbell, R.H., Liao, W.S.: Dynamic Cus-
             tomization in the μChoices Operating System. In: Proceedings of Reflec-
             tion 1996, San Francisco (April 1996)
[MPZ+98]   Mohindra, A., Purakayastha, A., Zukowski, D., Devarakonda, M.: Pro-
             gramming Network Components Using NetPebbles: An Early Report. In:
             Proceedings of the 4th USENIX Conference on Object-Oriented Technolo-
             gies and Systems, Santa Fe, New Mexico (April 1998)

[MRM06]   Mikic-Rakic, M., Medvidovic, N.: A Classification of Disconnected Oper-
            ation Techniques. In: Proceeding of 32nd EUROMICRO Conference on
            Software Engineering and Advanced Applications (EUROMICRO 2006),
            pp. 144–151. IEEE Computer Society, Los Alamitos (2006)
[Nai05]   Nair, R.: Virtual Machines: Versatile Platforms for Systems and Processes.
            Morgan Kaufmann, San Francisco (2005)
[PPE97]   Clements, P.E., Papaioannou, T., Edwards, J.: Aglets: Enabling the Vir-
            tual Enterprise. In: Proc. of the Managing Enterprises - Stakeholders, En-
            gineering, Logistics and Achievement Intl. Conference (ME-SELA 1997),
            Loughborough University, UK (1997)
[SC95]   Sane, A., Campbell, R.: Composite Messages: A Structural Pattern for
            Communication between Components. In: OOPSLA 1995 workshop on
            design patterns for concurrent, parallel, and distributed object-oriented
            systems (1995)
[SDP91]   Shrivastava, S.K., Dixon, G.N., Parrington, G.D.: An Overview of Ar-
            juna: A Programming System for Reliable Distributed Computing. IEEE
            Software 8(1), 63–73 (1991)
[Tid98]   Tidwell, J.: Interaction Design Patterns. In: Proceedings of the Confer-
            ence on Pattern Languages of Programs (PLoP 1998), Monticello, Illinois
            (1998)
[YJ02]   Yoder, J.W., Johnson, R.: The Adaptive Object Model Architectural
            Style. In: Proceeding of The Working IEEE/IFIP Conference on Soft-
            ware Architecture 2002 (WICSA3 2002). Kluwer Academic Publishers,
            Dordrecht (2002)

Design Patterns for Graceful Degradation

Titos Saridakis

Nokia Corporation, P.O. Box 226, FIN-00045, Finland
titos.saridakis@nokia.com

Abstract. Graceful degradation describes the smooth change of some
distinct system feature to a lower state as a response to an event that
prevents the system from exhibiting that feature in its full state. Such
system behavior has appeared in a variety of domains from image processing and telecommunications to shared memory multiprocessors and
multi-modular memory systems. In each domain, graceful degradation
has targeted a different system feature, e.g. image quality, voice quality, computational capacity, memory access throughput, etc. However,
irrespectively of the system feature that has been gracefully degraded,
the basic concepts behind the mechanisms responsible for this behavior
have been similar. This paper presents a design pattern that captures
the general idea behind graceful degradation, plus three more patterns
that describe how to smoothly reach a lower system state under different
circumstances.

1 Introduction

All hardware and software systems may experience various unsolicited events
during their execution. Such unsolicited events that lead a system, or part of it,
to failure are called *errors*. To deal with errors various fault tolerance techniques
have been devised, ranging from preventing an error from causing damage to its
environment by halting the system, to restoring an error-free state and continuing the system execution. Many of the techniques that restore an error-free state
and allow the system to continue its execution are using some form of redundancy, e.g. replicas of hosts, disks, memory units, network links, data records,
services, processes, and software components. Fault tolerance techniques like active replication, hot/cold stand-by and passive replication, use these replicas to
recover from errors and restore an error-free full system state. On the other hand,
there are techniques that allow a system to survive errors without using such
repliceas. This is achieved by removing the system part damaged by the error
and allowing the unaffected part to continue execution.

The smooth change of some distinct system feature to a lower state as a response to errors is called *graceful degradation*, and it has been used in a number
of domains to allow systems to survive errors by removing their damaged parts.
The system feature that degrades ranges from the content quality in image processing [4,7,10] and in telecommunications [22], to the system performance in
shared memory multiprocessors [15,20], multi-modular memory systems [5,6,11]

J. Noble and R. Johnson (Eds.): TPLOP I, LNCS 5770, pp. 67–93, 2009.

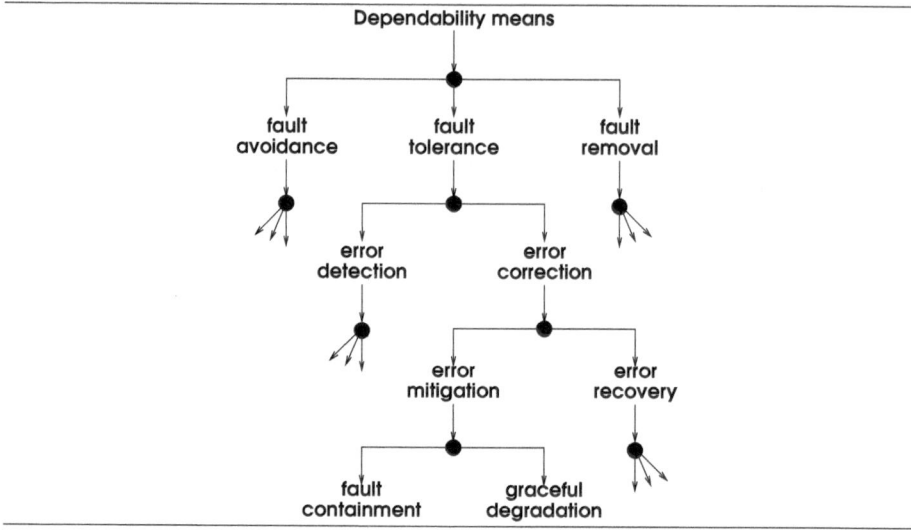

Fig. 1. Graceful degradation in the classification of fault tolerance techniques

and RAID systems [3], and to the delivered system functionality in distributed agreement protocols [12], systems specified using formal methods [9,21] and component-based software [16,18]. The Appendix contains a summary of the different domains where graceful degradation has been applied. As depicted in Figure 1, graceful degradation complements the fault containment techniques in error mitigation, a broad category of fault tolerance techniques that aims at reducing the impact of errors in a system execution.

To exemplify graceful degradation, let's consider the example of a simplified window manager $\mathcal{WM}$, which is responsible for drawing on a computer screen the graphical containers of application UIs, command shells, etc. In addition to the basic window management functionality (i.e. creating, moving, re-sizing, minimizing, restoring, maximizing, and destroying windows) $\mathcal{WM}$ also provides graphical functionality such as 3D shadows around the windows, cursor animation, frames that surround windows, and a menu-bar at the top-part of the window frame. $\mathcal{WM}$ is composed from a set of software components, each responsible for a different such graphical functionality. An error may cause the 3D shadowing component, or any other constituent component of $\mathcal{WM}$, to fail. Without a fault tolerant mechanism that could fix the damage (e.g. by instantiating a new 3D component), this error strips $\mathcal{WM}$ from the capability of drawing window shadows on the screen. But rather than behaving arbitrarily or just halting, $\mathcal{WM}$ can continue delivering the rest of its designated functionality except from the 3D shadows. As long as $\mathcal{WM}$ is able to convey the user input at each window to the corresponding application and the output of that application back to the corresponding window, the system may continue its execution. Thus, $\mathcal{WM}$ can survive such errors by removing the damaged components and gracefully degrading the functionality it provides to its users.

This paper presents four design patterns for graceful degradation. First, an overview of the system domain where graceful degradation applies presents the common characteristics and parameters of patterns presented later. Following that, the GRACEFUL DEGRADATION pattern captures the general idea behind smoothly reaching a lower system state after an error. Then, the OPTIMISTIC DEGRADATION pattern describes how to reach a lower state by removing the smallest part of the system that has been immediately affected by an error, under the optimistic assumption that no other parts of the system are affected by the error. The PESSIMISTIC DEGRADATION pattern describes how to reach a lower state by removing a group of adjacent system constituents to the one suffered the error, under the pessimistic assumption that they are also affected by the error. Finally, the CAUSAL DEGRADATION pattern captures the technique that identifies the constituents of the system that may experience errors causally related to a detected error and removes them in order to survive those errors.

2   Overview

Before describing the graceful degradation patterns, it is worthwhile presenting an overview of the system domain where these apply. This provides a better understanding about the invariants and the forces that relate to graceful degradation patterns, and allows a more compact and clear presentation of the individual patterns. The starting point of this overview is the definition of graceful degradation: *a smooth change of some distinct system feature to a lower state as a response to errors.* By analyzing this definition, one can deduce the following characteristics of the system domain to which graceful degradation can be applied:

- *"smooth change"* implies that the runtime cost of state transitions is acceptable, i.e. it does not violate the runtime behavior specification of the system.
- *"distinct features"* implies that the system is modular and consists of a number of distinct features, e.g. memory capacity, storage capacity, number of certain type of errors that it can mask, set of services it offers, etc.
- *"lower state"* implies that a system feature has different admissible states besides its full stage, e.g. the system can meaningfully continue its execution with smaller memory or storage capacity, lesser number of errors that can be masked, fewer services that it can offer, etc.
- *"response to errors"* implies that the system has error detection capabilities which allow it to realize the occurrence of errors.

In addition to these characteristics of the system domain where graceful degradation applies, there is a number of parameters that describe the system behavior during graceful degradation. The values that these parameters may take determine the variant of the graceful degradation that can be applied. These parameters include:

- The time cost of calculating a new, lower state for some system feature. This cost has two facets: the development-time cost needed to introduce into the system the knowledge about the admissible lower states of its various features, and the runtime cost of identifying a lower state after an error.

- The time cost of bringing some system feature to a new state. This cost too has two facets: the development-time cost associated to the development of the mechanism that loads new states to system features (which can potentially be a different mechanism for each system feature), and the runtime cost of loading the new state.
- The type of dependencies (strong or weak), which reflect the architectural ties among the system constituents and roughly correspond to mandatory and optional links among them [16]. For example, when a component X *requires* component Y this reflects a strong dependency; when a component X *uses* component Y this reflects a weak dependency. Strong dependencies propagate errors while weak dependencies do not.

The characteristics of the system domain discussed above describe the context of GRACEFUL DEGRADATION pattern (section 3), which captures the general idea of graceful degradation techniques. The combinations of values assigned to the above parameters of system behavior describe refinements of this pattern that apply to systems of different nature. For systems that have low time costs for calculating and loading a lower state of a feature after an error and have weak dependencies among adjacent system constituents, OPTIMISTIC DEGRADATION (section 4) fits best. Systems that have mostly strong dependencies among their constituents, hence an error in a constituent has high probability of causing failures in adjacent ones, can benefit most from PESSIMISTIC DEGRADATION (section 5). Finally, for systems that require minimum lowering of the corresponding state and have a clear distinction between strong and weak dependencies, CAUSAL DEGRADATION (section 6) is more suitable. These refinement relations are outlined in Figure 2. From another viewpoint, CAUSAL DEGRADATION can be seen as a specialization of PESSIMISTIC DEGRADATION under the condition of clear distinction between strong and weak dependencies among

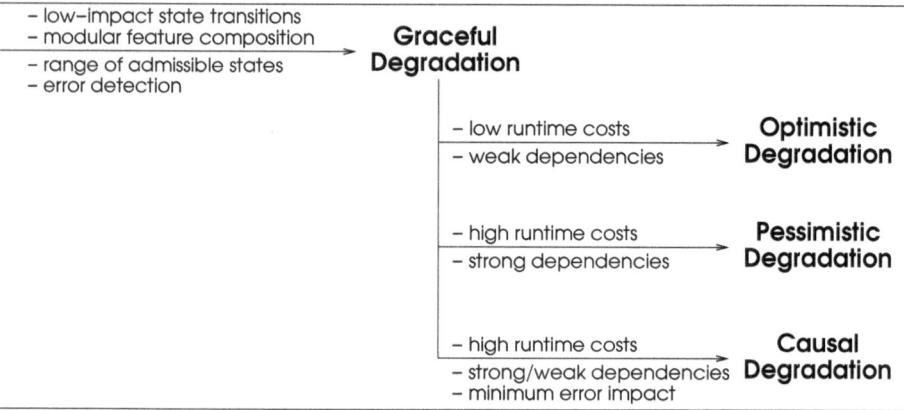

Fig. 2. GRACEFUL DEGRADATION and its refinements

system constituents. This condition allows the precise definition of the error propagation borders so that they contain only those system constituents that are really affected by a given error.

Both PESSIMISTIC DEGRADATION and CAUSAL DEGRADATION use the error propagation borders to identify a new state of a system feature after an error. The error propagation borders are constructed to contain the spanning tree rooted at the constituent where the error occurred and tp include all its dependencies for PESSIMISTIC DEGRADATION and only the strong dependencies for CAUSAL DEGRADATION. Some systems have fixed structure, like most hardware systems and some software systems (e.g. in the telecommunications domain) where constituents are not dynamically instantiated during the system execution. For such systems static analysis can be used at design time to identify the error propagation borders for various errors that the system may experience. The product of the static analysis is a table that maps errors on constituents to their corresponding error propagation borders. This table is loaded into the system at start-up and used after errors to identify the part of the system that must be removed. Consequently, the contribution to the runtime costs (in terms of time) of finding the new state after an error is fixed and small (equal to a table lookup).

However, for systems with dynamic structure where constituents are dynamically instantiated during system execution (e.g. many software systems in the component-based software domain), such static analysis is not feasible. In these cases a precise representation of the system structure is feasible only with a graph, which is dynamically created at system start up and updated at every change in the life-cycle of system constituents. This graph must also describe the dependency relations among the system constituents existing at any time during system execution. After an error, a traversal of the dependency graph starting at the constituent where the error occurred and following all its dependencies for PESSIMISTIC DEGRADATION and only the strong dependencies for CAUSAL DEGRADATION, leads to the identification of the error propagation borders. Consequently, the contribution to the runtime costs (in terms of time) of finding the new state after an error is variable and high (equal to a graph traversal). In addition, the data structure and the updating and traversing functionalities for this dependency graph must be part of the system, increasing the system development and runtime complexity. Unfortunately, in case of dynamic system structure there is no alternative for identifying the error propagation borders and applying CAUSAL DEGRADATION, while for PESSIMISTIC DEGRADATION the alternative static analysis produces too wide error propagation borders that are of no practical value. The impact of dynamic system structure on the costs and the applicability of PESSIMISTIC DEGRADATION and OPTIMISTIC DEGRADATION is discussed in the consequences of the corresponding patterns (sections 5.8 and 6.8 respectively).

3   Graceful Degradation

The GRACEFUL DEGRADATION pattern captures the basic idea behind graceful degradation.

3.1   Example

While the window manager WM is running, a memory leak causes an error in the 3D shadow component, when it is called to calculate the shadow of a re-sized window. The fault tolerance mechanism integrated with WM does not deal with such errors. It is expected that WM does not crash or halt its operation despite the error. Rather, it is desirable that WM continues executing and delivering at least its basic window management functionality plus, if possible, the rest of its designated functionality (i.e. cursor animation, window frames and menu-bars) except for the 3D shadows.

3.2   Context

The invariants describing the context in which the GRACEFUL DEGRADATION pattern can be applied are an 1-to-1 mapping of the system domain characteristics discussed in section 2:

- The runtime impact of state transitions is acceptable (i.e. it does not violate the runtime behavior specification of the system).
- The system is composed of distinct features (e.g. memory and storage capacity, set of services it offers, image resolution, voice quality, etc).
- System features have more admissible states beside their full state.
- Errors can be detected and mapped to the system constituent where they occurred.

3.3   Problem

In the above context, the following problem arises:

How can the system survive an error on some of its parts?

The GRACEFUL DEGRADATION pattern solves this problem by balancing the following forces:

- Removing completely from the system an feature that has been affected by an error has a high cost for the system as well as for its environment (e.g. user of the system).
- In certain cases it is not feasible to continue the system execution once an feature is completely removed.
- It is unacceptable to allow the system to continue its execution without removing its part that has been damaged by an error.

3.4   Solution

When an error is detected in the system and mapped to the constituent where it occurred, that constituent and possibly some of its adjacent environment must be removed, allowing the system to continue execution with the given feature being the resulting lower state.

3.5   Structure

The solution to the problem of surviving the occurrence of errors that is described by the GRACEFUL DEGRADATION pattern outlines the following entities:

- The system FEATURE, which is affected by an error. The FEATURE has more than one admissible state and each state may involve a different number of system constituents.
- The event NOTIFIER, which has the responsibility of detecting errors and mapping them to the system constituent where they occurred.
- The ASSESSOR, which is the runtime part of the system that calculates the new state of a FEATURE after an error has been reported.
- The LOADER, which is responsible for loading the new state decided by the ASSESSOR to the FEATURE.

Figure 3a provides an intuitive illustration of the structure of the GRACEFUL DEGRADATION pattern. The NOTIFIER monitors a given FEATURE of the system for errors and notifies the ASSESSOR when errors occur. The ASSESSOR calculates a new for the FEATURE and communicates it to the LOADER, which loads the new state onto the FEATURE. In this example, the error on x led the ASSESSOR to calculate a new state of the feature where not only x is removed but along with it the rightmost constituent of the FEATURE too. The logic implemented by the ASSESSOR may require that more system constituent than the one where an

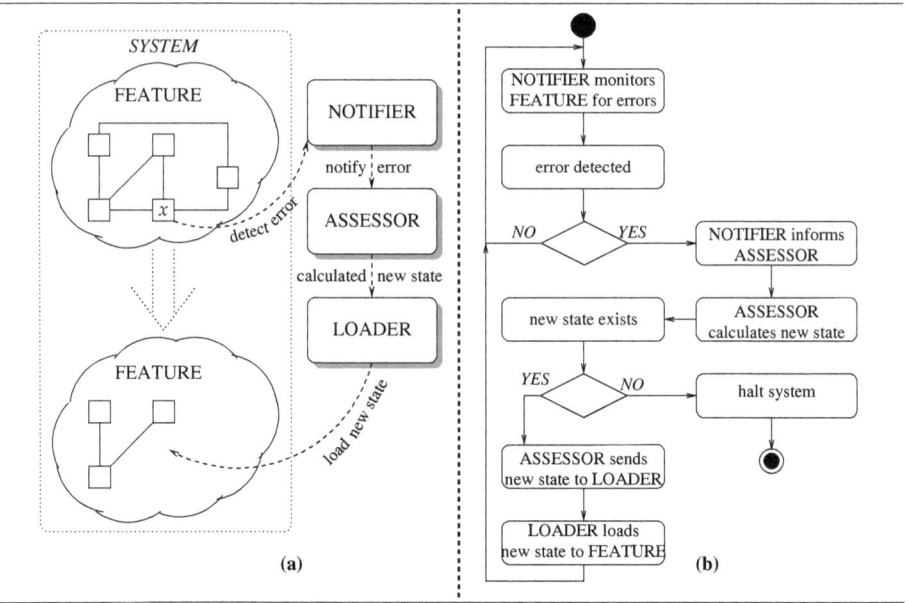

(a)   (b)

Fig. 3. The structure (a) and the activity diagram (b) of the GRACEFUL DEGRADATION pattern

error occurred have to be removed. This is further elaborated in the other three patterns presented in this paper. Figure 3b contains the activity diagram that describes the activities of the GRACEFUL DEGRADATION pattern that include the reporting of an error, the calculation of the new state and its loading onto the system.

3.6   Example Resolved

The $\mathcal{WM}$ is designed as a component-based system, where each of the additional features (i.e. 3D shadows, cursor animation, window frames and menu-bars) is provided by a different component. An error detection mechanism plays the role of the NOTIFIER by monitoring these components for errors. An error in those components is communicated to a separate component that implements the AS-SESSOR, which decides to remove from the system the components affected by the error. The LOADER role is played by the configuration subsystem of $\mathcal{WM}$, which provides the capability of hot-plugging and unplugging components to the system. The ASSESSOR instructs the $\mathcal{WM}$ configuration to remove the affected components. For the sake of this example we consider that the only component affected by the error is the one that provides 3D shadows. After its removal, any window that needs to be redrawn on the screen (e.g. following a moving or resizing operation) does not have a 3D shadow. Despite the decreased functionality of the $\mathcal{WM}$ after the error, the system continues provides all other functionalities (i.e. basic operations on windows plus cursor animation, window frames and menu-bars).

3.7   Implementation

The implementation of the GRACEFUL DEGRADATION pattern consists of the implementation of the three entities that are introduced by the pattern structure: the NOTIFIER, the ASSESSOR, and the LOADER. The implementation of the NOTIFIER depends on the events that it detects and reports. In practice, the NOTIFIER may not be a single entity but rather a set of entities which cooperate to provide error detection and notification, as well as reporting of other types of unsolicited events (e.g. power and temperature alarms). There are various patterns that can be used for developing the error detection mechanism of the NOTIFIER (see [14,8]). The implementation of the LOADER usually requires dynamic reconfiguration capabilities. In certain cases, system design may integrate state switching as part of its "normal" functionality, which means that no reconfiguration mechanism is necessary; employing this specific functionality is sufficient for loading the state calculated by the ASSESSOR.

The implementation of the ASSESSOR provides the identification of the new state after an error is reported on some system constituent. For this, the AS-SESSOR must have the knowledge of the admissible state of the system features. These admissible states are specific to the application domain and the system feature itself. One way to describe these admissible states is by means of a state transition diagram, which describes the states that a feature can reach after various errors that it may experience. This implies that admissible states are statically defined at system development time and included in the runtime system in some form of data structure. Another option is to describe the conditions that system constituents must satisfy in admissible system states and implement in the ASSESSOR the logic that checks these conditions. This results in dynamic identification of the new admissible state at runtime after an error occurs.

3.8   Consequences

The GRACEFUL DEGRADATION pattern has the following benefits:

- The GRACEFUL DEGRADATION pattern introduces lower costs in terms of system complexity, time and resource overheads during system execution compared to patterns for error recovery [8]. As a result, it offers an appealing alternative to the designers of systems that cannot afford the costs of error recovery, yet they must survive errors.
- The use of the GRACEFUL DEGRADATION pattern does not preclude the use of error recovery patterns in the system design. In fact, this pattern may share with such patterns the error detection capabilities, and deal with those errors that fall beyond the scope of error recovery. System can recover from critical errors, while events that have less significant impact on the system execution can lead to the graceful degradation of some system features. The resulting system would be able to tolerate a certain class of errors and survive another class of errors.
- The GRACEFUL DEGRADATION pattern does not introduce any time overhead to error-free system executions.

The GRACEFUL DEGRADATION pattern imposes also some liabilities:

- The GRACEFUL DEGRADATION pattern increases the complexity of the system design. When the system has already error detection and dynamic reconfiguration capabilities, the complexity increase is due to the introduction of the ASSESSOR. Otherwise, the GRACEFUL DEGRADATION pattern adds to the design complexity the cost of the NOTIFIER and LOADER too.
- Graceful degradation can be applied to features with more than one admissible state. Often, this is not feasible for all system features, limiting the applicability of graceful degradation.
- Often, bringing the system to a lower state implies dynamically reconfiguring the system during its execution. Dynamic reconfiguration mechanisms are shown to be costly to implement and they have significant implications on the system design and its performance during the reconfiguration time (e.g. see [2]).
- A system cannot gracefully degrade beyond a certain number of successive errors. In fact, most implementation of graceful degradation allow one or few successive degradations before the system crashes. That, along with the fact that a gracefully degraded system has lower qualities than its "normal" counterpart, implies that graceful degradation is a temporary solution to errors; it only allows the system to survive errors and possibly wait for the opportune moment to start an error recovery process.

3.9   Known Uses

The GRACEFUL DEGRADATION pattern has been applied in image processing to lower image quality, in telecommunication to lower voice quality, in shared memory multiprocessors to lower computational power, in multi-modular memory and RAID storage to lower memory and disk access throughput, in component-based software to lower the functionality of the system, and elsewhere. The Appendix provides a summary of these cases.

3.10   Related Patterns

The GRACEFUL DEGRADATION pattern is related to error detection patterns [14] and the other patterns presented in this paper, which elaborate on the way the ASSESSOR works.

4   Optimistic Degradation

The OPTIMISTIC DEGRADATION pattern describes a refinement of the GRACEFUL DEGRADATION pattern. In this pattern, the ASSESSOR calculates the new state of a system feature after an error by making the optimistic assumption that the error will affect only the constituent of the system where it occurred. The new state is derived by simply removing the failed constituent from the system.

4.1   Example

A window manager $\mathcal{WM}$ is designed as a component-based system. One component provides all the basic operations on windows (i.e. creating, moving, resizing, minimizing, restoring, maximizing, and destroying windows) each at a separate interface. A set of other components provide one additional feature each (e.g. 3D window shadows, window frames, cursor animation, menu-bars, etc) in a single interface per component. Each component executes in a separate thread inside the same process that hosts the entire $\mathcal{WM}$. The GRACEFUL DEGRADATION pattern has been applied on $\mathcal{WM}$ to allow it to degrade gracefully on errors, which cause services to crash or compute wrong results. An error detection mechanism monitors each service invocation for errors and plays the role of the NOTIFIER. The dynamic reconfiguration capabilities of the system play the role of the LOADER. Only the ASSESSOR needs to be designed in such a way that the gracefully degraded state does not cause any unnecessary loss of functionality to $\mathcal{WM}$.

4.2   Context

The context in which the OPTIMISTIC DEGRADATION pattern can be applied is defined in terms of the following invariants:

- The GRACEFUL DEGRADATION pattern has been applied to the system design.

- The runtime cost of LOADER is small and the system can afford to engage it more than once over some execution period where errors occur.
- There are weak dependencies among the system constituents, resulting in a low probability that an error on one constituent will cause its adjacent constituents to fail.

4.3   Problem

In the above context, a problem that arises is the following:

How to decide which will be the new state of a system after an error?

The OPTIMISTIC DEGRADATION pattern solves this problem by balancing the following forces:

- Removing the system constituent where an error occurred results in an admissible new state for the affected system feature.
- Calculating the new state after an error by removing only the system constituent where the error occurred is simple and fast.
- Removing only the system constituent where an error occurred may introduce a new fault in the system due to the absence of the functionality delivered by the removed constituent.
- The precise calculation of an error impact, i.e. identifying all system constituents directly and indirectly damaged by the error, can be very expensive and often impractical.
- In many systems that process dynamic input (e.g. human interaction), the propagation path of an error during a given execution depends on the input being processed. In such cases it is impossible to predict which adjacent constituents will be affected by an error occurring in a system constituent.

4.4   Solution

The new feature state after an error is calculated by removing from the system the constituent where the error occurred.

The new state after an error can be inconsistent, i.e. the error on a system constituent may have caused failures to adjacent constituents. This is acceptable in the suggested solution. Some systems may possess an error recovery mechanism that deals with these errors, and other system may consist of constituents robust enough to continue executing correctly despite these errors. For the rest of the systems, the new errors are reported to the ASSESSOR, which instructs the removal of the constituent where the error occurred. After a number of iterations, all the system constituents – and only those constituents – that have been damaged by the propagation of the initial error will be removed from the system. It is guaranteed that each time the graceful degradation mechanism is activated, it removes only the constituent on which the error occurred. But there is no guarantee that the system will survive all possible sequences of such errors. It may well happen that after a severe error the ASSESSOR removes one after another all system constituents that are essential for the system to continue a meaningful execution. Such cases have similar inconveniences as does the *"domino effect"* in rollback recovery [13].

4.5 Structure

The OPTIMISTIC DEGRADATION pattern does not introduce any new entities in the system where the GRACEFUL DEGRADATION pattern has already been applied. It only elaborates on the logic based on which the ASSESSOR calculates the new state. Figure 4a updates Figure 3a to reflect the exact result of this logic on the calculation of the new state of the system after an error. Similarly, Figure 4b updates the activity diagram of the GRACEFUL DEGRADATION pattern from Figure 3b with a more precise description of the ASSESSOR activities as described by the OPTIMISTIC DEGRADATION pattern. It is worth noticing that in practice, it is possible to simplify the shadowed part of the activity diagram in Figure 4b into a single activity, which is to instruct the LOADER to remove the system constituent where the error occurred.

4.6 Example Resolved

The ASSESSOR, which is responsible to gracefully degrade the functionality of *WM* when errors occur, is designed according to the OPTIMISTIC DEGRADA-TION pattern. The error detection mechanism reports to the ASSESSOR errors on

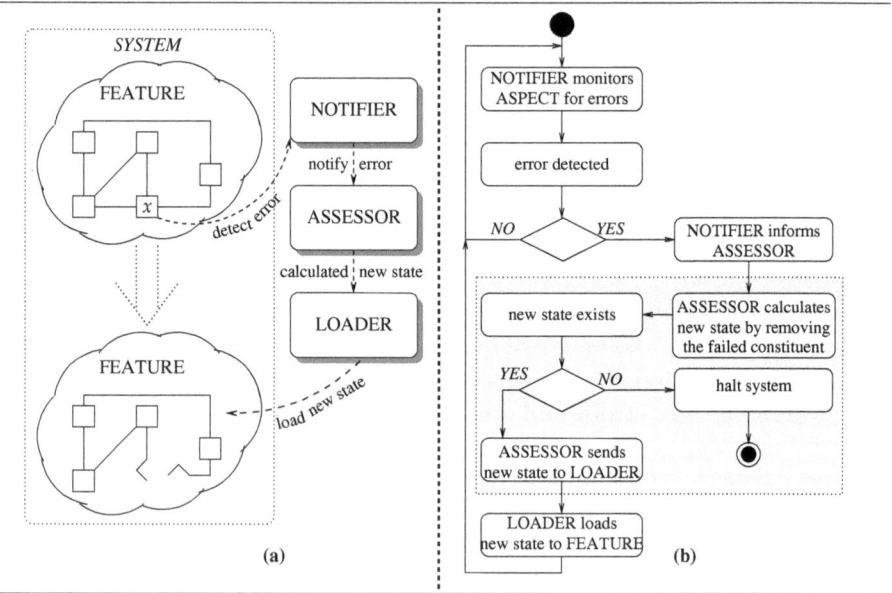

Fig. 4. The structure (a) and the activity diagram (b) of the OPTIMISTIC DEGRADA-TION pattern

individual interfaces. When the ASSESSOR is triggered by an error that occurred on interface X, it instructs the LOADER (i.e. the dynamic reconfiguration capabilities of WM) to replace the interface X by the NULL address in the system. As a result, subsequent attempts to invoke interface X result in an exception that indicates the lack of a binding.

After an error on the interface that provides 3D shadows, the ASSESSOR instructs the dynamic reconfiguration capabilities of WM to remove that interface from the system. When some application attempts to create a new window 3D shadows functionality is not accessible any more, but the window creation functionality is robust enough to continue operating (e.g. it can draw a window without any shadow). A different situation happens when the user of the system attempts to resize a window. The window resizing functionality attempts to invoke the 3D shadows functionality, which is not accessible after the error. The window resizing functionality is not robust enough to continue operating and a new error occurs in the system. The ASSESSOR is informed about that error and it instructs the dynamic reconfiguration capabilities of WM to remove the resizing interface from the system. The system continues operating in a gracefully degraded mode, without any 3D shadows or window resizing capabilities.

4.7   Implementation

The implementation of the ASSESSOR in the OPTIMISTIC DEGRADATION pattern is a fairly straightforward process. First, the designer must identify the errors for which OPTIMISTIC DEGRADATION will be applied. Some critical errors may require the use of a fault tolerance mechanism that fixes the damages they caused and recovers the system feature in its full state. But non-critical errors are good candidates for being treated by the less expensive OPTIMISTIC DEGRADATION. Second, the system constituents where different types of errors may occur must be identified. For example, in a component-based system, an expired timeout on a given binding instance (i.e. individual invocation of an operation inside an interface) can be caused by an intermittent fault on that given binding instance and can be dealt with by retrying the same invocation over the same binding. Hence, it would be wiser to associate a single expired timeout to the individual binding instance where it occurred, and associate with the entire binding only the occurrence of, say, three successive timeouts on that same binding. It can be more appropriate to associate other types of errors, like exceptions reporting severe internal errors, to entities such as interfaces or components.

The ASSESSOR implementation must contain the logic that calculates the new state after an error. In the OPTIMISTIC DEGRADATION pattern this logic is based on a condition that is dynamically evaluated at runtime. This condition is that the constituent where the error occurred must be removed from the system. In the WM example presented above, the interfaces on which errors occur are removed from the system. It is worth noting that the new state calculated by the ASSESSOR may contain *"garbage"*, as Figure 5 illustrates graphically. The error on x on the left-hand side of Figure 5 causes the ASSESSOR to instruct the its removal. The resulting new state is depicted on the right-hand side of Figure 5,

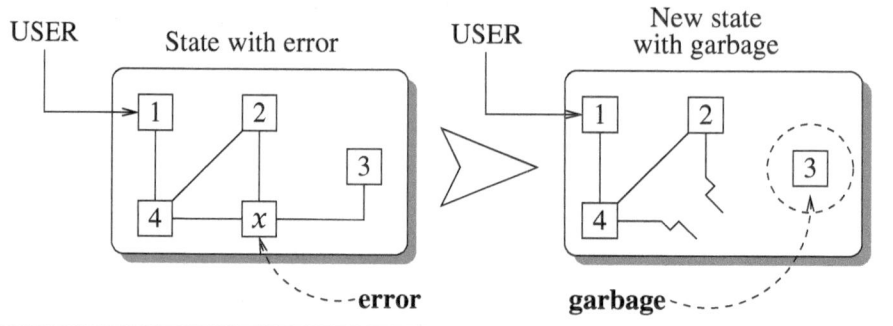

Fig. 5. Garbage in the new state calculated by the ASSESSOR

where x is no longer present, the bindings from constituents 2 and 4 to x are broken, and constituent 3 is left disconnected from the rest of the system.

4.8   Consequences

The OPTIMISTIC DEGRADATION pattern has the following benefits:

- The development-time and runtime costs of the ASSESSOR are low, because of the simplicity of the logic it implements.
- When the ASSESSOR is iteratively employed a successive number of times to deal with error propagation, it removes from the system the minimum part that could be subtracted from its full state and allow the system to survive the initial error.
- The exact impact of different types of errors on system features does not have to be known. During an iterative employment the ASSESSOR will gradual remove one after the other the system constituent that get affected by the initial error.
- Changes in the system design have no impact on the ASSESSOR.

The OPTIMISTIC DEGRADATION pattern imposes also some liabilities:

- The OPTIMISTIC DEGRADATION pattern has the risk of the *"domino effect"*.
- The ASSESSOR may leave garbage in the new state it calculates after an error, which consumes system resources without contributing to the correct execution of the system.
- The OPTIMISTIC DEGRADATION pattern does not apply to certain types of systems that do allow any period of inconsistent state during their execution.

4.9   Known Uses

The OPTIMISTIC DEGRADATION pattern has been widely applied in image processing, where pixel errors in the image analysis cause the quality of the image to degrade, but they do not prevent the system from rendering images [4,7,10]. Also, in the telecommunication domain packet errors in voice streams cause the quality of the voice to degrade, but they do not prevent the system from delivering voice [22]. Distributed agreement algorithms have employed the OPTIMISTIC DEGRADATION pattern too, where failed group members are simply excluded from the decision making process [12]. Finally, component-based software has employed the OPTIMISTIC DEGRADATION pattern to remove only the system constituent (e.g. component, interface, or binding) where the error has occurred [18].

4.10   Related Patterns

OPTIMISTIC DEGRADATION complements GRACEFUL DEGRADATION, for which it provides an elaborated solution to the way the ASSESSOR functions. In the same sense, it also relates to the other two patterns presented in the remainder of this paper, which provide alternative approaches on how develop the ASSESSOR of the GRACEFUL DEGRADATION pattern.

5   Pessimistic Degradation

The PESSIMISTIC DEGRADATION pattern describes an alternative design for the ASSESSOR of the GRACEFUL DEGRADATION pattern. In this pattern, the ASSESSOR decides on the new state of the system after an error occurrence by making the pessimistic assumption that the error will affect all system constituents that are related to the failed one. These relations are statically identified during design time, and the new state after the error is pre-defined by the system designer.

5.1   Example

A window manager $\mathcal{WM}$' consists of a number of components. Component A provides core functionality for creating/destroying a window, holding its descriptor, coordinates, associated process, etc and drawing its main panel. Component B provides functionality for moving, re-sizing, minimizing, restoring, and maximizing a window. Components C, D, E, and F provide functionality for creating a window frame, creating a menu-bar on the window frame, creating 3D shadows around the window frame, and animating the cursor respectively. Each component executes in a separate thread inside the same process that hosts the entire $\mathcal{WM}$' system. The GRACEFUL DEGRADATION pattern has been applied on $\mathcal{WM}$' to allow it to degrade gracefully on errors, which cause services to crash or compute wrong results. An error detection mechanism monitors each service invocation for errors and plays the role of the NOTIFIER. The dynamic reconfiguration capabilities of the system play the role of the LOADER. The ASSESSOR must be design so that, after an error, it identifies a new component configuration that is stable, i.e. the removal of some system functionality does not result in subsequent errors.

5.2 Context

The context in which the PESSIMISTIC DEGRADATION pattern can be applied is defined in terms of the following invariants:

- The GRACEFUL DEGRADATION pattern has been applied to the system design.
- The runtime cost of the LOADER is high and the system cannot afford to engage it frequently during its execution.
- There are strong dependencies among the system constituents, resulting in a high probability that an error on one constituent will cause its adjacent constituents to fail.
- It is feasible to calculate the error propagation borders for the different errors that the ASSESSOR will deal with.

5.3 Problem

In the above context, a problem that arises is the following:

How to decide which will be the new state of a system after an error?

The PESSIMISTIC DEGRADATION pattern solves this problem by balancing the following forces:

- Removing only the constituent where an error occurred does not eliminate the error propagation and hence results in a non-admissible state in the system.
- Removing all constituents inside the propagation borders of an error guarantees a single invocation of the LOADER as a direct or indirect consequence of that error.
- It is acceptable for the system to lose constituents after an error, even if there is no guarantee that these constituents would be affected by the error.

5.4 Solution

Based on the dependencies among system constituents, the error propagation borders are defined based on the largest amount of system constituents that can potentially be affected by an error occurring in one of them. The new state of the system for each such error is defined as the result of removing all constituents within the error propagation borders.

Opposite to the OPTIMISTIC DEGRADATION pattern, the new state produced by the PESSIMISTIC DEGRADATION pattern after an error is guaranteed to effectively stop the error propagation. Under the pessimistic assumption that all system constituents depending on the one where the error occurred may fail in the remainder of the system execution, all such constituents are removed from the system resulting in a significant lowering of this feature state. However, the pessimistic degradation mechanism will not be invoked again to deal with side effects and products of the propagation of the error in question.

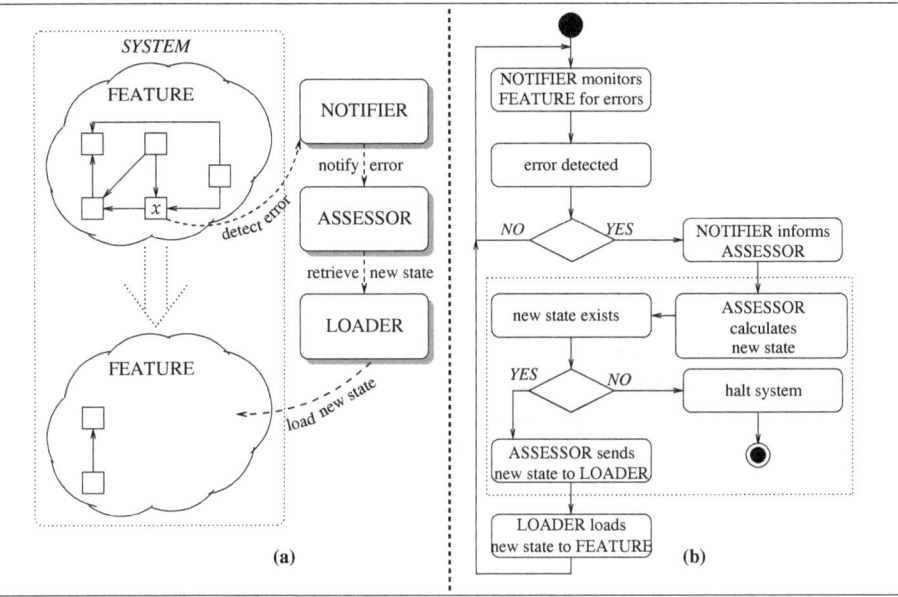

Fig. 6. The structure (a) and the activity diagram (b) of the PESSIMISTIC DEGRADA-
TION pattern

5.5 Structure

The PESSIMISTIC DEGRADATION pattern does not introduce any new entities
in the system where the GRACEFUL DEGRADATION pattern has already been
applied. It only elaborates on the logic based on which the ASSESSOR calculates
the new state. We can view the ASSESSOR as a table of mappings between errors
on system features and the gracefully degraded states of the features that have
been defined during design time. Figure 6a updates Figure 3a to reflect the exact
result of identifying the new state of the system after an error. Figure 6b updates
the activity diagram of the GRACEFUL DEGRADATION pattern from Figure 3b
with a more precise description of the ASSESSOR activities as described by the
PESSIMISTIC DEGRADATION pattern.

5.6 Example Resolved

The ASSESSOR is designed according to the PESSIMISTIC DEGRADATION pattern and the error detection mechanism reports to the ASSESSOR an error and
the identifier of the component where the error occurred. By static analysis of
the system structure and the dependencies among its constituents, the designer
creates the dependency graph shown in Figure 7. Based on this graph, the designer deduces that an error on components B, D, E, and F does not affect any
other component in the system, while an error on C affects both components D
and E, and an error on A affects the entire system. This mapping of errors on
components to new states is captured in a mapping table that is loaded to the

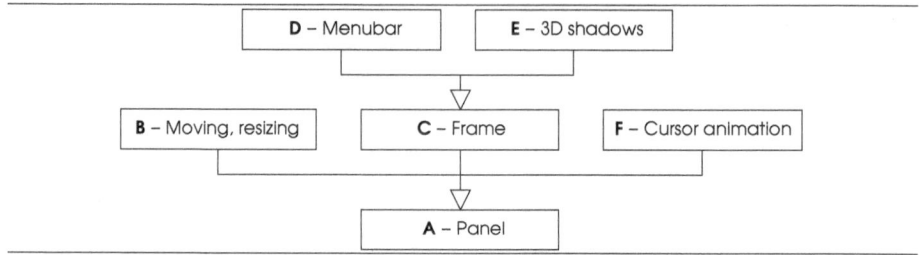

Fig. 7. The dependency graph of the $\mathcal{WM}$' example

$\mathcal{WM}$' system at start-up. After an error, the ASSESSOR instructs the LOADER to load a new state where the component on which the error occurred and all other components affected according to this mapping, are removed from the system.

5.7   Implementation

The implementation of the ASSESSOR in the PESSIMISTIC DEGRADATION pattern amounts to a mechanism that identifies all system constituents affected by an error and instructing the LOADER to remove them. There are two ways for implementing the logic that identifies such a new system state. One approach is to use static analysis at design time to create the dependency graph of the system and subsequently produce a mapping table between errors on constituents and new system states. The resolved example presented above is using such an approach based on static analysis. In many domains where systems have fixed structure during their execution, there are tools that facilitate such static analysis by creating the dependency graph of the system. However, dependency graphs are as complex as the system they represent, and the finer grained the system constituents are the more complex the dependency graphs become. Hence, although the runtime mechanism of the ASSESSOR that looks up the mapping table is simple, creating the mapping table at design time can be a complex task.

An alternative approach is to use dynamic analysis of the system dependencies to produce a dependency graph that captures a snapshot of the system structure the moment of an error. This approach is particularly valuable in domains of systems with dynamic structures that change during their execution. However, this option requires a higher development effort for developing the part of the ASSESSOR that perform the dynamic analysis of the system structure. In addition, it increases significantly the runtime overhead introduced by the ASSESSOR by performing the dependency analysis during the execution of the system.

5.8   Consequences

The PESSIMISTIC DEGRADATION pattern has the following benefits:

- Error propagation is effectively stopped in the new state, hence it does not suffer from the *"domino effect"*.

- The LOADER, which has high runtime cost, is invoked only once as a direct or indirect consequence of a single error.
- The ASSESSOR does not leave garbage in the new state of the system.
- The runtime cost for calculating the new state after an error is low when static analysis of system structure is used to identify the error propagation borders.

The PESSIMISTIC DEGRADATION pattern imposes also some liabilities:

- The development-time cost for the ASSESSOR is significantly higher than in the OPTIMISTIC DEGRADATION case, and includes the development of the mapping table (in case of static analysis of system structure) or the development of the mechanism for updating and traversing the dependency graph (in case of dynamic analysis of system structure).
- Simplifying the identification of error propagation borders results in including more system constituents than what would be really affected by the error. Consequently, unnecessarily large subsystems can be removed following an error.
- Changes in the system design (e.g. architectural re-factoring) have significant impact on the ASSESSOR, when it uses the results of static analysis of the system structure. As a result, reconstruction of the mapping table for the new system is required.

5.9   Known Uses

The PESSIMISTIC DEGRADATION pattern has been applied in shared memory multiprocessors [15,20], multi-modular memory [5,6,11], and RAID systems [3] where detected errors cause the entire processor, memory module or disk array to be excluded from the system execution without further consideration of the exact source of the error, i.e. process inside a processor, address block inside a memory module or track inside a disk array. Similarly, ABFT systems [21] have employed the PESSIMISTIC DEGRADATION pattern to remove entire processors from the system when errors are detected and re-organize the fault tolerance groups with the remaining processors. Finally, component-based software has employed the PESSIMISTIC DEGRADATION pattern to remove entire subsystems of components inside which an error is detected [19].

5.10   Related Patterns

PESSIMISTIC DEGRADATION complements GRACEFUL DEGRADATION, for which it provides an elaborated solution to the way the ASSESSOR functions. It describes an alternative solution to that proposed by the OPTIMISTIC DEGRADATION pattern presented in the previous section, and to the one proposed by the CAUSAL DEGRADATION pattern described in the next section.

6   Causal Degradation

The CAUSAL DEGRADATION pattern describes yet another alternative design for the ASSESSOR of the GRACEFUL DEGRADATION pattern. In this pattern, the ASSESSOR dynamically analyzes the dependencies of the system constituents on the one where the error has occurred, and calculate the new state by removing all those constituents that strongly depend on the failed one.

6.1   Example

A window manager $\mathcal{WM}$" dynamically creates a different instance of the window component for every window that is created in the system. Every window component depends strongly on the component that contains the application logic the receives input from this window and sends to it output. Also, every window depends weakly on the parent window through which it has been created. For example, if one application launches another application, then the window of the former application is the parent of the window of the latter application. The GRACEFUL DEGRADATION pattern has been applied on $\mathcal{WM}$" to allow it to degrade gracefully on errors that occur on windows and their associated applications. An error detection mechanism monitors each service invocation for errors and acts as the NOTIFIER. The dynamic reconfiguration capabilities of the system play the role of the LOADER. The ASSESSOR must be designed so that it stops the error propagation without removing more system constituents than the strict minimum to guarantee the elimination of error propagation.

6.2   Context

The context, in which the CAUSAL DEGRADATION pattern can be applied to calculate the gracefully degraded state of a system after an error occurrence, is defined in terms of the following invariants:

- The GRACEFUL DEGRADATION pattern has been applied in the system design.
- The runtime cost of the LOADER is high and the system cannot afford to engage it frequently during its execution.
- There is a clear distinction between strong and weak dependencies among the system constituents.
- It is feasible to construct the dependency graph of the system distinguishing the strong from the weak dependencies among its constituents.

6.3   Problem

In the above context, a problem that arises is the following:

How to decide which will be the new state of a system after an error?

The CAUSAL DEGRADATION pattern solves this problem by balancing the following forces:

- Removing only the constituent where an error occurred does not eliminate the error propagation and hence results in a non-admissible state in the system.
- Removing all constituents inside the propagation borders of an error guarantees a single invocation of the LOADER as a direct or indirect consequence of that error.
- It is not acceptable for the system to lose constituents after an error, if there is no guarantee that these constituents would be affected by the error.

6.4 Solution

Based on the dependency graph of the system and the clear distinction between strong and weak dependencies, the error propagation borders are defined by the spanning tree that is rooted on the constituent where the error occurred and contains all the links that represent strong dependencies. The new state of the system for each such error is defined as the result of removing all constituents within the error propagation borders.

Similar to the PESSIMISTIC DEGRADATION pattern, the new state produced by the CAUSAL DEGRADATION pattern after an error is guaranteed to effectively stop the error propagation. However, in this case only the strict minimum of constituents has been removed to guarantee the elimination of error propagation. Hence, the system does not lose more of its functionality than what is absolutely necessary in order to stop the error propagation.

6.5 Structure

The CAUSAL DEGRADATION pattern does not introduce any new entities in the system where the GRACEFUL DEGRADATION pattern has already been applied. It only elaborates on the logic based on which the ASSESSOR calculates the new, error-free state where error propagation is stopped by removing from the state where the error occurred a strict minimum of constituents. To achieve this, the ASSESSOR must be able to identify those constituents, and only those, that can participate in the propagation of the error. This is achieved based on the clear distinction between strong and weak dependencies among system constituents. Figure 8a updates Figure 3a to reflect the exact result of identifying the new state of the system after an error. In this figure, solid and dashed arrows depict strong and weak dependencies respectively. The failed constituent and all its strong dependencies have been removed from the system, while its weak dependencies, e.g. the far right constituent, remain in the new state of the system. Figure 8b updates the activity diagram of the GRACEFUL DEGRADATION pattern from Figure 3b with a more precise description of the ASSESSOR activities as described above.

6.6 Example Resolved

The ASSESSOR keeps in its memory a runtime representation of the dependency graph (DG) of the system constituents, which is dynamically updated every time

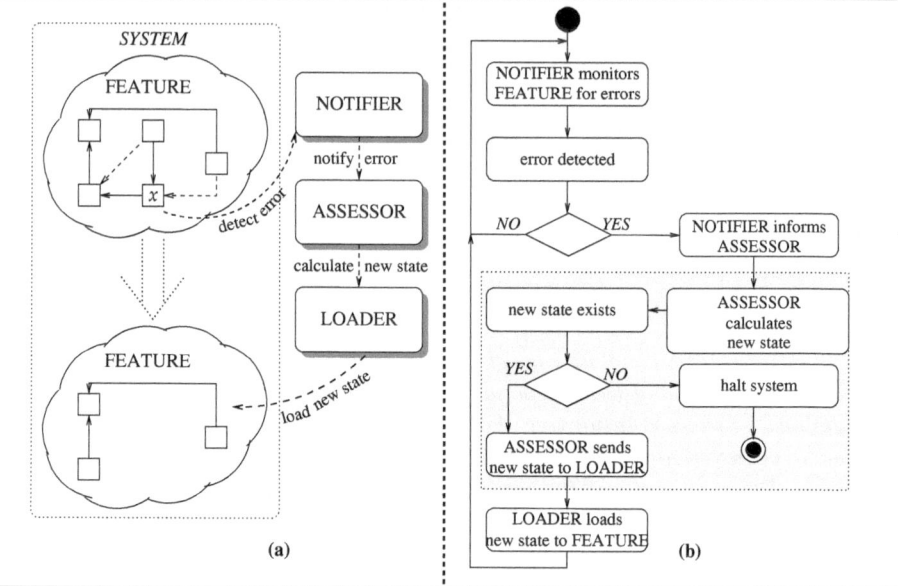

Fig. 8. The structure (a) and the activity diagram (b) of the CAUSAL DEGRADATION pattern

a new window is created or a new application is launched. Windows depend weakly on their parent windows in order to return screen and input focus when exiting, and they depend strongly on the application from which they receive output and to which the send their input. When an error is reported on one component, the ASSESSOR identifies the corresponding node in the DG it keeps in memory, and marks. Then, the ASSESSOR initiates a depth-first reverse traversal of the DG from the marked node and following the edges that represent strong dependencies. This way, all the nodes that corresponds to system constituents that recursively depend strongly on the failed one are visited and marked. Once the traversal is over, the ASSESSOR calculates the new system state by removing from the current state all the constituents that are represented by DG nodes that have been marked during the traversal. The new state is then communicated to the dynamic reconfiguration mechanism of the system, which plays the role of the LOADER.

6.7   Implementation

The implementation of the ASSESSOR as outlined by the CAUSAL DEGRADATION pattern is based on the distinction between strong and weak dependencies among the system constituents. As mentioned earlier, for component-based systems this can be described in the interface definition by the use of the clauses *"requires"* and *"uses"*. In formal system specification, the difference between strong and weak dependencies can be captured in *"mandatory"* and *"optional"* constructs of an assertion. Similar to the PESSIMISTIC DEGRADATION pattern, there are two ways of implementing the ASSESSOR logic. One approach is to use static analysis at design time to create the dependency graph of the system that distinguishes between strong and weak dependencies. The spanning trees based on strong dependency link in this graph are used to produce a mapping table between errors on constituents and new system states. In many domains where systems have fixed structure during their execution, there are tools that facilitate such static analysis by creating the dependency graph of the system. However, dependency graphs are as complex as the system they represent, and the finer grained the system constituents are the more complex the dependency graphs become. Hence, although the runtime mechanism of the ASSESSOR that looks up the mapping table is simple, creating the mapping table at design time can be a complex task.

The alternative is to use dynamic analysis of the system dependencies to produce a dependency graph that captures a snapshot of the system structure the moment of an error. The resolved example presented above is using such an approach based on dynamic analysis. This approach is particularly valuable in domains of systems with dynamic structures that change during their execution. However, this option requires a higher development effort for developing the part of the ASSESSOR that perform the dynamic analysis of the system structure. In addition, it increases significantly the runtime overhead introduced by the ASSESSOR by performing the dependency analysis during the execution of the system.

6.8 Consequences

The CAUSAL DEGRADATION pattern has the following benefits:

- Error propagation is effectively stopped in the new state, hence it does not suffer from the *"domino effect"*.
- The LOADER, which has high runtime cost, is invoked only once as a direct or indirect consequence of a single error.
- The runtime cost for calculating the new state after an error is low when static analysis of system structure is used to identify the error propagation borders.
- Only the minimum number of the system constituents that are affected by an error is removed from the system.

The CAUSAL DEGRADATION pattern imposes also some liabilities:

- The development-time cost for the ASSESSOR is significantly higher than in the OPTIMISTIC DEGRADATION case, and includes the development of the mapping table (in case of static analysis of system structure) or the development of the mechanism for updating and traversing the dependency graph (in case of dynamic analysis of system structure).
- Changes in the system design (e.g. architectural re-factoring) have significant impact on the ASSESSOR, when it uses the results of static analysis of the system structure. As a result, reconstruction of the mapping table for the new system is required.
- The ASSESSOR may leave garbage in the new state of the system.

6.9 Known Uses

The CAUSAL DEGRADATION pattern has been applied mainly in component-based systems [16,17], where the *"requires"* and *"uses"* clauses in the interface definition are used to distinguish between strong and weak dependencies, and removal of components after an error occurrence follows the reverse DG traversal described by the CAUSAL DEGRADATION pattern. Also, the CAUSAL DEGRADATION pattern has been applied in formal system specification [9], where weak dependencies are expressed as optional assertions and strong dependencies are the normal (mandatory) assertions.

6.10 Related Patterns

CAUSAL DEGRADATION complements GRACEFUL DEGRADATION, for which it provides an elaborated solution to the way the ASSESSOR functions. It describes an alternative solution to that proposed by the OPTIMISTIC DEGRADATION and PESSIMISTIC DEGRADATION patterns presented in the previous sections.

7 Summary

This paper presented four design patterns that capture the most widely used methods for graceful degradation. The GRACEFUL DEGRADATION pattern describes the context and problem where graceful degradation techniques apply, and outlines a general design approach to smoothly change the system state by removing its damaged parts. The remaining three patterns describe different methods for calculating the damaged part to be removed from the system state.

In the OPTIMISTIC DEGRADATION pattern the damaged part is considered to be the system constituent where the error occurred. As a result, a simple and quick calculation determines this constituent is the only part of the system that must be removed. On the negative side, this pattern may leave "garbage" in the system state, i.e. parts of the system on which no error was reported but they are not any more used in the system's execution after the removal of the damaged part. It may also cause a "domino effect" when other parts of the system fail due to the initial removal of the damaged part, causing the repetitive activation of the graceful degradation mechanism.

In the PESSIMISTIC DEGRADATION pattern the damaged part is the subset of the system that relates in some way to the constituent where the error occurred. This eliminates the "domino effect" risks and results in a new, garbage-free system state. On the down side, the mechanism that identifies the new state after an error is substantially more complex than in the previous case, and the removed part of the system state often includes constituents that will not have been affected by the error during the system execution.

Finally, in the CAUSAL DEGRADATION pattern the damaged part is the subset of the system identified by the spanning tree rooted at the constituent where the error occurred and following only strong dependency links. As a result, the removed part is exactly the part of the system state that must be removed without risk for "domino effect". However, the resulting state may contain garbage plus the mechanism that identifies the new state after an error is substantially more complex than in the OPTIMISTIC DEGRADATION pattern.

References

1. Avizienis, A., Laprie, J.-C., Randell, B., Landwehr, C.: Basic Concepts and Taxonomy of Dependable and Secure Computing. IEEE Transactions on Dependable and Secure Computing 1(1), 11–33 (2004)
2. Bidan, C., Issarny, V., Saridakis, T., Zarras, A.: A Dynamic Reconfiguration Service for CORBA. In: Proceedings of the 4th International Conference on Configurable Distributed Systems, pp. 35–42 (1998)
3. Chen, P.M., Lee, E.K., Gibson, G.A., Katz, R.H., Patterson, D.A.: RAID: High-Performance, Reliable Secondary Storage. ACM Computing Surveys 26(2), 145–185 (1994)
4. Chen, Y.-C., Sayood, K., Nelson, D.J.: A Robust Coding Scheme for Packet Video. IEEE Transactions on Communications 40(9), 1491–1501 (1992)
5. Cherkassky, V., Malek, M.: A Measure of Graceful Degradation in Parallel-Computer Systems. IEEE Transactions on Reliability 38(1), 76–81 (1989)
6. Cheung, K., Sohi, G., Saluja, K., Pradhan, D.: Organization and Analysis of a Gracefully-Degrading Interleaved Memory System. In: Proceedings of the 14th Annual International Symposium on Computer Architecture, pp. 224–231 (1987)
7. Dang, P.P., Chau, P.M.: Robust Image Transmission over CDMA Channels. IEEE Transactions on Consumer Electronics 46(3), 664–672 (2000)
8. Hanmer, R.S.: Patterns for Fault Tolerant Software. Wiley Software Patterns Series. John Wiley & Sons, Chichester (2007)
9. Herlihy, M.P., Wing, J.M.: Specifying Graceful Degradation. IEEE Transactions on Parallel and Distributed Systems 2(1), 93–104 (1991)
10. Lafruit, G., Nachtergaele, L., Denolf, K., Bormans, J.: 3D Computational Graceful Degradation. In: Proceedings of the IEEE International Symposium on Circuits and Systems, pp. 3.547–3.550 (2000)
11. Lee, Y.-H., Shin, K.G.: Optimal Reconfiguration Strategy for a Degradable Multimodule Computing System. Journal of the ACM 34(2), 326–348 (1987)
12. Mahaney, S.R., Schneider, F.B.: Inexact Agreement: Accuracy, Precision, and Graceful Degradation. In: Proceedings of the 4th Annual ACM Symposium on Principles of Distributed Computing, pp. 237–249 (1985)
13. Randell, B.: System Structure for Software Fault Tolerance. IEEE Transactions on Software Engineering 1(2), 220–232 (1975)
14. Renzel, K.: Error Detection. In: Proceedings of the 2nd European Conference on Pattern Languages of Programs (1997)
15. Saheban, F., Friedman, A.D.: Diagnostic and Computational Reconfiguration in Multiprocessor Systems. In: Proceedings of the ACM Annual Conference, pp. 68–78 (1978)
16. Saridakis, T.: Graceful Degradation for Component-Based Embedded Software. In: Proceedings of the 13th International Conference on Intelligent and Adaptive Systems and Software Engineering, pp. 175–182 (2004)
17. Saridakis, T.: Towards the Integration of Fault, Resource, and Power Management. In: Proceedings of the 23rd International Conference on Computer Safety, Reliability and Security, pp. 72–86 (2004)

18. Saridakis, T.: Surviving Errors in Component-Based Software. In: Proceedings of the 31st Euromicro Conference on Software Engineering and Advances Applications – Component-Based Software Engineering Track (2005)
19. Shelton, C.P., Koopman, P.: Improving System Dependability with Functional Alternatives. In: Proceedings of the International Conference on Dependable Systems and Networks, pp. 295–304 (2004)
20. Thomasian, A., Avizienis, A.: A Design Study of a Shared Resource Computing System. In: Proceedings of the 3rd Annual Symposium on Computer Architecture, pp. 105–112 (1976)
21. Yajnik, S., Jha, N.K.: Graceful Degradation in Algorithm-Based Fault Tolerant Multiprocessor Systems. IEEE Transactions on Parallel and Distributed Systems 8(2), 137–153 (1997)
22. Zaruba, G.V., Chlamtac, I., Das, S.K.: A Prioritized Real-Rime Wireless Call Degradation Framework for Optimal Call Mix Selection. Mobile Networks and Applications 7(2), 143–151 (2002)

Appendix: Applications of Graceful Degradation

Image processing. Rather than discarding a compressed image that cannot be reconstructed to its original resolution, the *image quality* can be gracefully degraded to lower levels [4,7,10].

Telecommunications. Rather than closing a connection that is dropping some packets of voice data, the *voice quality* delivered to the end-points is gracefully degraded to lower levels [22].

Shared memory multiprocessors. Instead of stopping a computation on a multiprocessor system when a processor fails, the tasks assigned to the failed processor can be rescheduled on the remaining processors resulting in the graceful degradation of the *computational power* of the system [15,20].

Multi-modular memory. Instead of rendering inaccessible the entire memory when a single module fails, the data of the failed module are recovered from stable storage and distributed among the remaining modules, gracefully degrading, thus, the *memory access throughput* of the system [5,6,11].

Redundant Arrays of Inexpensive Disks (RAID). Rather than rendering a RAID system inaccessible when a disk fails, the data of the failed disk are reconstructed from the error correction codes on the remaining disks and distributed among those resulting in the graceful degradation of the *disk access throughput* of the RAID system [3].

Distributed agreement. Instead of failing to reach an agreement when a member of the distributed agreement group fails, the group can reach an agreement on a value less close to the expected one resulting in a graceful degradation of the *computational accuracy* of the agreed value [12].

Algorithm-Based Fault Tolerance (ABFT). Instead of dropping the fault tolerance degree of an ABFT system when a processor fails, the remaining processors form a smaller number of fault tolerant groups with the same degree of fault tolerance, gracefully degrading, thus, the *computational throughput* of the ABFT system [21].

Formal specification. Rather than causing a system failure when a set of constraints that enable some system functionality is not met, an alternative, weaker set of constraints that still hold can enable an alternative system functionality resulting in the graceful degradation of the *constraint strictness* satisfied by the system during its execution [9].

Component-based software. Rather than letting the whole system to fail when an error occurs on a component of the system, the error affects only those components in the system that directly or indirectly depend the failed component. This results in the graceful degradation of the *system functionality* to a subset of it that has not been affected by the error [16,17,18,19].

Meeting Real-Time Constraints Using "Sandwich Delays"

Michael J. Pont, Susan Kurian, and Ricardo Bautista-Quintero

Embedded Systems Laboratory, University of Leicester,
University Road, LEICESTER LE1 7RH, UK

Abstract. This short paper is concerned with the use of patterns to support the development of software for reliable, resource-constrained, embedded systems. The paper introduces one new pattern (SANDWICH DELAY) and describes one possible implementation of this pattern for use with a popular family of ARM-based microcontrollers.

Keywords: Embedded system, design pattern, time-triggered architecture, balanced code.

1 Introduction

In this paper, we are concerned with the development of embedded systems for which there are two (sometimes conflicting) constraints. First, we wish to implement the design using a low-cost microcontroller, which has – compared to a desktop computer – very limited memory and CPU performance. Second, we wish to produce a system with extremely predictable timing behaviour.

To support the development of this type of software, we have previously described a "language" consisting of more than seventy patterns (e.g. see Pont, 2001).

This brief paper describes one new pattern (SANDWICH DELAY) and illustrates – using what we call a "pattern implementation example" (e.g. see Kurian and Pont, 2005) - one possible implementation of this pattern for use with a popular family of ARM-based microcontrollers.

SANDWICH DELAY

{pattern}

Context

- You are developing an embedded system.
- Available CPU and / or memory resources are – compared with typical desktop designs – rather limited.
- Your system is based on a time-triggered scheduler rather than a "real-time operating system".
- Your system involves running two or more periodic tasks.
- Predictable timing behaviour is a key design requirement.

Problem

You are running two activities, one after the other. How can we ensure that the interval between the release times of the two activities is known and fixed?

J. Noble and R. Johnson (Eds.): TPLOP I, LNCS 5770, pp. 94–102, 2009.

Background

In many embedded applications (such as those involving control or data acquisition) variations in the start times of tasks or functions can have serious implications. Such timing variations are known as "release jitter" (or simply "jitter").

For example, Cottet and David [1] show that – during data acquisition tasks – jitter rates of 10% or more can introduce errors which are so significant that any subsequent interpretation of the sampled signal may be rendered meaningless. Similarly Jerri discusses the serious impact of jitter on applications such as spectrum analysis and filtering [3]. Also, in control systems, jitter can greatly degrade the performance by varying the sampling period [9,5].

In many embedded systems, we wish to keep the levels of jitter to a minimum.

Solution

A SANDWICH DELAY can be used to solve this type of problem. More specifically, a SANDWICH DELAY provides a simple but highly effective means of ensuring that a particular piece of code *always takes the same period of time to execute*: this is done using two timer operations to "sandwich" the activity you need to perform.

To illustrate one possible application of a SANDWICH DELAY, suppose that we have a system executing two functions periodically, as outlined in Listing 1.

```
// Interrupt Service Routine (ISR) invoked by timer overflow every 10 ms
void Timer_ISR(void)
  {
  Do_X();   // WCET¹ approx. 4.0 ms
  Do_Y();   // WCET approx. 4.0 ms
  }
```

Listing 1. Using a timer ISR to execute two periodic functions.

According to the code in Listing 1, function Do_X() will be executed every 10 ms. Similarly, function Do_Y() will be executed every 10 ms, after Do_X() completes. For many resource-constrained applications (for example, control systems) this architecture may be appropriate. However, in some cases, the risk of jitter in the start times of function Do_Y() may cause problems. Such jitter will arise if there is any variation in the duration of function Do_X(). In Figure 1, the jitter will be reflected in differences between the values of *ty1* and *ty2* (for example).

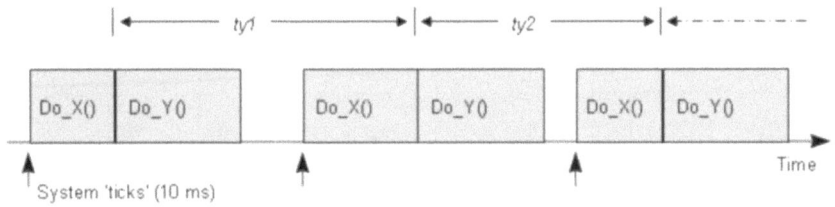

Fig. 1. The impact of variations in the duration of Do_X() on the release jitter of Do_Y().

---

¹ WCET = Worst-Case Execution Time. If we run the task an infinite number of times and measure how long it takes to complete, the WCET will be the longest execution time which we measure.

We can use a SANDWICH DELAY to solve this problem: please refer to Listing 2.

```
// ISR invoked by timer overflow every 10 ms
void Timer_ISR(void)
    {
    // Execute Do_X() in a 'Sandwich Delay' - BEGIN
    Set_Sandwich_Timer_Overflow(5);        // Set timer to overflow after 5 ms
    Do_X();                                // Execute Do_X - WCET approx. 4 ms
    Wait_For_Sandwich_Timer_Overflow();    // Wait for timer to overflow
    // Execute Do_X() in a 'Sandwich Delay' - END

    Do_Y();  // WCET approx. 4.0 ms
    }
```

Listing 2. Employing a SANDWICH DELAY to reduce release in function Do_Y().

In Listing 2, we set a timer to overflow after 5 ms (a period slightly longer than the worst-case execution time of Do_X()). We then start this timer before we run the function and – after the function is complete – we wait for the timer to reach the 5 ms value. In this way, we ensure that – as long as Do_X() does not exceed a duration of 5 ms - Do_Y() runs with very little jitter[2].

Figure 2 shows the tick graph from this example, with the SANDWICH DELAY included.

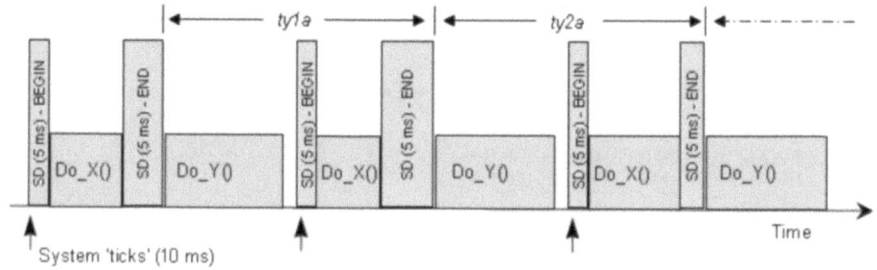

Fig. 2. Reducing the impact of variations in the duration of Do_X() on the release jitter of Do_Y() through use of a SANDWICH DELAY

2   Related Patterns and Alternative Solutions

In some cases, you can avoid the use of a SANDWICH DELAY altogether, by altering the system tick interval. For example, if we look again at our Do_X() / Do_Y() system, the two tasks have the same duration. In this case, we would be better to reduce the tick interval to 5 ms and run the tasks in alternating time slots (Figure 3).

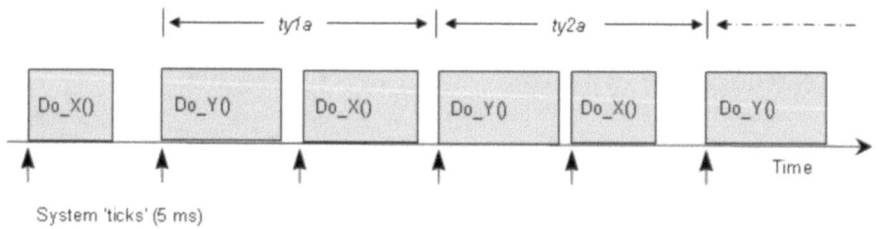

Fig. 3. Avoiding the use of SANDWICH DELAYS through changes in the scheduler tick interval

---

[2] In general, it is not possible to remove all jitter using this approach: we explain why under the heading "Reliability and safety implications".

Please note that this solution will only work (in general) if the tasks in your system have similar durations. Where the tasks do not have the same duration, a scheduler involving multiple timer interrupts may be more appropriate: such a solution is beyond the scope of this paper.

3   Reliability and Safety Implications

Use of a SANDWICH DELAY is generally straightforward, but there are three potential issues of which you should be aware.

First, you need to know the duration (WCET) of the function(s) to be sandwiched. If you underestimate this value, the timer will already have reached its overflow value when your function(s) complete, and the level of jitter will not be reduced (indeed, the SANDWICH DELAY is likely to slightly increase the jitter in this case).

Second, you must check the code carefully, because the "wait" function may never terminate if the timer is incorrectly set up. In these circumstances a watchdog timer (e.g. see [7, 8]) or a "task guardian" [2] may help to rescue your system, but relying on such mechanisms to deal with poor design or inadequate testing is – of course - never a good idea.

Third, you will rarely manage to remove all jitter using such an approach, because the system cannot react instantly when the timer reaches its maximum value (at the machine-code level, the code used to poll the timer flag is more complex than it may appear, and the time taken to react to the flag change will vary slightly). A useful rule of thumb is that jitter levels of around 1 µs will still be seen using a SANDWICH DELAY.

4   Overall Strengths and Weaknesses

☺   A simple way of ensuring that the WCET of a block of code is highly predictable.

☹   Requires (non-exclusive) access to a timer.

☹   Will only rarely provide a "jitter free" solution: variations in code duration of around 1 µs are representative.

5   Example: Application of Dynamic Voltage Scaling

As we note in "Context", we are concerned in this pattern with the development of software for embedded systems in which (i) the developer must adhere to severe resource constraints, and (ii) there is a need for highly predictable system behaviour. With many mobile designs (for example, mobile medical equipment) we also need to minimise power consumption in order to maximise battery life.

To meet all three constraints, it is sometimes possible to use a system architecture which combines time-triggered co-operative (TTC) task scheduling with a power-reduction technique know as "dynamic voltage scaling" (DVS). To achieve this, use of a SANDWICH DELAY is a crucial part of the implementation (and is used to ensure that the complex DVS operations do not introduce task jitter).

The use of SANDWICH DELAYS in this context is described in detail elsewhere [6].

SANDWICH DELAY (C, LPC2000)

{pattern implementation example}[3]

Context

- You wish to implement a SANDWICH DELAY [this paper]
- Your chosen implementation language is C[4].
- Your chosen implementation platform is the NXP LPC2000 family of (ARM7-based) microcontrollers.

Problem

How can you implement a SANDWICH DELAY for the NXP LPC2000 family of microcontrollers?

Background

As with all widely-used microcontrollers, the LPC2000 devices have on-chip timers which are directly accessible by the programmer. More specifically, all members of this family have two 32-bit timers, known as Timer 0 and Timer 1. These can each be set to take actions (such as setting a flag) when a particular time period has elapsed.

In the simplest case, these timers (and other peripheral devices) will be driven by the "peripheral clock" (plck) which - by default - runs at 25% of the rate of the system oscillator (Figure 4).

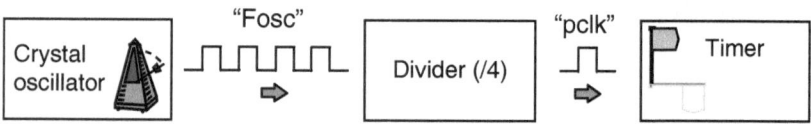

Fig. 4. The link between oscillator frequency and timer updates in the LPC2000 devices (default situation)

By taking into account the link between the oscillator frequency and the timer hardware, the timers can be configured so that (for example) a flag is set after a period of 10ms has elapsed. The resulting delay code can be made highly portable.

Both Timer 0 and Timer 1 are 32-bit timers, which are preceded by a 32-bit pre-scalar. The pre-scalar is in turn driven by the peripheral clock. This is an extremely

---

[3] As the name might suggest, PIEs are intended to illustrate how a particular pattern can be implemented. This is important (in the embedded systems field) because there are great differences in system environments, caused by variations in the hardware platform (e.g. 8-bit, 16-bit, 32-bit, 64-bit), and programming language (e.g. assembly language, C, C++). The possible implementations are not sufficiently different to be classified as distinct patterns: however, they do contain useful information (please see [5] for further information about the use of PIEs).

[4] The examples in the pattern were created using the GNU C compiler, hosted in a Keil uVision 3 IDE.

flexible combination. As an example, suppose that we wished to generate the longest possible delay using Timer 0 on an LPC2100 device with a 12 MHz oscillator. The delay would be generated as follows:

- Both the pre-scalar and the timer itself begin with a count of 0.
- The pre-scalar would be set to trigger at its maximum value: this is 2^{32}-1 (=4294967295). With a 12 MHz oscillator (and the default divider of 4), the pre-scalar would take approximately 1432 seconds to reach this value. It would then be reset, and begin counting again.
- When the pre-scalar reached 1432 seconds, Timer 0 would be incremented by 1. To reach its full count (4294967295) would take approximately 200,000 years.

Clearly, this length of delay will not be required in most applications! However, very precise delays (for example, an hour, a day – even a week) can be created using this flexible hardware.

As a more detailed example, suppose that we have a 12 MHz oscillator (again with default divider of 4) and we wish to generate a delay of 1 second. We can omit the prescalar, and simply set the match register on Timer 1 to count to to the required value (3,000,000 – 1).

We can achieve this using the code shown in Listing 3.

```
// Prescale is 0 (in effect, prescalar not used)
T1PC = 0;

// Set the "Timer Counter Register" for this timer.
// In this register, Bit 0 is the "Counter Enable" bit.
// When 1, the Timer Counter and Prescale Counter are enabled for counting.
// When 0, the counters are disabled.
T1TCR &= ~0x01;    // Stop the timer by clearing Bit 0

// There are three match registetrs (MR0, MR1, MR2) for each timer.
// The match register values are continuously compared to the Timer Counter
value.
// When the two values are equal, actions can be triggered automatically
T1MR0 = 2999999;   // Set the match register (MR0) to required value

// When the match register detects a match, we can choose to:
// Generate an interrupt (not used here),
// Reset the Timer Counter and / or
// Stop the timer.
// These actions are controlled by the settings in the MCR register.
// Here we set a flag on match (no interrupt), reset the count and stop the
timer.
T1MCR = 0x07;      // Set flag on match, reset count and stop timer

T1TCR |= 0x01;     // Start the timer

// Wait for timer to reach count (at which point the IR flag will be set)
while ((T1IR & 0x0001) == 0)
    {
    ;
    }

// Reset the timer flag (by writing "1")
T1IR |= 0x01;
```

Listing 3. Configuring Timer1 in the LPC2000 family. See text for details.

Solution

A code example illustrating the implementation of a SANDWICH DELAY for an
LPC2000 device is given in Listing 4 and Listing 5.

```
/*-------------------------------------------------------------------*-

    Main.C (v1.00)

    -------------------------------------------------------------------

    Simple "Sandwich Delay" demo for NXP LPC2000 devices.

-*-------------------------------------------------------------------*/
#include "main.h"

#include "system_init.h"

#include "led_flash.h"
#include "random_loop_delay.h"

#include "sandwich_delay_t1.h"
/*-------------------------------------------------------------------*-

  int main (void)

-*-------------------------------------------------------------------*/
int main(void)
    {
    // Set up PLL, VPB divider, MAM and interrupt mapping
    System_Init();

    // Prepare to flash LED
    LED_FLASH_Init();

    // Prepare for "random" delays
    RANDOM_LOOP_DELAY_Init();

    while(1)
        {
        // Set up Timer 1 for 1-second sandwich delay
        SANDWICH_DELAY_T1_Start(1000);

        // Change the LED state (OFF to ON, or vice versa)
        LED_FLASH_Change_State();

        // "Random" delay
        // (Represents function with variable execution time)
        RANDOM_LOOP_DELAY_Wait();

        // Wait for the timer to reach the required value
        SANDWICH_DELAY_T1_Wait();
        }

    return 1;
    }
/*-------------------------------------------------------------------*-
    ---- END OF FILE ------------------------------------------------
-*-------------------------------------------------------------------*/
```

Listing 4. Implementing a SANDWICH DELAY for the LPC2000 family (main.c)

```
/*-----------------------------------------------------------------*-

     sandwich_delay_t1.c (v1.00)

   -------------------------------------------------------------------

     "Sandwich delay" for the LPC2000 family using Timer 1.


   -*-----------------------------------------------------------------*/

#include "main.h"

/*-----------------------------------------------------------------*-

     SANDWICH_DELAY_T1_Start()

     Parameter is - roughly - delay in milliseconds.

     Uses T1 for delay (Timer 0 often used for scheduler)

   -*-----------------------------------------------------------------*/
void SANDWICH_DELAY_T1_Start(const unsigned int DELAY_MS)
     {
     T1PC = 0x00;     // Prescale is 0
     T1TCR &= ~0x01;  // Stop timer

     // Set the match register (MR0) to required value
     T1MR0 = ((PCLK / 1000U) * DELAY_MS) - 1;

     // Set flag on match, reset count and stop timer
     T1MCR = 0x07;

     T1TCR |= 0x01;    // Start timer
     }

/*-----------------------------------------------------------------*-

     SANDWICH_DELAY_T1_Wait()
     Waits (indefinitely) for Sandwich Delay to complete.

   -*-----------------------------------------------------------------*/

void SANDWICH_DELAY_T1_Wait(void)
     {
     // Wait for timer to reach count
     while ((T1IR & 0x01) == 0)
        {
        ;
        }

     // Reset flag (by writing "1")
     T1IR |= 0x01;
     }

/*-----------------------------------------------------------------*-
   ---- END OF FILE -------------------------------------------------
   -*-----------------------------------------------------------------*/
```

Listing 5. Implementing a SANDWICH DELAY for the LPC2000 family (example): file (sandwich_delay_t1.c)

Acknowledgements

This paper was originally reviewed through EuroPLoP 2006. Many thanks to Bob Hanmer, who provided numerous useful suggestions during the shepherding process.

We also thank the contributors to our workshop session (Joe Bergen, Frank Buschmann, Neil Harrison, Kevlin Henney, Andy Longshaw, Klaus Marquardt, Didi Schütz and Markus Völter) for further comments on this paper at the conference itself.

References

1. Cottet, F., David, L.: A solution to the time jitter removal in deadline based scheduling of real-time applications. In: 5th IEEE Real-Time Technology and Applications Symposium - WIP, Vancouver, Canada, pp. 33–38 (1999)
2. Hughes, Z.M., Pont, M.J.: Reducing the impact of task overruns in resource-constrained embedded systems in which a time-triggered software architecture is employed. Transactions of the Institute of Measurement and Control 30, 427–450 (2008)
3. Jerri, A.J.: The Shannon sampling theorem: its various extensions and applications a tutorial review. Proc. of the IEEE 65, 1565–1596 (1997)
4. Kurian, S., Pont, M.J.: Building reliable embedded systems using Abstract Patterns, Patterns, and Pattern Implementation Examples. In: Koelmans, A., Bystrov, A., Pont, M.J., Ong, R., Brown, A. (eds.) Proceedings of the Second UK Embedded Forum, Birmingham, UK, October 2005, pp. 36–59. University of Newcastle upon Tyne (2005) ISBN: 0-7017-0191-9
5. Mart, P., Fuertes, J.M., Ramamritham, K., Fohler, G.: Jitter Compensation for Real-Time Control Systems. In: 22nd IEEE Real-Time Systems Symposium (RTSS 2001), London, England, pp. 39–48 (2001)
6. Phatrapornnant, T., Pont, M.J.: Reducing jitter in embedded systems employing a time-triggered software architecture and dynamic voltage scaling. IEEE Transactions on Computers 55(2), 113–124 (2006)
7. Pont, M.J.: Patterns for Time-Triggered Embedded Systems: Building Reliable Applications with the 8051 Family of Microcontrollers. Addison-Wesley/ACM Press (2001) ISBN: 0-201-331381
8. Pont, M.J., Ong, H.L.R.: Using watchdog timers to improve the reliability of TTCS embedded systems. In: Hruby, P., Soressen, K.E. (eds.) Proceedings of the First Nordic Conference on Pattern Languages of Programs (VikingPloP 2002), September 2002, pp. 159–200. Microsoft Business Solutions (2003) ISBN: 87-7849-769-8
9. Torngren, M.: Fundamentals of implementing real-time control applications in distributed computer systems. Real-Time Systems 14, 219–250 (1998)

Synchronization Patterns for Process-Driven and Service-Oriented Architectures

Carsten Hentrich

CSC Deutschland Solutions GmbH, Abraham-Lincoln-Park 1
65189 Wiesbaden, Germany
chentrich@csc.com

Abstract. This paper introduces a small pattern language for solving different kinds of synchronization problems in the area of process-driven and service-oriented architectures. The paper addresses synchronization issues in terms of coordinating the order of actions in technically independent process instances. Synchronization is thus addressed in terms of event-, control flow-, and object access synchronization. The patterns are related to the Service Composition and Service Provider Layers in an SOA.

Keywords: SOA, pattern language, software architecture, process-driven, service-oriented, synchronization.

1 Introduction

The key principle of process-driven architecture approach is separation of business logic from process logic. Practically, this principle means that the process logic will be taken out of applications and will be flexibly controlled by a process-driven middleware. Flexibility is achieved by introducing an abstraction layer for process control with such process-driven middleware that allows changing the process flow definition more easily compared to static process implementation within application program code. That means a process-driven architecture employs a process engine to coordinate and execute process activities according to a defined process model. These activities are either automatically executed system-activities or involve human interaction. Yet, both types require any sort of program or system that implements the logic to be executed by the activity, as the process engine only orchestrates the activities, but does not implement the functionality represented by them. Rather these functions are executed by systems integrated in the process flow.

Service-oriented architectures (SOA) [1] understand these activity implementations as services that offer a defined functionality which is clearly expressed by its commonly accessible interface description (see also [2]) and that may be invoked from any high-level orchestration independently from the involved technology.

An SOA is typically represented as a layered architecture that separates the different responsibilities of the involved components or tasks in order to reach this goal. Figure 1 shows such a layered representation [3].

The Service Composition Layer denotes the high-level orchestration of services that may be accomplished by a process engine. In this case we speak of a process-driven

J. Noble and R. Johnson (Eds.): TPLOP I, LNCS 5770, pp. 103–135, 2009.

Orthogonal Aspects   *Layers*

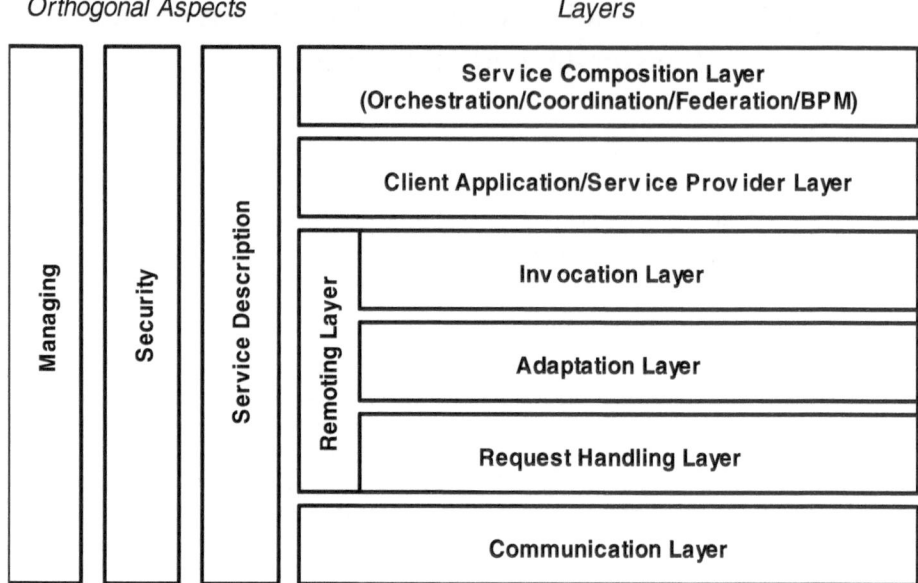

Fig. 1. SOA Layers

SOA. The Client Application and Service Provider Layer include both service consumption on client side and service offering on server side. The lower layers deal with remoting of service calls to and from the service providers and with low-level communication. This paper deals with the Service Composition and the Service Provider Layer as all considerations are motivated by problems that mainly occur at their boundaries.

Even though a clean separation of layers might suggest that almost none or at least very little coupling or interaction exists between process flow and service execution, there are still links and dependencies that are wanted and needed in order to assemble a working solution.

Besides identifying and invoking a service via a name when a process activity is scheduled, parameters will have to be supplied or references to business objects [4] need to be passed, as addressed by the BUSINESS OBJECT REFERENCE PATTERN [5]. The process flow might have to wait at some point for an event to occur asynchronously after a service has been invoked by a previous activity or even by another process. Moreover, if processes are executed in parallel and invoke services that will operate on the same business object, how will the access be synchronized, so that both processes operate with valid data and do not block their execution?

Wherever a service is invoked by a process instance an interaction takes place that may require different degrees of synchronization and that may bear different consequences. The patterns described in this paper tackle the problems that arise from interactions which require some sort of synchronization of the process flow and the service execution. In other words: synchronization of the process flow within the process engine itself as well as synchronization of the process execution and interacting system components is essential for a seamless integration and a functioning process-driven architecture.

In this paper a collection of patterns is introduced which offer solutions to different sorts of synchronization problems in process-driven and service-oriented architectures. Some of these patterns mainly deal with business process modeling and are therefore of interest for business analysts or process modelers. Yet, the scope of this paper is not only to present patterns for organizing process flows. Quite some work has been done in this area [5, 6, 7, 8, 9] and also some patterns for process flow synchronization within single processes and among several process instances exist [7].

This paper does not only take process design into account, i.e. the design time view on problem situations, but rather tries to see the problems from an architectural point of view. That means that not only process models are considered, but also the environment and its underlying software architecture in which the process engine is integrated to execute the business processes. This integration aspect will mainly be of interest for software architects who have to integrate a process engine into an existing or newly designed application or system architecture. Thus, the problem domains for system-wide event synchronization and synchronization of data access, which are presented later on, are addressed rather to software architects than business analysts.

2 Pattern Language Overview

The patterns are related to each other as shown in Figure 2. Figure 2 also denotes different categories of synchronization that further group related patters. Table 1 provides thumbnails of the patterns covering problems and solutions. The patterns are divided in three different categories according to the covered problem domain as shown in Figure 2. The categories are just briefly outlined at this point and will be explained in more detail later in the context of the patterns descriptions:

- *Process Flow Synchronization:* Patterns of this class address synchronization issues in the control flow of one or among several processes.

- *Event Synchronization:* Patterns of this class address synchronization problems in the area of business processes and external events.

- *Business Object Access Synchronization:* Patterns of this class deal with synchronization problems of business object access form parallel processes.

Figure 2 illustrates that Process Flow Synchronization patterns and Event Synchronization patterns can be combined. That means the WAITING ACTIVITY and TIMEOUT HANDLER patterns may be based on external events. For this reason, the patterns can be combined with the EVENT-BASED ACTIVITY pattern, which deals with handling external events. The relationships between the patterns indicate that in this case the patterns can be applied together. The relationship between EVENT DISPATCHER and EVENT-BASED ACTIVITY points out that an EVENT-DISPATCHER might manage external events that are captured by an EVENT-BASED ACTIVITY in a process. Analogously the EVENT DISPATCHER can also manage events for an EVENT-BASED PROCESS INSTANTIATOR, which captures external events to create process instances on a process engine. A corresponding relationship is thus defined between

Table 1. Problem/solution overview of the patterns

Pattern	Problem	Solution
EVENT-BASED ACTIVITY	How can events that occur outside the space of a process instance be handled in the process flow?	Model an EVENT-BASED ACTIVITY that actively waits for events to occur and that terminates if they do so.
EVENT-BASED PROCESS INSTANTIATOR	How can process instances be created on a process engine on the basis of occurring events?	Use an EVENT-BASED PROCESS INSTANTIATOR that instantiates processes if corresponding events occur.
EVENT DISPATCHER	Often events are fired from various event sources. These event sources have different lifecycles and may change over time. Registering to concrete event sources thus implies an issue of inflexibility.	Use a central EVENT DISPATCHER That manages occurring events and which offers a central access point for event-based process components.
TIMEOUT HANDLER	How can timeouts of process activities be managed in a process?	Model a TIMEOUT HANDLER that defines behaviour in the process model in case a timeout has occurred.
WAITING ACTIVITY	A process only consists of activities, such that it is actually a problem how to model such a waiting position, which is rather passive than active in nature.	Model a WAITING ACTIVITY which uses an internal timer and actively waits for a defined time frame to elapse until it terminates.
PRIVATE-PUBLIC BUSINESS OBJECT	When business processes access business objects in parallel, concurrency issues occur. Thus, the problem arises how business processes can access shared business objects in a controlled way to avoid concurrent updates and to limit the visibility of uncommitted changes.	Introduce PRIVATE-PUBLIC BUSINESS OBJECTS, which expose two separate images, a private and a public image of the contained data.

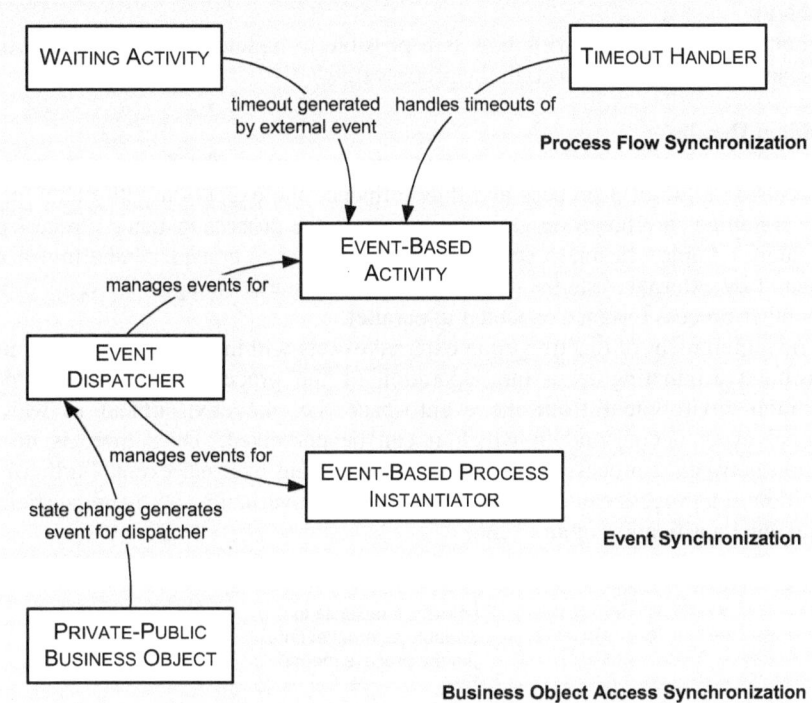

Fig. 2. Relationships of simple synchronisation patterns

the EVENT DISPATCHER and the EVENT-BASED PROCESS INSTANTIATOR. The PRIVATE-PUBLIC BUSINESS OBJECT may act as event source and create events that are handled by an EVENT DISPATCHER. For this reason, a relationship is defined between those patterns as well. There is no fixed sequence to apply the patterns.

3   Event Synchronization

A process instance runs in its own data and event space. If events outside the context of a process instance occur that need to be considered by the process instance, problems may occur how to capture those events by the process instance. Patterns of this class provide solutions to consider events that occur outside the event space of a process instance.

3.1   Pattern: Event-Based Activity

Context
Business process design becomes more complex and involves interaction with other business applications and external data sources. Handling of external events needs to be considered in the process design. A process instance running on a process engine has an own data and event space.

Problem
In complex business scenarios how is it possible to handle events that occur outside the space of a process instance in the process flow?

Problem Details
During the execution of a process instance the evaluation of defined conditions shape the decision logic of a process and thus influence the execution path of the process. Such conditions are based on variables known in the process instance. Process design in a more complex business scenario may also have to consider handling of events triggered by external systems, e.g. business object status changes or events produced by another process instance executed in parallel.

The requirement of reacting upon external events within a process instance implies a problem originating from the separation of the process space, i.e. the process execution environment from the event space, i.e. the environment in which the external event occurs and in which it can be perceived. Thus, there is no direct relation between a process instance and an occurring external event. Furthermore, a condition in a process can evaluate process instance variables, but is not sufficient for retrieving a notification of an event.

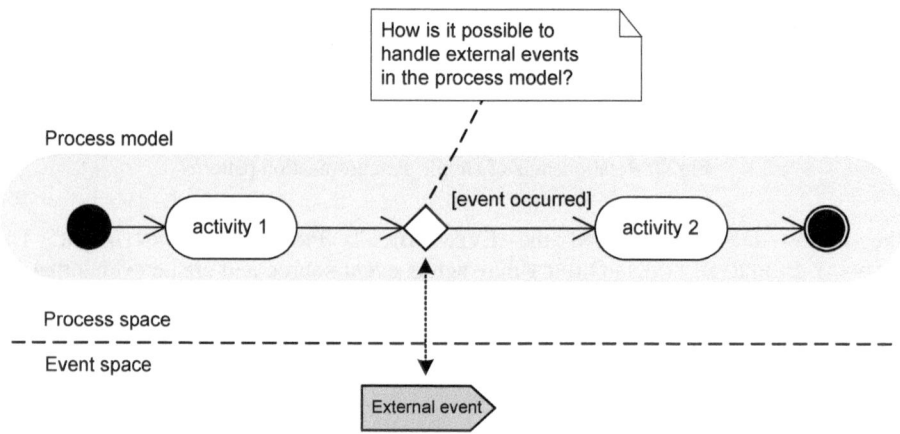

Fig. 3. Problem illustration for handling external events

Consider an asynchronous print job that is sent to an output system when a user finishes an activity. In case a subsequent activity of the process instance depends on the newly created document it shall not be scheduled as long as the document is not available. Since the state of the document creation is not known in the scope of the process engine, it cannot be evaluated by the process in an internal condition. Additionally, such a condition could not be simply evaluated once, but would have to be iteratively checked until it is satisfied, as the process does not know when an event occurs. The problem in this scenario is that the creation of the document is an event that occurs outside the process event space. Therefore the scheduling of the activity cannot be easily influenced by this external event.

The scenario above can be summarized to the basic problem that a process instance shall wait at a defined process-step for an external event to occur before continuing the process execution. This problem also brings up two closely related aspects that need to be considered: How are errors handled while waiting for an event and what happens if the event never occurs? A strategy for error and timeout handling has to be considered in this context as well.

Solution
Model an EVENT-BASED ACTIVITY that actively waits for external events to occur and that terminates if they do so. The EVENT-BASED ACTIVITY implementation acts as an event listener to report occurring events to the process instance.

Solution Details
An EVENT-BASED ACTIVITY acts as an event listener and registers to event sources from which it would like to retrieve notifications about occurring events. In case it is notified of the events that the activity is waiting for, the activity terminates and the process execution continues.

The activity implementation of an EVENT-BASED ACTIVITY represents an event listener that observes another component, i.e. the event source, by registering as an OBSERVER [10]. The event source simply notifies all registered observers in case an event (e.g. a change of its state) occurs. The subjects to observe, i.e. the event sources, must be known by the activity implementation of an EVENT-BASED ACTIVITY. Thus, the problem is solved outside the space of the process engine. The activity implementation literally connects the event space of the process instance with an external event space. An EVENT-BASED ACTIVITY being modelled in a process is related to its activity implementation when it is instantiated by the process engine. The implementation being an event listener receives notifications of the occurring events. If it is notified of the events it has been waiting for, the activity implementation will terminate the activity in the process.

The pattern shown in Figure 4 decouples the process from the event space. A coupling is only present in terms of a reference from the activity to its implementation. This has the advantage that the process engine and also the process designer are

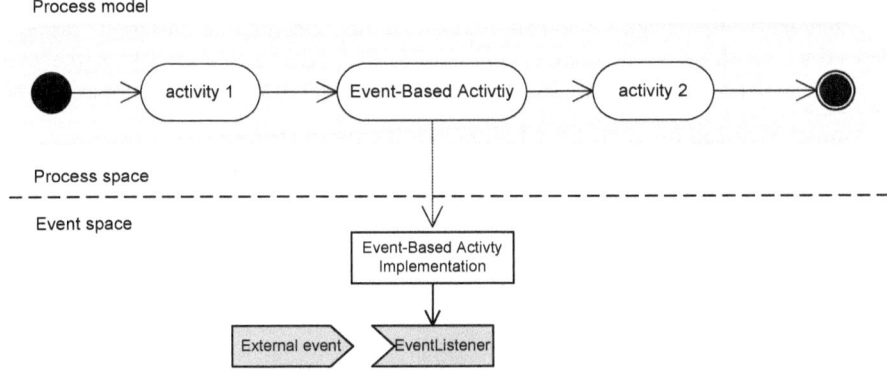

Fig. 4. An event-based activity to handle external events

independent of concrete events and event sources. On the other hand all logic concerning which events to wait for until the process flow continues is contained in the event-based activity implementation outside of the process space. If a common knowledge about events and event source is desirable, corresponding identifiers can be supplied in the activity's data container during design time and evaluated in the implementation during runtime.

As a consequence of this pattern the process flow is interrupted and its further execution depends on the occurrence of one or more defined external events. Business process design can integrate a broad range of enterprise system resources like external business applications or data sources, as the process flow may be synchronized with external systems. Additional effort has to be paid to timeout and error handling in order not to block the process execution for an undefined amount of time. As a negative consequence the handling of events and modelling event-based activities makes the processes more complex. For this reason, this complexity and thus increased development and maintenance efforts should only be considered if the business scenarios actually require external events to be handled in the process.

The EVENT DISPATCHER pattern introduces a possibility to decouple event listeners from event sources and thereby added a higher degree of abstraction from concrete implementations. Apply the pattern in this context if the system has to deal with many event sources and frequent changes are expected.

Applying the pattern requires consideration of timeout and error handling, since a controllable process execution highly depends on a deterministic behaviour of such EVENT-BASED ACTIVITIES. The process designer is responsible for handling these situations within the process model. For this purpose, the related TIMEOUT HANDLER pattern can be applied. The TIMEOUT HANDLER pattern describes a solution for handling timeouts that are reported by components integrated in the process flow. EVENT-BASED ACTIVITIES are typically considered as such components, as listening for an event should include a defined timeout value. The PROCESS-BASED ERROR MANAGEMENT pattern [5] provides a solution for dealing with reported errors.

The WAITING ACTIVITY pattern describes a solution for controlling process execution based on a dynamic or static timer. In the context of EVENT-BASED ACTIVITIES the timer can be perceived as an event source and the waiting activity as a special type of EVENT-BASED ACTIVITY.

Moreover, the pattern is related to the OBSERVER pattern [10] known from object oriented software design. The pattern can be implemented in different variations depending on the process engine being used, the environment in which the event occurs, and depending on how generic or specific the solution design is required to be.

Example: Waiting for a Status Change in a Business Object
The following example assumes a process engine according to the WfMC [11, 12] standards denoted as the process space and any object oriented application execution environment for the activity implementations in the event-space, e.g. offered by a J2EE application server [4]. For instance, if the process flow often has to wait for a specific status change of business objects managed outside the process engine, a generic EVENT-BASED ACTIVITY implementation will be considered for this purpose.

This specific implementation registers as a listener at a business object that is referenced by the activity using a unique ID (also compare the BUSINESS OBJECT REFERENCE pattern [5]).

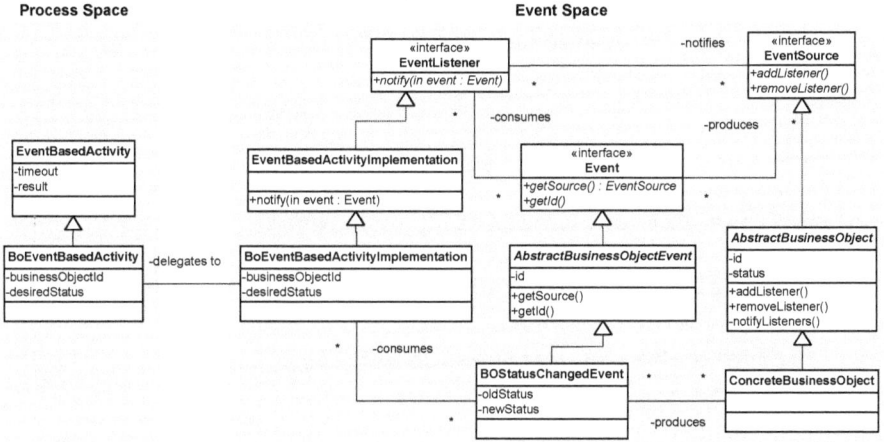

Fig. 5. Example of a generic implementation for business object status change events

Once notified of a BoStatusChangedEvent the EVENT-BASED ACTIVITY implementation compares the new status to the one specified in the activity's input data. If the new status is equal to the desired status, the activity implementation terminates the activity and the process execution continues. The code fragment below gives a more detailed insight into the implementation of such an EVENT-BASED ACTIVITY implementation:

```
public abstract class EventBasedActivityDelegate
implements EventListener {
        // field initialized from activity's input data
        // container
        private int timeout;

        // Initialization
        public EventBasedActivityDelegate() {
                // Create a timeout event source
                EventSource source = new
                        TimeOutEventSource(timeout);
                // Register as listener
                source.addListener(this);
        }

        public synchronized void notify(Event event) {
                if (event.getId() == TIMEOUT_EVENT) {
```

```
                    // Terminate the activity
                    terminate(TIMEOUT);
            }
      }
      ...
}
public class BoEventBasedActivityDelegate extends
EventBasedActivityDelegate{
      // fields initialized from activity's input
      // container
      private String businessObjectId;
      private int desiredStatus;
      // Initialization
      public BoEventBasedActivityDelegate() {
            // Initialize timeout counter
            super();
            // Get the business object to register to
            EventSource source =
            BoManager.getBusinessObject(
                                   businessObjectId());
            // Register as listener
            source.addListener(this);
      }
      public synchronized void notify(Event event) {
            if (event.getId() == BO_STATUS_CHANGED_EVENT)
      {
                    BoStatusChangedEvent statusEvent =
                    (BoStatusChangedEvent) event;
                    // Compare new status to desired status
                    if (statusEvent.getNewStatus() ==
                    desiredStatus) {
                            // Terminate the activity
                            terminate(SUCCESS);
                    }
            } else {
                    // handle the event in the super class
                    super.notify(event);
            }
      }
      ...
}
```

Known Uses

- Leading BPEL engines like BEA Agualogic Fuego, Tibco WebMethods, or IBM WebSphere Process Server, and Oracle Fusion provide event handling mechanisms.
- The pattern has also been implemented with older workflow engines such as IBM WebSphere MQ Workflow or Staffware. In this case the event handling implementation was delegated to an external program and not directly integrated into the features of the engine. As a result an implementation from scratch has been necessary.
- Also message busses and support this kind of event handling. Examples are WebSphere Advanced ESB, or the former version WebSphere Business Integration Message Broker.

3.2 Pattern: Event-Based Process Instantiator

Context
Processes are executed on a process engine and need to be modelled in complex business scenarios.

Problem
How can process instances be dynamically created by a process engine on the basis of occurring external events?

Problem Details
In a typical process-driven environment process instances are instantiated and started by the process engine due to user interaction, e.g. a user triggers the creation of a process instance from within an application. Process instances are also created during execution of the process model if it involves sub-processes, which will be instantiated dynamically by the process engine once the execution has reached the corresponding process-step to start a sub-process.

These types of process creation either involve human interaction or require the processes to be statically modelled as sub-processes that will be called from within another process model.

In some situations it will not be possible to statically define the processes to be started from within another process model. For example, this may be the case if the amount of instances, or the type of processes to be instantiated, depends on dynamic parameters that are only available during runtime. Furthermore, it may not always be desirable to start processes from other process instances, as this requires the "super processes" to run during that time, as it wraps the sub-process.

If the creation of process instances shall neither be triggered directly by a user interaction nor due to a static model, it will be necessary to automatically instantiate a process if an external event takes place within the system environment.

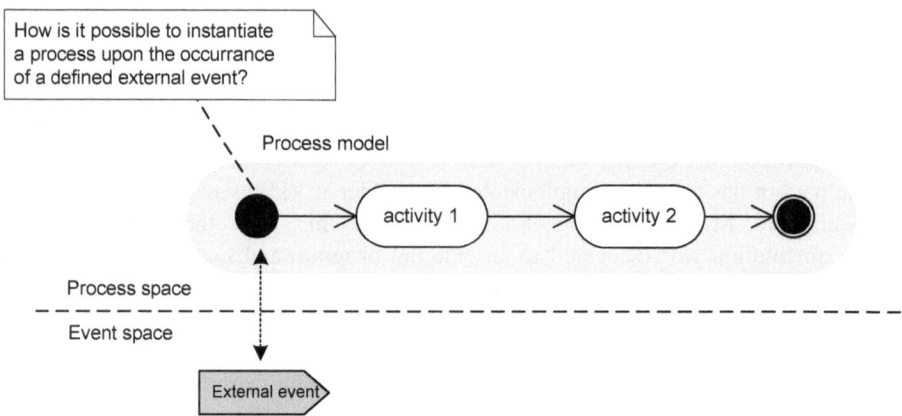

Fig. 6. Problem illustration for the instantiation of a process upon events

The basic problem to achieve this goal is that the event to occur will not always be visible in the scope of the process engine and the engine may not support dynamic process instantiation. How is it possible to create instances of defined process models when an event occurs outside of the scope of the process engine? How can the instantiated process be supplied with correct input data?

Solution
Introduce an EVENT-BASED PROCESS INSTANTIATOR, which acts as an event listener and instantiates a process or a set of processes once the defined events occur.

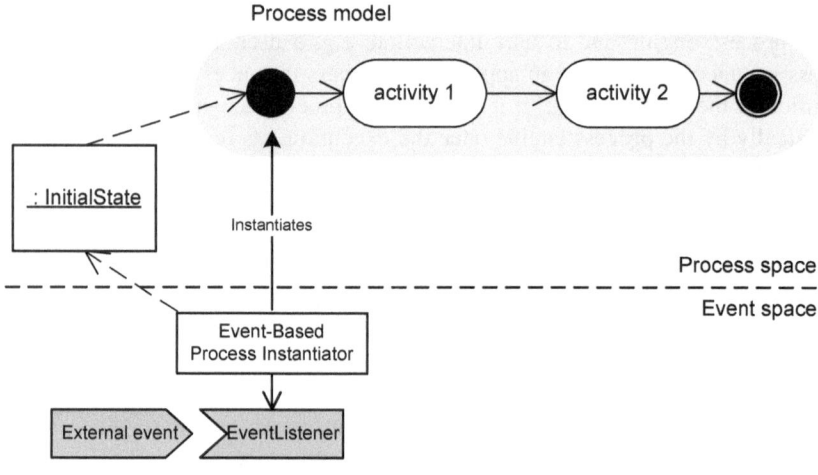

Fig. 7. Solution employing an event-based process instantiator

Solution Details
An EVENT-BASED PROCESS INSTANTIATOR is responsible for instantiating one or more processes and starting them with a defined initial state upon the occurrence of

an external event. It acts as an event listener, i.e. it waits to be notified about occurring events from defined event sources that it registers to.

Since external events will occur outside the scope of the process engine, the EVENT-BASED PROCESS INSTANTIATOR resides within the external event space, i.e. the space in which the events occur or where the events can be perceived. If the process to be started requires a predefined set of information, the EVENT-BASED PROCESS INSTANTIATOR is responsible for supplying this initial state to the newly created process instance. This is either possible by the means of an external configuration or any other data storage.

Example: Implementation of the Pattern in a Component Structure

Figure 8 shows an example component structure of an EVENT-BASED PROCESS INSTANTIATOR as it has been implemented in practice. The EVENT-BASED PROCESS INSTANTIATOR uses a process adapter that offers a programming interface to the process engine to start a process instance. The pattern distinguishes between event listeners and event sources. An event source is a component that fires events and notifies all listeners that have registered to this source about the events. When notified, the event listener checks whether the event is of interest using its unique ID or checking the event source it was emitted from.

As a consequence to this pattern, process instances can be dynamically instantiated and started depending on external events. If the process to start requires an initial state to be supplied, the EVENT-BASED PROCESS INSTANTIATOR resides is responsible for supplying it, and, therefore, the corresponding information has to be stored outside the process engine. This may result in additional effort for ensuring data consistency. It also needs to be considered, however, that again the business requirements should be the driver to implement this pattern, as it increases complexity of the architecture. This added complexity is a negative consequence, if the business scenario does not require event-based process instantiation. In this case the additional development effort might be avoided.

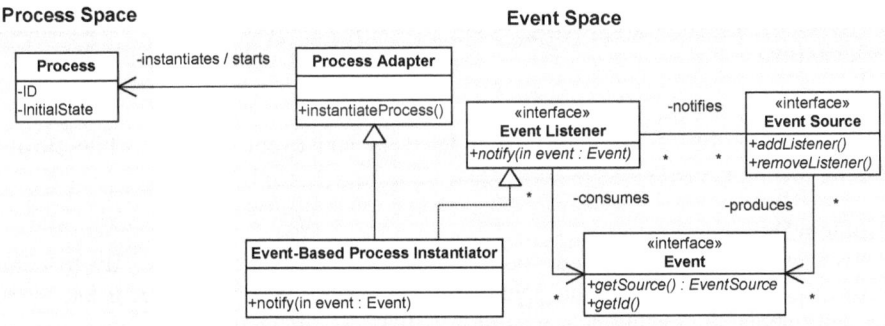

Fig. 8. Structural concept of an event-based process instantiator

The EVENT DISPATCHER is a related pattern that introduces a possibility to decouple event listeners from event sources and thereby adds a higher degree of abstraction from concrete implementations. Applying this pattern in this context allows to flexibly dealing with many event sources. The EVENT-BASED ACTIVITY pattern employs the same event listener / event source mechanism and describes, like the EVENT-BASED PROCESS INSTANTIATOR resides pattern, an event-based component.

The EVENT-BASED PROCESS INSTANCE pattern [5] is a specialization of this pattern. It offers a solution for the problem of processes that are suspended for a long time, because of an EVENT-BASED ACTIVITY waiting for an external event. The process is split into two parts and EVENT-BASED PROCESS INSTANCE can be used to instantiate the second process when the event occurs. This special usage requires the state of the first process to be stored and used as initial the state for the instantiated process.

Known Uses

- Leading BPEL engines like BEA Agualogic Fuego, Tibco WebMethods, or IBM WebSphere Process Server, and Oracle Fusion provide process instantiation features based on events. The engines implement the pattern as a feature of the engine.
- The pattern has also been implemented with older workflow engines such as IBM WebSphere MQ Workflow or Staffware. In this case an external program has been implemented that has used the API of the engine to create processes based on events.
- Also message busses and support this kind of message flow instantiation based on events. Examples are WebSphere Advanced ESB, or the former version WebSphere Business Integration Message Broker.

3.3 Pattern: Event Dispatcher

Context
External events are occurring outside the scope of the process engine. Often events are fired from various event sources. These event sources have different lifecycles and may change over time. Registering to concrete event sources thus implies an issue of inflexibility.

Problem
How is it possible to decouple event listeners and event sources, while flexibly linking them together?

Problem Details
If each event-based component has to register at event sources directly to obtain notifications from events of this source, this implies the component needs knowledge not only about the events it is waiting for, but also about the source that fires this event. Problems arise when there are several sources for the same event. The event observer has to know these concrete sources and register to all of them. If event sources change, this will consequently have an impact on the event observing components. As a result, this is not a flexible architectural solution.

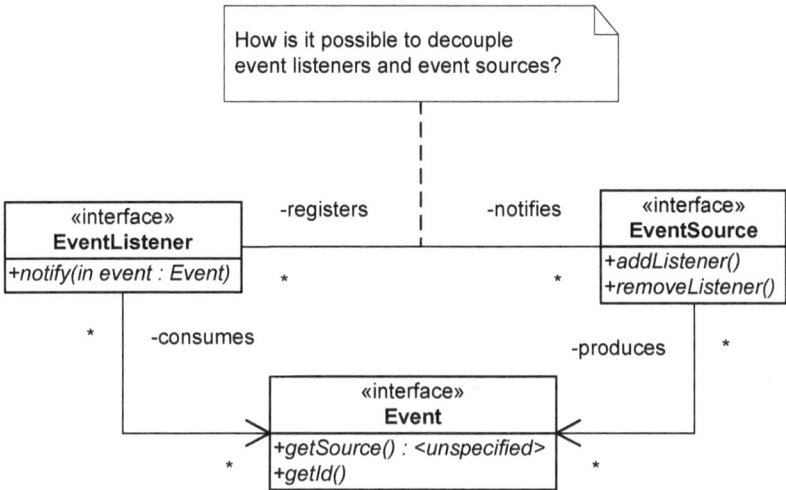

Fig. 9. Problem illustration for decentralized event handling

Another problem arises if one takes the runtime aspect into account. For instance, if an event-based component is instantiated, i.e. an EVENT-BASED ACTIVITY implementation or an EVENT-BASED PROCESS INSTANTIATOR, it may register immediately to the event source in order not to miss an occurring event during its lifetime. This may be a problem if the concrete event source is not always present. In case an event source is implemented by a component that has limited lifetime, i.e. an instance of the component will be created and destructed several times during the application's runtime, an event listener might not always have the chance to register.

Consider a scenario in which a process shall wait for a business object state to change. If the process designer employs an EVENT-BASED ACTIVITY to realize this requirement, this component will have to register with an event source that fires such a business object event. In case the business object is defined as the event source itself, listeners would have to register directly with it. This will be a problem if the business objects are only instantiated on demand.

The scenario above can be summarized to the basic problem that event listeners not only need knowledge of the concrete event source to register to, but also depend on runtime aspects that may not always suite flexibility requirements.

Solution
Use a central EVENT DISPATCHER that manages occurring events and which offers a central access point for event-based components.

Solution Details
An EVENT DISPATCHER is a central architectural component that is responsible for gathering, managing and delegating events from event sources to event listeners. It offers a common interface for event listeners and sources to register to and to remove from the EVENT DISPATCHER.

In order to be able to act as such a central component all event sources of the considered application or system must register at the EVENT DISPATCHER, thereby offering their service of event notification in the system. When an event source registers, the EVENT DISPATCHER itself registers as a listener at that source. Consequently the EVENT DISPATCHER does not initially have to know about all concrete event sources, yet is informed about each event that will occur in the system. If the event source no longer fires events, or if it will be destructed, it removes itself from the repository.

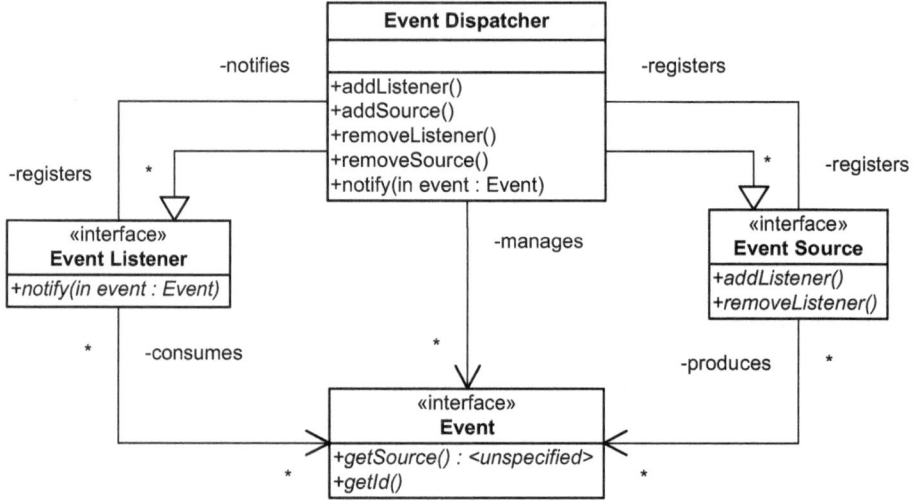

Fig. 10. The event dispatcher

All event listeners, i.e. event-based components waiting for defined events to occur, simply have to register at the EVENT DISPATCHER. The EVENT DISPATCHER is responsible for delegating the events to event listeners having registered for them. For this to work the listeners must provide a system-wide unique identifier of the events that they are interested in. In case the event source is known, the listener may also state to be notified about all events of that specific source. Information which events to route to which listener must be provided by the listeners or may be centrally configured.

Furthermore, introduction of an EVENT DISPATCHER allows a centralized common handling for all events. This includes aspects such as centrally configured logging, verification, or filtering.

By introducing an EVENT DISPATCHER event listeners and event sources of the application or system can be decoupled. This also decouples process components from other application resources. Concrete implementations of event sources may be changed without any impact on defined listeners, i.e. event-based components, because these listeners do not directly register with these components any more. Event listeners no longer depend on runtime aspects of the event sources they request to be notified by. The introduction of system-wide unique event identifiers and event source identifiers is essential for central event management.

This added complexity introduced by an EVENT DISPATCHER is actually a negative consequence. For this reason, the pattern should only be applied if the business requirements point to using the pattern. If flexible dispatching of events is not required from the business point of view then applying the pattern involves unnecessary development and maintenance effort.

The EVENT-BASED ACTIVITY and the EVENT-BASED PROCESS INSTANTIATOR pattern introduce process components that act as event listeners and that register to defined event sources. Introducing an EVENT DISPATCHER for these components offers the possibility to exchange event sources without any major impacts. The pattern is similar to the PUBLISHER-SUBSCRIBER [14] pattern and may be viewed as a speciality of this pattern. The speciality about the EVENT DISPATCHER is that it focuses in events and not components. That means different components may fire the same events. The dispatcher is registering events and not components. Moreover, subscribing for events is selective, i.e. event-listeners only listen to a subset of all registered events, which represents the dispatching rule.

Example: Dispatching Business Object State Change Events
The example introduced in the EVENT-BASED ACTIVITY pattern includes business objects as event sources and an EVENT-BASED ACTIVITY registering at such an event source in order to react upon a state change event of a certain business object. The example is suited in any object oriented application scenario (e.g. a J2EE environment). As already mentioned it might be the case that the business objects are instantiated and destructed by the application on demand. An EVENT-BASED ACTIVITY might fail registering at the business object directly.

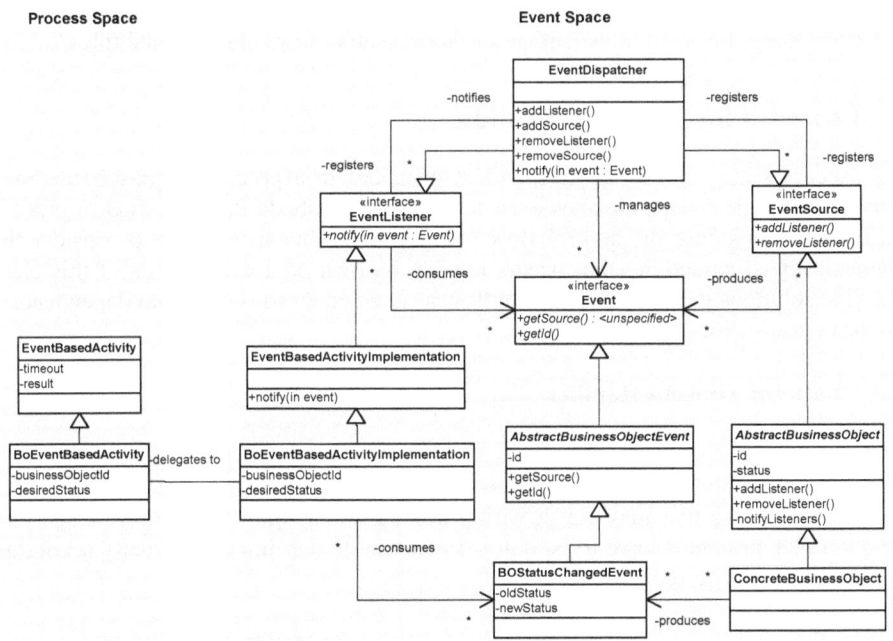

Fig. 11. Example employing an event dispatcher

The example shown in Figure 11 introduces an EVENT DISPATCHER in this context. The EVENT-BASED ACTIVITY registers at the EVENT DISPATCHER and supplies an identifier for the event source it is interested in. The example uses a business object ID, which serves as an event source ID in this case.

Once other application components access business objects, the business objects will be instantiated and register at the EVENT DISPATCHER during initialization. If the application component commits a modification that results in a change of the business object's state then the event source, i.e. the business object, will fire an according event and will notify its listeners (the EVENT DISPATCHER). The EVENT DISPATCHER checks the event source and compares all registered listeners. It forwards the event to the EVENT-BASED ACTIVITY, which now checks for the desired state it is waiting for.

Known Uses

- Leading BPEL engines like BEA Agualogic Fuego, Tibco WebMethods, or IBM WebSphere Process Server, and Oracle Fusion provide event dispatching mechanisms.
- The pattern has also been implemented with older workflow engines such as IBM WebSphere MQ Workflow or Staffware. In this case the event dispatching implementation was delegated to an external program and not directly integrated into the features of the engine. As a result an implementation from scratch has been necessary.
- Also message busses and support this kind of event dispatching. Examples are WebSphere Advanced ESB, or the former version WebSphere Business Integration Message Broker. Special routing flows are usually designed to implement the dispatching rules and to instantiate further reusable flows based on the rules.

4   Process Flow Synchronization

As processes are running as independent instances in a process engine, issues may arise when logical dependencies exist to something outside the context of a process instance. In this case the control flow of the process instance needs to consider the dependency to something that occurs outside its own context. Patterns of this class provide solutions to model the control flow as to consider those external dependencies in the control flow.

4.1   Pattern: Timeout Handler

Context
Processes are modelled for execution on a process engine. If the process model contains activities that may finish with a timeout, this situation has to be taken into account and structures have to be defined that handle the timeout correctly according to the business requirements.

Problem
How can a timeout be handled generically in a process model?

Problem Details

During the execution of a process instance activities are scheduled according to the definition of the process model. Once an activity is instantiated and started by the process engine the execution of the process path suspends until the activity is finished. If an activity implementation contains a rather time consuming logic or if it waits for an event to occur (see the EVENT-BASED ACTIVITY pattern) it is often desired to introduce a timeout mechanism, to add an additional level of control.

The process model that contains such an activity has to handle this situation in a defined way in order to continue the process execution. Normally the process flow shall not continue, as if the activity was finished regularly. On the other hand this might be desired in some cases. However, it is necessary to handle these timeouts somehow.

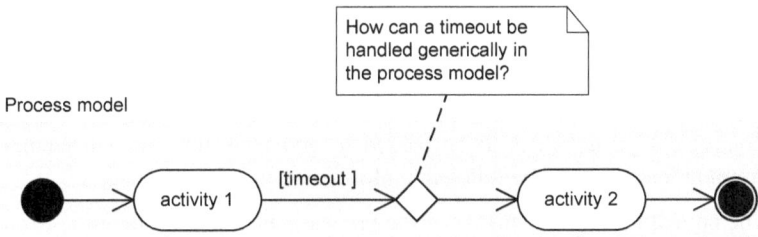

Fig. 12. Problem illustration for handling timeouts in the process model

Solution

Model a reusable timeout handler activity that allows reacting in defined ways in the process model in case a timeout has occurred.

Solution Details

A TIMEOUT HANDLER is an activity in a process that is responsible for handling timeout situations in a process model. Wherever an activity that may raise a timeout is defined in a process, model a decision point that checks whether a timeout has taken place or not. In case of a timeout it branches to the timeout handler.

When the TIMEOUT HANDLER is instantiated it evaluates the given situation, processes this input according to its configuration and terminates with the resulting decision how to handle the situation. This result is either to retry the execution of the activity that caused the timeout, to ignore the timeout and proceed in the process flow, or to abort the process execution and clean up any process resources.

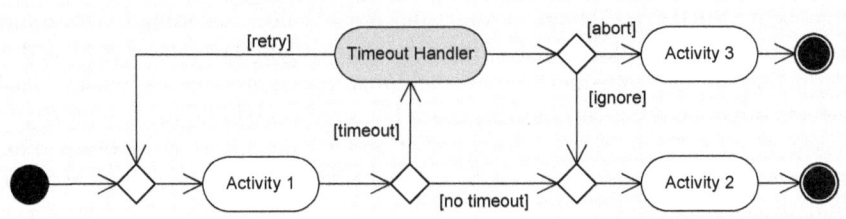

Fig. 13. An activity causing a timeout and branching to a timeout handler

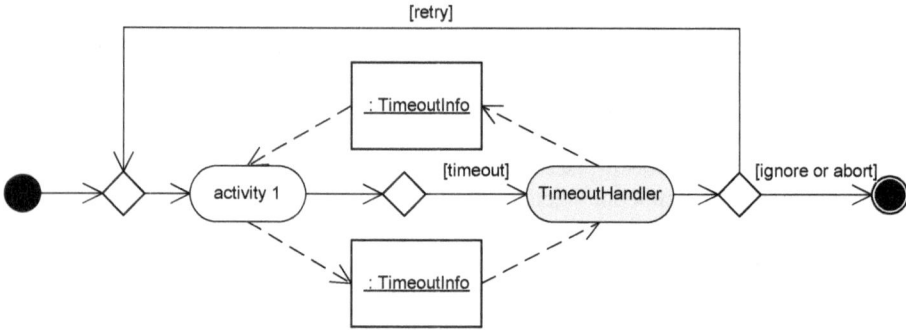

Fig. 14. Passing timeout information to and from the timeout handler

In order to determine an appropriate result (retry, ignore, or abort) the timeout handler depends on information about the timeout situation. Figure 14 depicts that an appropriate process control data structure is to be passed to and from the timeout handler. This structure must at least contain the following information to make a decision:

- The name or unique identifier of the process causing the timeout.

- The name or unique identifier of the activity that caused the timeout.

- A retry count that is initially zero and will be incremented with each retry by the timeout handler.

- The context in which the timeout occurred, e.g. a business object reference, or the ID of an event source the activity was registered to, or the ID of an external system, which was not accessible, etc.

Provided with this information the TIMEOUT HANDLER is be able to decide. The decision can be made by human interaction or fully automatically. To achieve a high degree of reuse it makes sense to externalize some handling logic in configurations of the timeout handler. For instance, this may include a configuration for each activity that states the maximum retry count before aborting the process or a configuration that ignores timeouts of certain event sources.

Using this pattern, timeouts reported by activities during process execution can be handled generically within the process model according to defined rules. Activities that may finish with a timeout are not responsible for handling the timeout themselves. Furthermore, the process designer does not need to evaluate each single timeout situation and model the process respectively; rather the timeout handler component will be configured to direct the process flow accordingly (separation of concerns). Activities that finish with a timeout might have to supply additional information to the timeout handler such that decisions can be made. Handling timeouts might be necessary in many cases but also involves higher complexity of the process models. Thus higher development and testing effort is involved. For this reason, it should be considered case by case whether handling timeouts is necessary to avoid unnecessary effort.

The PROCESS-BASED ERROR MANAGEMENT [5] pattern describes a solution for handling errors that are reported by components integrated in the process flow. The TIMEOUT HANDLER pattern functions in a similar way, yet exclusively handles timeout situations. Thus, the TIMEOUT HANDLER can be viewed as a special subset of the PROCESS-BASED ERROR MANAGEMENT. The EVENT-BASED ACTIVITY pattern introduces activities that listen for events occurring outside the scope of the process instance. Activities of that type will usually be defined with a timeout value and might require the use of a TIMEOUT HANDLER.

Example: Timeout Handling with IBM WebSphere Process Server
Most recent BPEL engines like Oracle Fusion, or IBM WebSphere Process Server allow handling exceptions. Handling timeouts is just one case of an exception in this context. As a result, the exception handling mechanisms of those BPEL engines can be used for timeout handling. In IBM WebSphere Process Server a timeout is actually a built-in fault and a corresponding off-the-shelf fault handler can be used, i.e. a timeout handler. Figure 15 shows an example of modelling a timeout exception with WebSphere Process Server.

Fig. 15. Modelling a timeout handler using WebSphere Process Server

Known Uses

- Leading BPEL engines like BEA Agualogic Fuego, IBM WebSphere Process Server, and Oracle Fusion provide exception handling mechanisms that provide timeout handling.
- The pattern has also been implemented with older workflow engines such as IBM WebSphere MQ Workflow or Staffware.
- Also message busses and support this kind of timeout handling. Examples are WebSphere Advanced ESB, or the former version WebSphere Business Integration Message Broker.

4.2 Pattern: Waiting Activity

Context
Processes are modelled to be executed on a process engine. When modelling business processes it is often required to suspend the process for a defined period of time.

Problem
How to model a waiting position in a process, which is rather passive than active in nature?

Problem Details
Consider a process for order entry and order processing. Regulatory constraints might force the order processing not to be started before the defined period of legal order revocation has passed. The execution of the process instance has to wait a defined period of time before the next activities are scheduled.

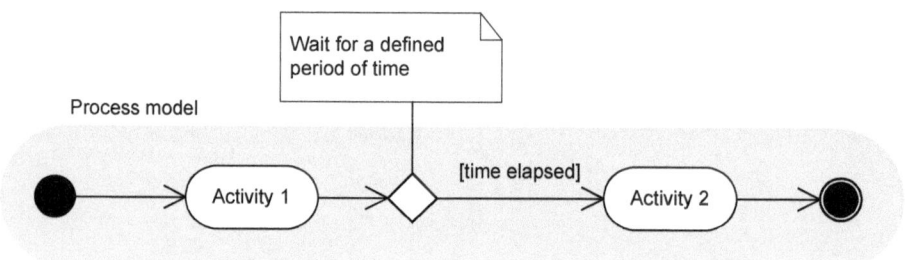

Fig. 16. Problem illustration of defining wait-states in the process flow

The scenario mentioned above deals with a fixed or static time frame which does not change depending on other data processed in the system. The period is known during process design time and it can be supplied within the process model or in an external configuration. Yet, the time to wait may not always be known during process design, e.g. because it depends on a user input during process execution. In that case the process execution has to wait for a time that has to be evaluated during runtime.

Solution
Model a waiting activity which uses an internal timer and actively waits for a defined time frame to elapse until it terminates. The termination causes the process execution to continue.

Solution Details
A WAITING ACTIVITY implements a statically or dynamically configured timer. The waiting activity is responsible for starting the timer when the activity is instantiated and automatically terminates when the timer reaches the configured value. Thus, the process flow will be suspended for the desired time at that process step if the process engine schedules this activity.

The value specifying the time frame to wait for is either statically supplied to the activity, for example, as metadata within the process model, or is supplied from an external configuration source, or is dynamically calculated during runtime and supplied from within the process instance via the activity's input data. Correspondingly, we distinguish static and dynamic timers. A static timer is configured during design time, a dynamic timer is configured during runtime, e.g. by a previously executed activity (see Figure 17).

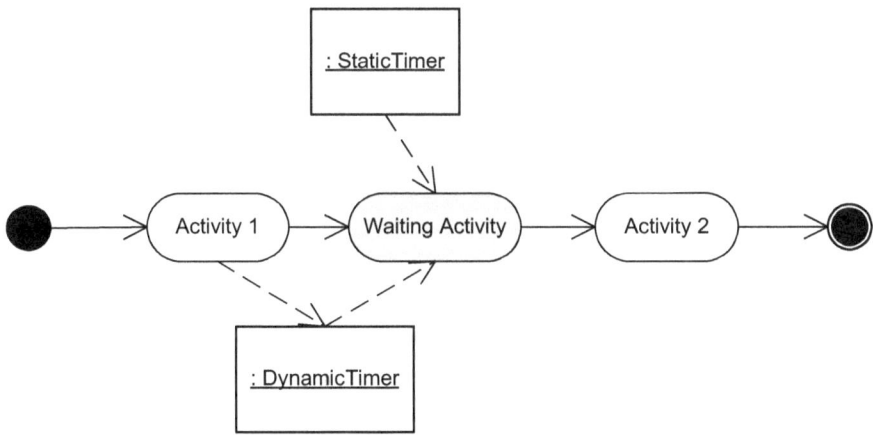

Fig. 17. Concept of a waiting activity

Use a static timer in case the time to elapse is not influenced by any measure within the system environment. Model a dynamic timer in case the timer's value can only be evaluated during runtime or will undergo changes initiated through other system components.

As a consequence of this pattern, when modelling a WAITING ACTIVITY the process flow can be actively suspended for a defined period of time at a defined process step. When using a dynamic timer, it must be ensured that the evaluated time frame is reasonable. A wrong evaluation could result in an unexpected long suspension of the process execution. Waiting activities delay the flow of activities, which can be viewed as a negative consequence. Choosing the right waiting interval might be crucial to avoid unnecessary delay. For this reason the business requirements need to be clear to avoid such unnecessary delay and defining the wait-logic might be of considerable effort that needs to planned and developed. The pattern should for this reason only be applied when the business requirements and wait-logic is clear and the additional development effort introduced by this additional complexity needs to be considered.

The EVENT-BASED ACTIVITY pattern describes a general event-aware activity. An activity of that kind terminates upon the occurrence of a defined external event. One variation of a WAITING ACTIVITY pattern can be perceived as a special EVENT-BASED ACTIVITY. The event the activity subscribes to is created by a timer. This is only valid, though, if the timer is not known in the scope of the process instance and has to be seen as an external event source.

Example: Implementation with WebSphere MQ Workflow

Many process engines offer integrated support for implementing EVENT-BASED ACTIVITY with static or dynamic timers. The example illustrated in Figure 18 is an implementation using the expiration mechanism of IBM WebSphere MQ Workflow. The model and configuration shown in Figure 18 and Figure 19 are defined with MQ Workflow Buildtime [13].

Figure 19 shows the configuration dialog for the expiration mechanism, which offers support for both static and dynamic implementations. The input value for a dynamic configuration can be obtained from the activity's input data. In order to implement a dynamic waiting activity using the expiration mechanism, model a sequence of two activities, the first is responsible for acquiring the value for the timer and passing it to the second one that uses this value available in its input data for the expiration configuration.

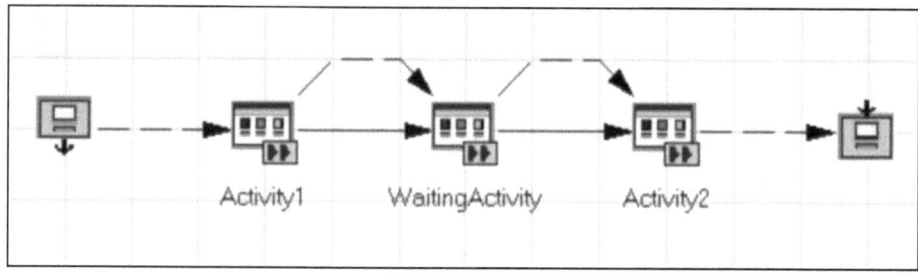

Fig. 18. Example of a waiting activity

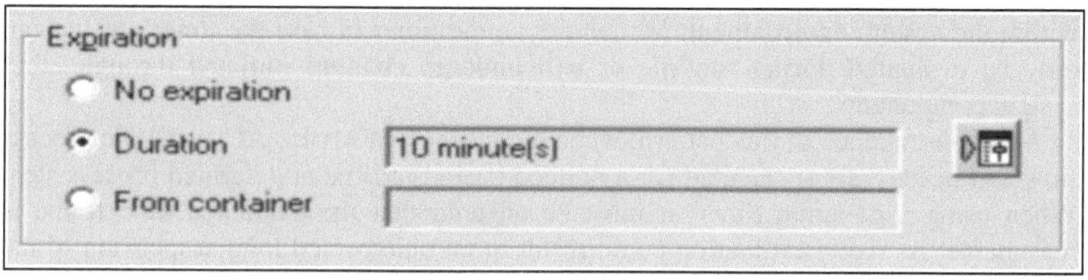

Expiration

     No expiration

     Duration   10 minute(s)

     From container

Fig. 19. WebSphere MQ Workflow's expiration mechanism to implement a waiting activity

Known Uses

- Leading BPEL engines like BEA Agualogic Fuego, Tibco WebMethods, or IBM WebSphere Process Server, and Oracle Fusion provide modeling of waiting activities.
- The pattern has also been implemented with older workflow engines such as IBM WebSphere MQ Workflow or Staffware. Those engines also provide modeling wait states according to defined rules, e.g. to wait for a certain period of time. This can be done with a static value of from a prior set variable.
- Also message busses and support this kind of waiting states. Examples are WebSphere Advanced ESB, or the former version WebSphere Business Integration Message Broker.

5   Business Object Access Synchronization

Business objects often serve as a central resource for many process instances that run in parallel. In this context issues may occur when different process instances try the access the same business object, e.g. a write operation to the same business object should be performed by two different process instances. Patterns of this class thus deal with synchronizing the access to the business objects that serve as central resources to many process instances.

5.1   Pattern: Private-Public Business Object

Context
Business processes are concurrently accessing business objects. When business processes access business objects in parallel, concurrency issues occur.

Problem
How can business processes access shared business objects in a controlled way to avoid concurrent updates and to limit the visibility of uncommitted changes?

Problem Details
Business objects representing a company's or system's business data are usually accessed from within defined business process activities. Such objects are typically managed and persistently stored in central data stores or business applications. Activities that process business objects during their execution may access these with a reference uniquely identifying the object.

If such activities are executed in parallel, conflicts will arise by parallel write access, but will also arise by parallel read access to a business object that is currently being processed by another activity. Parallel read access can result in a problem, because business object modifications made in the context of one activity will be visible immediately to other system activities when the corresponding business object transaction is committed. If a business activity involves user interaction, for example, a referenced business object may be modified subsequently by multiple user invoked transactions actually representing only intermediate states of a business object.

The modifications and thus intermediary states are immediately accessible by parallel activities if the changes are committed after each interaction. This behaviour is usually not desired, because only the final state shall be visible but not the intermediary states. A microflow may also offer a user to undo modifications, for example. If a parallel activity reads the processed business object it may operate on a temporary and thus invalid business object state.

The problem of parallel read access to a business object is especially given in the context of ACTIVITY INTERRUPTS [5]. Considering business object modifications in this scenario, it is rather obvious that it is necessary to save the current work done on business objects in order not to lose information and to be able to re-establish the context when resuming the activity at a later point in time.

When the user interrupts his/her work, modified business objects may not always be in a consistent state. Consider an activity which involves entering a large amount of data, for example, a detailed customer feedback form. When the user processing the activity wants to interrupt his work, the data entered so far shall not be lost, but shall not be publicly visible either, because not all data of the feedback form has been entered. Thus, it may be necessary that interruptible activities allow saving inconsistent states of associated business objects. These states shall not be publicly visible, i.e. not become available in the system, until all data is consistent and the activity is finished. The read access to the business object shall be limited to the state it had before the changes were made.

Furthermore, parallel changes to a business object shall be prohibited. If an activity processes a business object and another activity performs parallel changes the object will enter an inconsistent state.

In the context of the ACTIVITY INTERRUPT [5] pattern, if an object has been modified before an ACTIVITY INTERRUPT, the corresponding user expects to resume at the same point, i.e. the activity's context has to remain consistent. Therefore, a business object modified within this interruptible activity shall be locked by the activity to prohibit parallel changes. In other words, write access shall be limited to the processing activity in order to guarantee a deterministic behaviour of the business transaction spanned by the activity.

These fundamental problems are related to existing mechanisms in the area of transactional systems, like, for example, database transaction and locking features that prevent parallel updates by write locks and ensure limited data visibility during a running transaction. Yet, these technical solutions to data visibility and write control do not provide a solution within the context of more complex business scenarios as we have them in process-driven systems.

Solution

Introduce PRIVATE-PUBLIC BUSINESS OBJECTS, which expose two separate images of the contained data: a private and a public image. A business object of that kind allows making changes on its "private" image prior to publishing the changes to its "public" state and enforces a write-lock for other activities as long as a private image exists.

Solution Details

The concept of separation of business logic from process logic implies that the modification of business data is done on business objects that are managed outside the process engine. Even if business objects are stored via a database management system (DBMS), updates to a business object from within a business activity will often be performed in more than one single database transaction. That means processing of a business activity can involve several user interactions. Each user interaction typically spans a database transaction in this scenario. The activity itself, though, spans a business transaction that shall not be committed until the activity is finished.

A PRIVATE-PUBLIC BUSINESS OBJECT has a public and a private image. Both images contain the same business object attributes. The private image is created during a business transaction and reflects the object's state, which is only visible from within this transaction, i.e. the processing activity. The public image of the object reflects its state which is always publicly visible. When the activity commits the first modifications on a PRIVATE-PUBLIC BUSINESS OBJECT, a private image is created that exposes the business object's data including the changes. Any read access to the business object from within another business activity returns the object's public image that does not contain these modifications. Any parallel write access will be prohibited if a private image exists.

Read access to the business object issued from the activity, which initially performed the changes, will return the private image and thus reflects all modifications made in that business transaction so far. When the activity is finished it explicitly publishes these modifications. The changes stored in the private image are merged into the public image and will then be accessible by all system activities.

To be able to differentiate between the activities that access the object, a unique activity or business transaction identifier (ID) has to be introduced. The identifier has to be compared with the owning transaction ID during each read and write request. Thus, the business transaction, which created the private image, is stored in that image (see attribute transactionId in Figure 20).

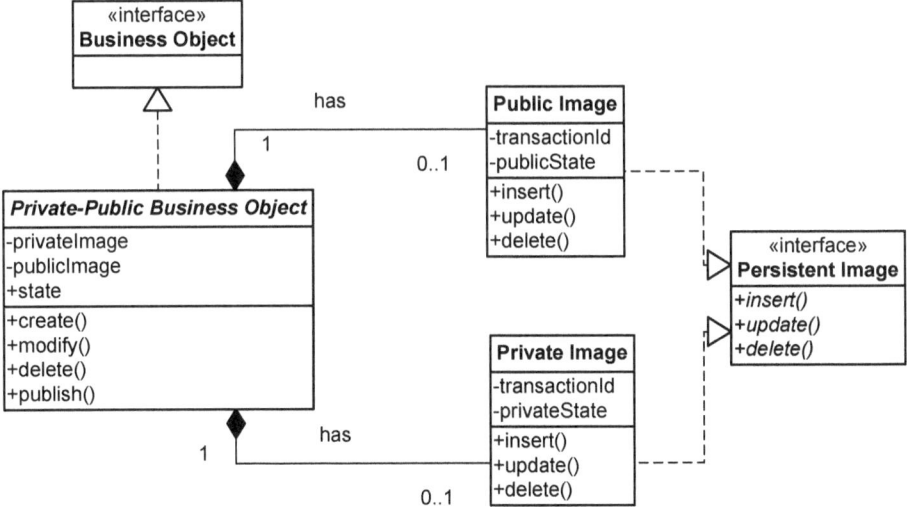

Fig. 20. Conceptual structure of a private-public business object

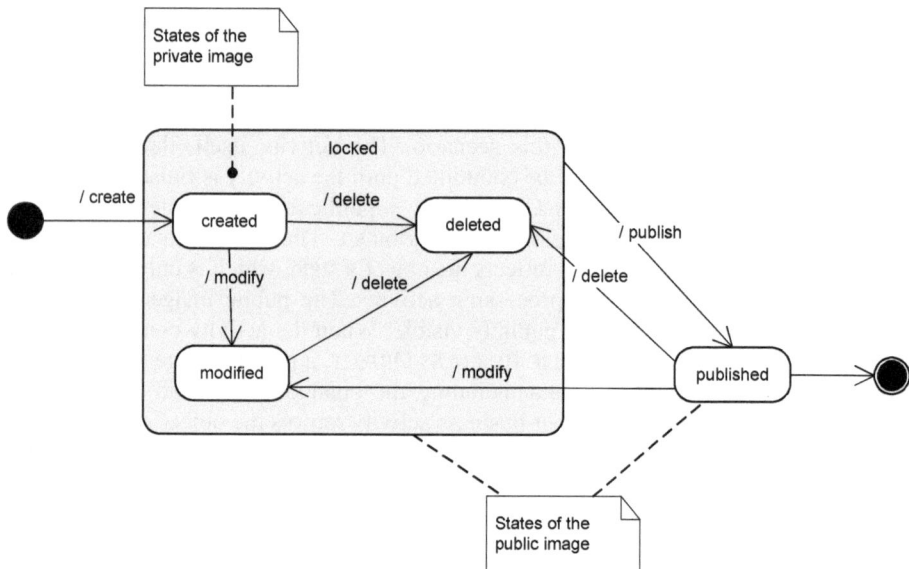

Fig. 21. State transitions of a private-public business object

Figure 21 shows the possible transitions between private and public states of PRIVATE-PUBLIC BUSINESS OBJECTS. The object is in a private state if a private image of the object exists and in a public state if it has no private image. A PRIVATE-PUBLIC BUSINESS OBJECT is either in one of the private states (*created, modified* and *deleted*) or it is in public (*published*) state. Figure 21 also shows the state *locked* which is the state of the public image once a private image exists.

The differentiation between the private states created, modified and deleted allows applying the appropriate merge operation when publishing the changes. When the object is initially created no public image exists. The publish operation will invoke the public image to be created. If the object is being deleted before the first publish operation is called then no public image has to be created. Once a public image exists, the business object can either enter the states private-modified, or private-deleted. If a private image exists or the business object is not in the published state, its public image is write-locked.

The pattern introduces significant additional logic and implementation effort, which is a negative consequence. For this reason, one needs to be clear whether access synchronisation to business objects is a must-have requirement in order to avoid unnecessary development effort.

Example: Parallel Access to a Business Object
Figure 22 gives an example of parallel access to a PRIVATE-PUBLIC BUSINESS OBJECT, which is modified during the execution of a business process activity represented as a microflow. The first modification of the object within the activity (process instance A in Figure 22) creates a private image reflecting the changes and enforces a write-lock on the object's public image. Parallel activities can still read the objects public state, but are not eligible to perform any changes (process instance B in Figure 22). The public image

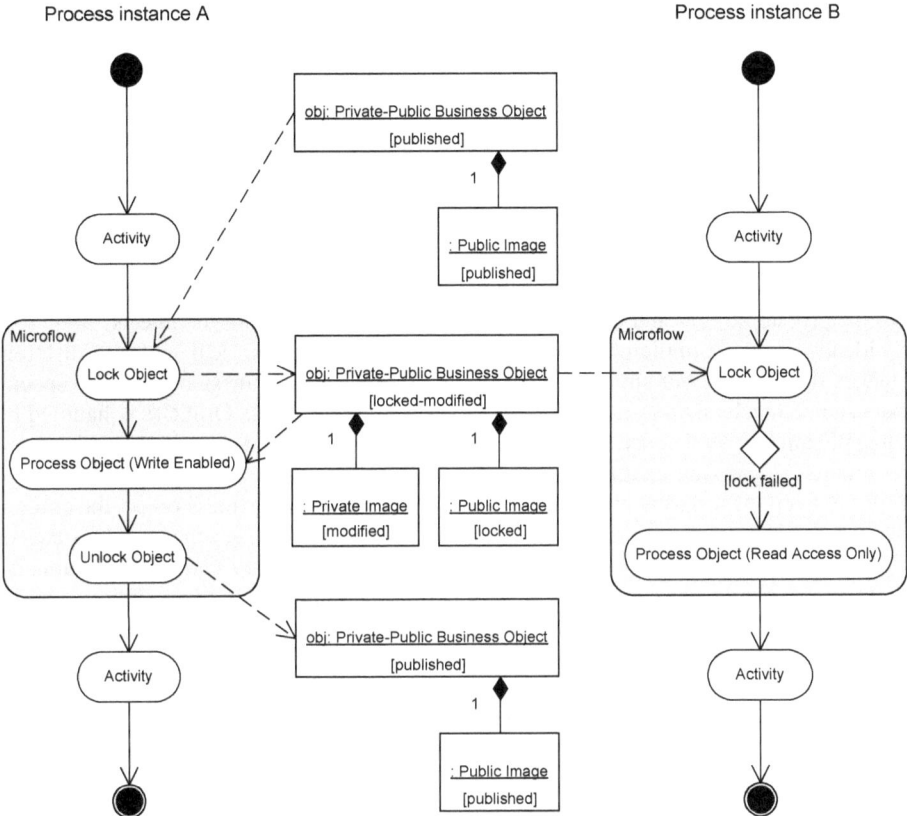

Fig. 22. Parallel access to private-public business objects

remains in state "locked" during the processing and interruption of the activity. The activity may modify the object's private image until the user finishes the activity. When finishing the activity the private image is merged into the public image and deleted afterwards. The write-lock is freed and the object is in state "published" again.

The pattern offers a concept for accessing a business object from within different activities. The business object is publicly write-locked by the first activity that creates a persistent private image. Business objects may be write-locked for a long time, which may block execution of parallel processes. As a consequence, this aspect enforces a clear and integrated design of business processes and business objects. Users of a process management system involving ACTIVITY INTERRUPT [5] may save modifications on business objects made within the activity in inconsistent states prior to finishing the activity. The realization of the pattern requires implementing a custom persistence framework for such business objects or extension of existing frameworks, which causes implementation effort.

The ACTIVITY INTERRUPT pattern describes activities that allow interrupting and resuming work done on business objects within the activity. Thus, this pattern is used in conjunction with PRIVATE-PUBLIC BUSINESS OBJECTS. The BUSINESS OBJECT REFERENCE pattern [5] takes the separation of business data and process engine into account. The BUSINESS OBJECT REFERENCES can point to PRIVATE-PUBLIC BUSINESS OBJECTS. Considering these concepts the PRIVATE-PUBLIC BUSINESS OBJECT pattern introduces a way to handle business objects referenced by and modified in activities, especially in the context of the ACTIVITY INTERRUPT pattern. The change of a state of a PRIVATE-PUBLIC BUSINESS OBJECT can represent an event that is fired and processed by an EVENT DISPATCHER.

The pattern can be implemented in several ways depending on the technology used to store business objects in the system and the way services access these objects. When using a relational database to store business objects, the concept of a PRIVATE-PUBLIC BUSINESS OBJECT can be realized by introducing two database schemas, one for the private images and one for the public images of the business objects.

Ideally, activity implementations (services) do not have to deal with the different images themselves, but simply perform operations on the business object. The special persistence mechanism required for PRIVATE-PUBLIC BUSINESS OBJECTS is handled by an application's persistence layer that encapsulates the required write and read logic.

Figure 23 gives an example of the persistence logic using a relational database. In order to keep information about the transaction locking of a business object the column TransactionId is contained in each table of the public and private schema. The states of the private and public images are stored in the *PrivateState* and *PublicState* column.

In the example, a customer object is being updated and another object is being deleted during a long running transaction, e.g. via an ACTIVITY INTERRUPT. The changes performed during this activity are logged in a transaction log table. This is needed to keep track of the operations to be executed when the long running transaction is committed, i.e. the business objects are published.

The code fragment below gives a high level example of an implementation of the PRIVATE-PUBLIC BUSINESS OBJECT's publish method. Depending on the state, a database row in the public schema will be inserted, updated, or deleted for an existing private image. The database operations (e.g. executed via JDBC) are supposed to be encapsulated within the implementation of the *PublicImage* class.

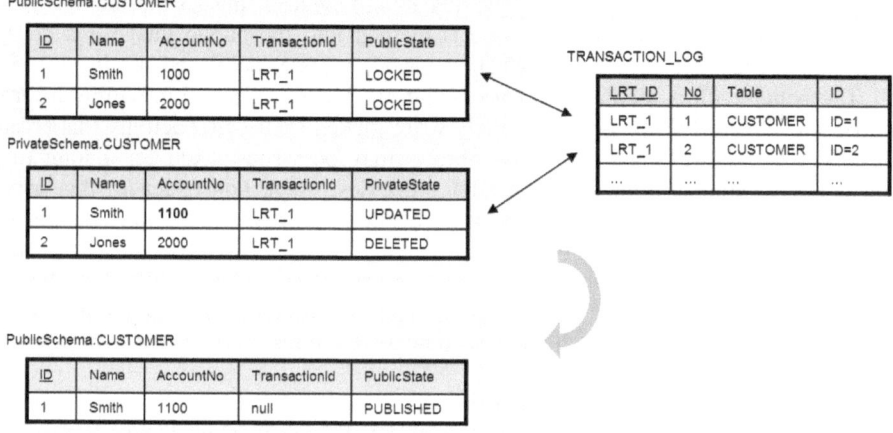

Fig. 23. Realization of private-public business objects with a relational database

```java
public abstract class PrivatePublicBusinessObject
implements BusinessObject {
      private PersistentImage privateImage;
      private PersistentImage publicImage;
      private int state;

      public synchronized void publish() {
        if (state==STATE_CREATED) {
            publicImage = new PublicImage();
            // Copy all attributes of private to
            // public image
            copyAttributes(privateImage, publicImage);
            // Set the state and insert the row
            publicImage.setState(STATE_PUBLISHED);
            publicImage.setTransactionId(null);
            publicImage.insert();
            // Delete private image
            privateImage.delete();
        } else if (state==STATE_MODIFIED) {
            // Merge all changes of private to
            // public image
            mergeAttributes(privateImage, publicImage);
            // Set the state and update the row
            publicImage.setState(STATE_PUBLISHED);
            publicImage.setTransactionId(null);
            publicImage.update();
            // Delete private image
            privateImage.delete();
        } else if (state==STATE_DELETED) {
            // Persistently delete public and
            // private images
            publicImage.delete();
            privateImage.delete();
        }
      }
      ...
}
```

Simple data access becomes more complex in this scenario. Imagine all *Customer* objects visible in the context of a specific long running transaction are to be retrieved by a simple query like this:

```
SELECT NAME FROM CUSTOMERS WHERE ((NAME LIKE 'AB%'))
```

This query has to be changed to retrieve all public images except the ones currently processed in this long running transaction (identified by *<current_LRT_ID>*) and perform a union with the private images that are in this transaction, but are not marked as deleted:

```
SELECT NAME FROM PublicSchema.CUSTOMERS
WHERE (NAME LIKE 'AB%') AND TransactionId <>
<current_LRT_ID>
OR TransactionId is null
UNION
SELECT NAME FROM PrivateSchema.CUSTOMERS
WHERE (NAME LIKE 'AB%') AND TransactionId =
<current_LRT_ID>
AND PrivateState <> <deleted>
```

This query to retrieve the correct data depending on the current scope (within a long running transaction or not) should be encapsulated in an adequate way, e.g. by offering special database union views.

Known Uses

- In a Supply Chain Management solution in the automotive industry the pattern has been implemented in a programming framework to control the access to central business objects.
- In the insurance industry the pattern has been implemented in a Claims Management solution to control concurrent access to claims as business objects during parallel running business processes that handle the claim.
- In the context of Enterprise Content Management solutions the pattern has been used in projects in insurance and banking to control the access to central documents using IBM FileNet.

6 Conclusion

In this article we have documented six patterns that deal with different kinds of synchronization issues when designing and implementing process-driven SOAs. We have defined three different categories for the patterns:

- Process Flow Synchronization
- Event Synchronization
- Business Object Access Synchronization

The patterns can be used individually or in combination to solve synchronization issues that occur in these three categories. This article thus documents a small pattern language of related patterns. The patterns aim at providing generic and flexible solutions when implementing architectures that require dealing with changing or evolving requirements over time.

References

[1] Barry, D.K.: Web Services and Service-oriented Architectures. Morgan Kaufmann Publishers, San Francisco (2003)

[2] Voelter, M., Kircher, M., Zdun, U.: Remoting Patterns. Pattern Series. John Wiley and Sons, Chichester (2004)

[3] Zdun, U., Hentrich, C., van der Aalst, W.M.P.: A Survey of Patterns for Service-Oriented Architectures. International Journal of Internet Protocol Technology (2006)

[4] Alur, D., Malks, D., Crupi, J.: Core J2EE Patterns: Best Practices and Design Strategies. Prentice Hall PTR, Englewood Cliffs (2003)

[5] Hentrich, C.: Six patterns for process-driven architectures. In: Proceedings of the Conference on Pattern Languages of Programs, EuroPLoP 2004 (2005)

[6] van der Aalst, W.M.P., ter Hofstede, A.H.M., Kiepuszewski, B., Barros, A.P.: Workflow Patterns. BETA Working Paper Series, WP 47 (2000)

[7] van der Aalst, W.M.P., ter Hofstede, A.H.M., Kiepuszewski, B., Barros, A.P.: Advanced workflow patterns. In: Scheuermann, P., Etzion, O. (eds.) CoopIS 2000. LNCS, vol. 1901, pp. 18–29. Springer, Heidelberg (2000)

[8] Russell, N., ter Hofstede, A.H.M., Edmond, D., van der Aalst, W.M.P.: Workflow Resource Patterns. BETA Working Paper Series, WP 127, Eindhoven University of Technology, Eindhoven (2004)

[9] Lawrence, P. (ed.): Workflow Handbook 1997, Workflow Management Coalition. John Wiley and Sons, New York (1997)

[10] Gamma, E., Helm, R., Johnson, R., Vlissides, J.: Design Patterns: Elements of Reusable Object-Oriented Software. Addison-Wesley, Reading (1994)

[11] WMFC. The Workflow Reference Model (WFMC-TC-1003), Workflow Management Coalition (1995)

[12] WMFC. Terminology and Glossary (WFMC-TC-1011), Technical report, Workflow Management Coalition (1996)

[13] IBM corporation. WebSphere MQ Workflow 3.4 – Getting Started with Buildtime, IBM corporation (2003)

[14] Buschmann, F., Meunier, R., Rohnert, H., Sommerlad, P., Stal, M.: Pattern-Oriented Software Architecture: A System Of Patterns. John Wiley & Sons Ltd., West Sussex (1996)

A Pattern Language for Process Execution and Integration Design in Service-Oriented Architectures

Carsten Hentrich[1] and Uwe Zdun[2]

[1] CSC Deutschland Solutions GmbH, Abraham-Lincoln-Park 1, 65189 Wiesbaden, Germany
chentrich@csc.com
[2] Distributed Systems Group, Information Systems Institute, Vienna University of Technology,
Argentinierstrasse 8/184-1, A-1040 Vienna, Austria
zdun@infosys.tuwien.ac.at

Abstract. Process-driven SOAs are using processes to orchestrate services. Designing a non-trivial process-driven SOA involves many difficult design and architectural decisions. Examples are: Different kinds of processes exist: long-running, business-oriented and short-running, technical processes. How to best integrate them and how to map them to execution platforms? A SOA has many different stakeholders, such as business analysts, management, software designers, architects, and developers, as well as many different types of models these stakeholders need to work with. How to present each of them with the best view on the models they need for their work? A realistic process-driven SOA contains many systems that need to be integrated, such as various process engines, services, and backend systems, running on heterogeneous technologies and platforms. How to perform integration in a way that is maintainable and scalable? This article introduces a pattern language that deals with process modeling, execution, and integration. Its main goal is to help solution architects, as well as process and service designers, to master the challenges in designing a stable and evolvable process-driven SOA.

Keywords: Process-Driven Architecture, SOA, Integration Architecture.

1 Introduction

Service-oriented architectures (SOA) can be defined as an architectural concept or style in which all functions, or services, are defined using a description language and have invokable, platform-independent interfaces that are called to perform business processes [Channabasavaiah 2003 et al., Barry 2003]. Each service is the endpoint of a connection, which can be used to access the service, and each interaction is independent of each and every other interaction. Communication among services can involve simple invocations and data passing, or complex activities of two or more services. Though built on similar principles, SOA is not the same as Web services, which is a collection of technologies, such as SOAP and XML. SOA is more than a set of technologies and runs independent of any specific technologies.

Even though this definition and scoping of SOA gives us a rough idea what SOA is about, many important aspects are still not well defined or even misleading. For

J. Noble and R. Johnson (Eds.): TPLOP I, LNCS 5770, pp. 136–191, 2009.

instance, the definition is centered on SOAP-style services (so-called WS-* services) and seems to exclude other service technologies such as REST. More importantly, the definition does not explain the main purposes of SOAs in an organization such as supporting business agility or enterprise application integration, to name a few. To get a clearer picture on what SOA is about and which proven practices exist, we provide in this article a pattern language describing proven knowledge for an important part of many SOAs: the process execution and integration design in SOAs.

A SOA is typically organized as a layered architecture (see Figure 1), both on client and server side [Zdun et al. 2006]. At the lowest layer, low-level communication issues are handled. On top of this layer, a Remoting layer is responsible for all aspects of sending and receiving of remote service invocations, including request creation, request transport, marshalling, request adaptation, request invocation, etc. Above this layer comes a layer of service client applications on the client side and a layer of service providers on server side. The top-level layer is the Service Composition Layer at which the service clients and providers from the layer beneath are used to implement higher-level tasks, such as service orchestration, coordination, federation, and business processes based on services.

In this article we view the SOA concept from the perspective of a Service Composition Layer that is process-driven. That is, the Service Composition Layer introduces a process engine (or workflow engine) which invokes the SOA services to realize individual activities in the process (aka process steps, tasks in the process). The goal of decoupling processes and individual process activities, realized as services, is to introduce a higher level of flexibility into the SOA: Pre-defined services can flexibly be assembled in a process design tool. The technical processes should reflect and perhaps optimize the business processes of the organization. Thus the flexible assembly of services in processes enables developers to cope with

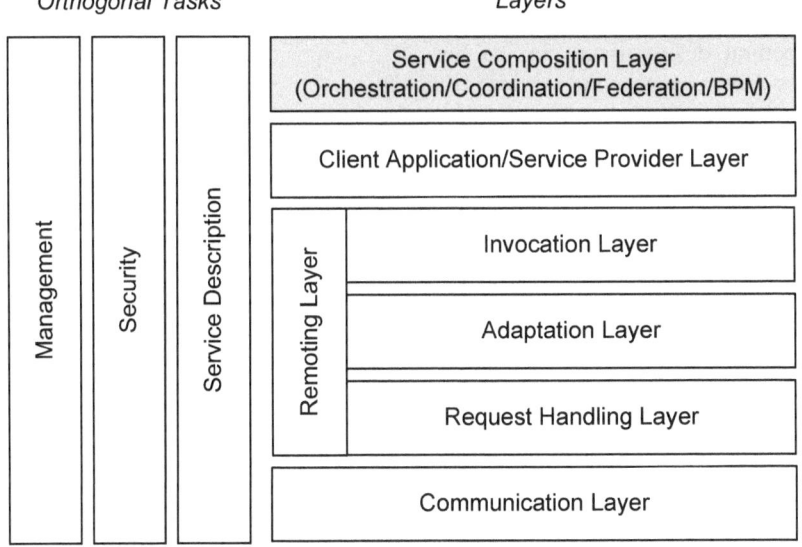

Fig. 1. SOA Layers

required changes to the organizational processes, while still maintaining a stable overall architecture.

In a process-driven SOA the services describe the operations that can be performed in the system. The process flow orchestrates the services via different activities. The operations executed by activities in a process flow thus correspond to service invocations. The process flow is executed by the process engine. In SOAs different communication protocols and paradigms, such as synchronous RPC, asynchronous RPC, messaging, publish/subscribe, etc. can be used and are supported by SOA technologies, such as Web Service frameworks or Enterprise Service Bus implementations. For a process-driven SOA, it can generally be assumed, however, that mainly asynchronous communication protocols and paradigms are used. This is because it cannot generally be assumed that a business process blocks until a service invocation returns. In most cases, in the meantime other sensible activities can be performed by the process. In addition, there are many places in a process-driven SOA where invocations must be queued (e.g. legacy systems that run in batch mode). It is typically not tolerable that central architectural components of the process-driven SOA, such as a central dispatcher, block until an invocation returns. Hence, synchronous service invocations are only used in exceptional cases, where they make sense.

This article is structured as follows. In Section 2 we give an overview of the pattern language presented in this article. Section 3 introduces the challenges in modeling and executing business-driven and technical processes. We present two conceptual and two architectural patterns in this context. Integration and adaptation issues in process-driven SOAs are introduced in Section 4, and four architectural patterns are presented. In Section 5 we provide a literature review and overview of related patterns. Finally, in Section 6 we conclude.

2 Pattern Language Overview

The pattern language presented in this article basically addresses conceptual and architectural design issues in the Service Composition Layer, when following a process-driven approach to services composition.

The patterns and pattern relationships for designing a Service Composition Layer are shown in Figure 2. The MACRO-/MICROFLOW[1] pattern conceptually structures process models in a way that makes clear which parts will be run on a process engine as long running business process flows (below called *macroflows*) and which parts of the process will be run inside of higher-level business activities as rather short running, technical flows (below called *microflows*). The DOMAIN-/TECHNICAL-VIEW pattern explains how to split models in a SOA into two views: A high-level, domain-oriented view and a low-level, technical view. This pattern solves the problem that executable models sometimes must be designed so that both technical and non-technical stakeholders can participate in model creation and evolution. This problem is especially in the context of long-running process flows. In this context, we require – at some point in the design – a link or translation between conceptual flows and executable flows. The pattern can also be applied for other models in a process-driven SOA, such as business object models or component models.

---

[1] We use SMALLCAPS font to highlight pattern names.

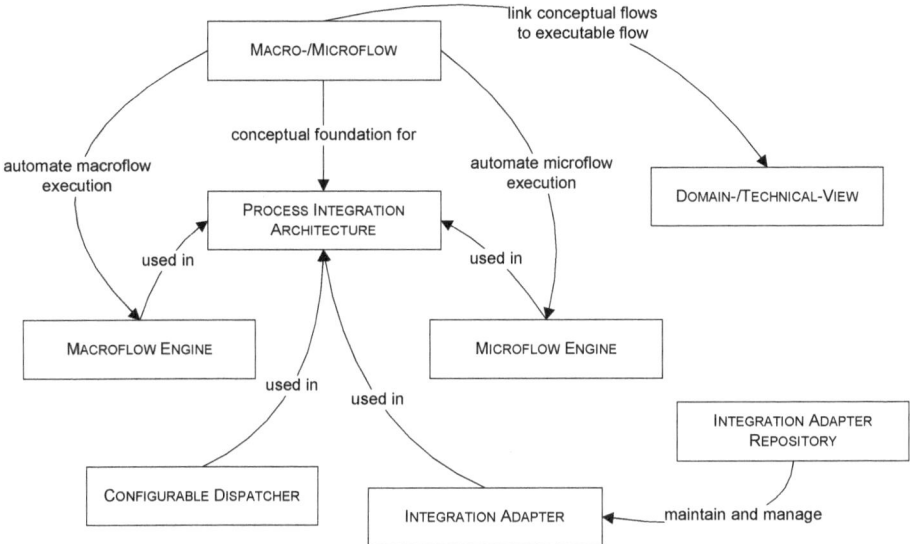

Fig. 2. Pattern relationships overview

The PROCESS INTEGRATION ARCHITECTURE pattern describes how to design a MACRO-/MICROFLOW architecture in detail. It is based on a number of tiers. In particular, two kinds of process engines can be used in a PROCESS INTEGRATION ARCHITECTURE. With regard to the macroflows, you can delegate the business process execution to a dedicated MACROFLOW ENGINE that executes the business processes described in a business process modeling language. The engine allows developers to configure business processes by flexibly orchestrating execution of macroflow activities and the related business functions. With regard to microflows, you can delegate the execution to a dedicated MICROFLOW ENGINE that allows developers to configure microflows by flexibly orchestrating execution of microflow activities and the related services.

The INTEGRATION ADAPTER pattern explains how to connect the various parts of the SOA, such as process engines and backend systems, in a maintainable and evolvable fashion. The INTEGRATION ADAPTER REPOSITORY pattern describes how to manage and maintain INTEGRATION ADAPTERS.

The CONFIGURABLE DISPATCHER pattern explains how to connect client and target systems using a configurable dispatch algorithm. Hence, it enables us to postpone dispatch decisions until runtime. It uses configurable dispatching rules that can be updated at runtime.

3 Modeling and Executing Business-Driven and Technical Processes

In many business domains, there is a need to model the processes of the business. A process model defines the behavior of its process instances. The process model is the

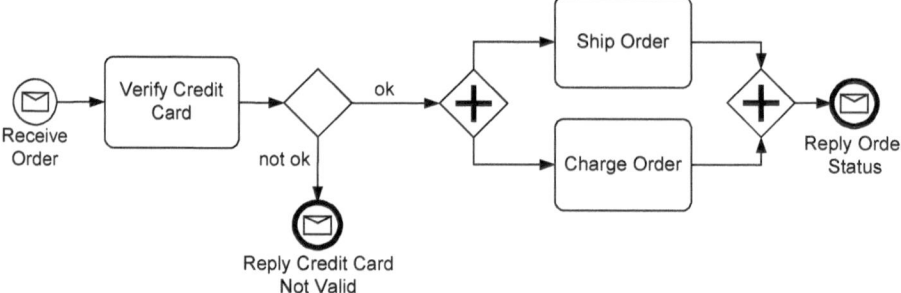

Fig. 3. Example BPMN process

type of the process instances. That is, process instances are instantiations of the same kind of behavior. Process models are usually expressed in a process modeling language or notation. There are more high-level, domain-oriented languages and notations, such as BPMN, EPC, Adonis process flows, UML activity diagrams, and so on. These focus on expressing the behavior of a business or a domain. In addition, there are technical process modeling or workflow languages that define how a process behavior can be executed on a process or workflow engine. Examples are the Business Process Execution Language (BPEL), the jBPM Process Definition Language (JPDL), Windows Workflow Foundation models, or the XML Process Definition Language (XPDL)[2]. In both cases, the process modeling languages define which elements can be used in the process models.

Consider the process model example in BPMN depicted in Figure 3. It shows a very simple order handling process in which first an order is received, then the credit card is verified, and only if it is valid, the process proceeds. Otherwise, the customer is informed of the invalid credit card. Next, in parallel, the order shipment and charging for the order happens. Finally, the order status is reported to the customer.

This process model can describe different things with regard to an organization, depending on the purpose of the business process modeling, such as:

- The process model describes how order handling should be handled, as a guideline or documentation of the business. The people involved in the execution of the process instances can deviate from the predefined process, where it makes sense. For instance, in some exceptional cases, shipment might be postponed, but once the shipment date is fixed, the order status reply can already be sent. This makes for instance sense in a small business, where people fulfill the order handling process and have an overview of the orders they handle.
- The process model defines how exactly the process instances must behave. An automated process management system ensures that each process instance follows the process model. This makes for instance sense in an

---

[2] XPDL actually is not an execution language, but a process design format that can be used to store and exchange process diagrams. However, XPDL elements can have attributes which specify execution information. Some process engines, such as Enhydra Shark [Enhydra 2008], use XPDL directly as their execution language.

organization where a high volume of similar orders with only a few exceptions must be processed, and the activities in the process are mostly automated. People only handle exceptional cases.

- The process model defines how the process instances should behave in the future. Process modeling is part of a business change initiative, for example with the goal to improve the business performance. This is one goal of many SOA initiatives. Such initiatives aim to make the business processes explicit, optimize them, and then support them through technology.
- The process model has explanatory purposes, such as the following. It defines the rationale for what happens in an information system. It links to the requirements of the IT system. It defines the data of the process that can be used for reporting purposes. It enables management or other non-technical stakeholders to analyze and plan the IT system.

Many combinations of these reasons for process modeling are possible and many other reasons exist. This section deals with the situation that you model your business processes and also want to implement them using IT support.

The first issue that must be addressed is the semantic difference between a domain-oriented business processes like the one depicted above and an executable process. *Executable* in this context means that the process contains all technical information that is needed to run it on a computer. The BPMN order handling example is not executable because many technical details are omitted. Some examples in the sample process are:

- It is unclear how the activities of the process are realized. For instance, the credit card verification could be realized as a service, a sub-process, a piece of programming language code, a script, etc. For a service, for example, we need the endpoint information that is needed to access it, such as host and port, but this technical information is missing in the BPMN example process.
- It is unclear how the data is passed from the incoming message to the process activities. For instance, which credit card information is provided and how is it used in the process?
- It is unclear how the data is mapped to the interface of a component or service that performs activities, such as credit card verification? How are interface and data differences handled? It is also unclear how the results are mapped into the process, so that the process' control structures, such as the decision node following the credit card verification in the BPMN example process, can use it.

All this information is provided in technical modeling languages, such as BPEL. Please note that some executable processes include human tasks. Others are machine-executable, meaning that no human tasks are part of the process. In both cases, we need to add the technical details to the domain-oriented processes executable.

For instance, below you see a very small excerpt from a simplistic BPEL process, implementing the BPMN process above. The example excerpt just shows the code needed to receive the initial message, copy some variables to an input type for the VerifyCreditCard service, and then invoke that service.

```
<sequence>
  <receive name="ReceiveOrder" createInstance="yes"
    partnerLink="Customer"
    operation="OrderHandlingOperation"
    xmlns:tns=
      "http://j2ee.netbeans.org/wsdl/OrderHandling"
    portType="tns:OrderHandlingPortType"
    variable="OrderHandlingOperationIn"/>
  <assign name="AssignCreditCardInfo">
    <copy>
      <from>$OrderHandlingOperationIn.
        orderHandlingInputMessage/ns0:creditCardNumber
      </from>
      <to>$IsValidIn.parameters/number</to>
    </copy>
    <copy>
      <from>$OrderHandlingOperationIn.
        orderHandlingInputMessage/ns0:creditCardHolder
      </from>
      <to>$IsValidIn.parameters/holder</to>
    </copy>
    <copy>
      <from>$OrderHandlingOperationIn.
        orderHandlingInputMessage/
        ns0:creditCardSecurityCode
      </from>
      <to>$IsValidIn.parameters/securityNumber</to>
    </copy>
  </assign>
  <invoke name="VerifyCreditCard"
    partnerLink="VerifyCreditCard"
    operation="isValid" xmlns:tns="http://orderHandling/"
    portType="tns:VerifyCreditCard"
    inputVariable="IsValidIn"
    outputVariable="IsValidOut"/>
```

In addition to the BPEL code, we require the WSDL files that describe the interfaces of the services and of this process, and the XML Schema definitions of the data types that are passed.

All these technical specifications are even hard to understand and complex for technical experts. For that reason, many modeling tools exist. For example, the following Figure 4 shows a simplistic BPEL process implementation of our order handling process modeled in the BPEL modeler of the NetBeans IDE. In addition to modeling BPEL graphically, designer tools offer support for designing WSDL interfaces, XML Schema definitions, and data mappings. The typical tooling around process engines has been described in pattern form by Manolescu (see [Manolescu 2004]).

In cases where process execution is the main goal of the process modeling, it seems to make sense to model the processes directly in BPEL using such a modeling

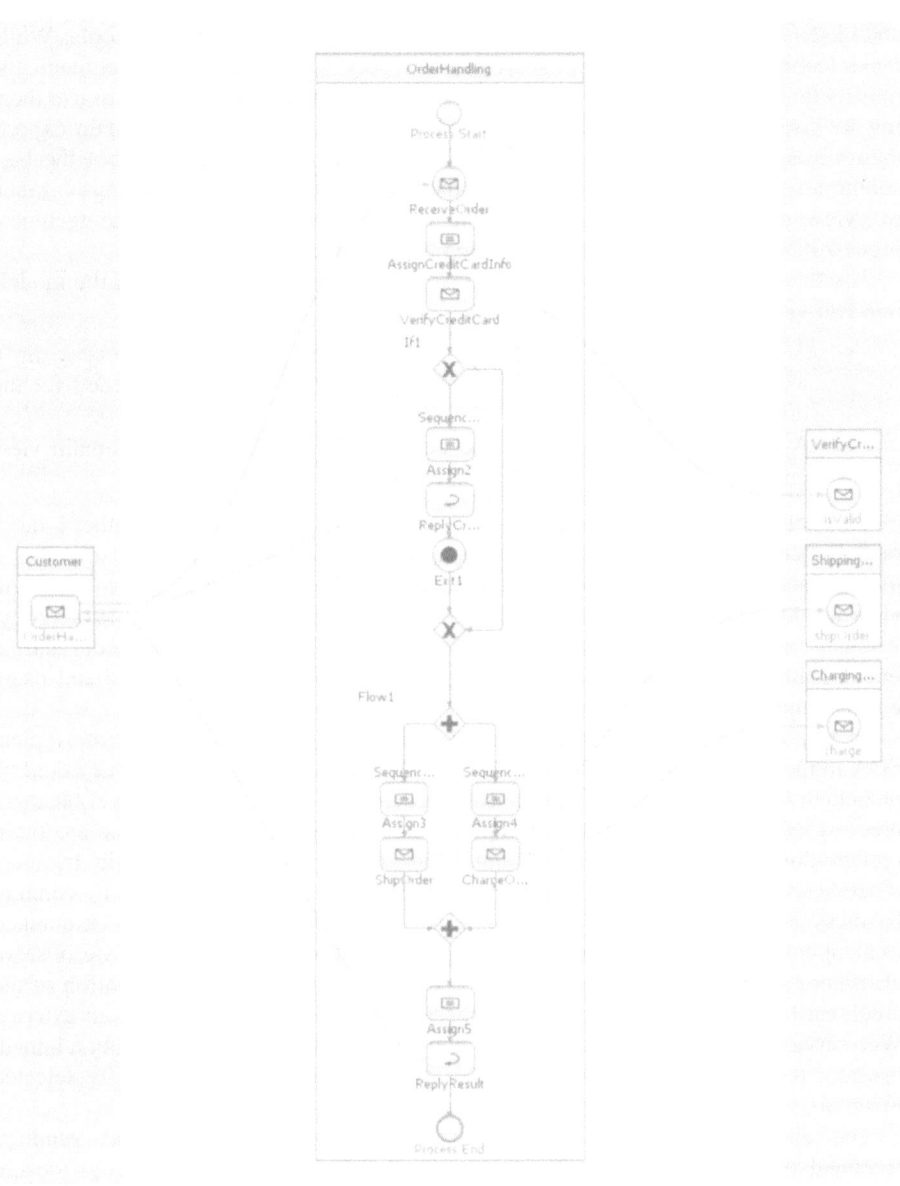

Fig. 4. Example BPEL Process

tool, instead of modeling in BPMN. However, it is rather seldom the case that process execution is the only goal that process modeling is needed for. Usually, the technical experts are not domain experts and hence need to discuss the processes with the domain experts to incorporate the domain knowledge in the right way. BPEL is usually not a good representation for tasks that involve domain experts because BPEL processes are overloaded with technical details. This is certainly valid for the BPEL code itself. But it is also the case for what is shown in BPEL modeling tools: While these technical process modeling tools are a very helpful aid for developers, the models they expose are still pretty technical and complex. It is awkward to use them for the discussion with domain experts and usually impossible to let domain experts themselves work with these tools. For the same reasons, they are also not the best solution for technical stakeholders, if their work requires only getting a quick overview of the existing processes. The technical process code or the technical process modeling tools should only be used for in-depth technical work.

The DOMAIN-/TECHNICAL-VIEW pattern solves this problem by splitting the models into two views:

- A high-level, domain-oriented view that represents the process in a technology-independent fashion leaving away all details not needed for the domain task.
- A low-level, technical view that contains the elements of the domain view and also contains additional technical details.

This pattern is not only applicable for process models, but also for all other kind of models that must be shown in two views. An example is a data model that has a logical data view and a technology-dependent view. Here, the technology-dependent view would model the mapping of the logical view to a database (access) technology. Another example is a class model that represents a high-level domain model and an implementation model showing how the domain model elements are realized using e.g. a component technology.

So far, we did not distinguish different kinds of processes. However, in a typical SOA in the enterprise field we can observe different kinds of behaviour that could be modelled as process flows. For instance, there are strategic, very high-level business processes that are hard to automate or support through technology. These are often broken down – sometimes in a number of steps – into more specific business processes, such as the order handling example above. The result is long-running business processes, perhaps with human involvement, which can possibly be mapped to a supporting technology. Finally, when implementing these processes, we observe also more short-running and technical processes. For instance, the verification of the credit card in the example above could consist of three steps, each calling an external Web service. Or the shipping of an order could require to a few steps guiding a human operator through a number of GUI dialogs for approving the automatically selected inventory items, approving the sending of an invoice, and so on.

The distinction between long-running, business-oriented and short running, technical processes is an important conceptual distinction that helps us to design process activities at the right level of granularity. In addition, the technical properties of the two kinds of processes are different. For instance, for long-running processes it is typically not appropriate to use ACID (Atomicity, Consistency, Isolation, Durability) transactions because it is infeasible to lock resources for the duration of the whole process, while this might be perfectly feasible for more short running processes of only a few service invocations.

The MACRO-/MICROFLOW pattern provides a clear guideline how to design process models following these observations. In the pattern, we refer to the long-running process using the term *macroflow*. We use the term *microflow* to refer to the short running, technical processes. The pattern advises to refine macroflows in a strictly hierarchical fashion – starting from high-level, strategic process to long-running, executable processes. The activities of these executable macroflows can further be refined by microflows. Microflow activities can be refined by other microflows. That is, an activity of a higher-level process model is refined by a lower-level process model in form of a sub-process.

The pattern is closely related to the DOMAIN-/TECHNICAL-VIEW pattern: The highest level macroflows usually only have domain views. The lowest level microflows often only have a technical view. But the models in between – in particular the executable macroflows as in the example above – have both views as they are relevant to both technical and non-technical stakeholders.

Refinements, as described in MACRO-/MICROFLOW and DOMAIN-/TECHNICAL-VIEW patterns, can be performed in general following processes such as or similar to Catalysis [D'Souza and Wills 1999]. Catalysis is a method for component-based development that defined traceable refinements from business requirements through component specifications and design, down to code.

The MACRO-/MICROFLOW pattern advises to use a suitable technology for realizing macroflows and microflows. Of course, it is possible to implement both macroflows and microflows using ordinary programming language code. But often we can provide better support. For instance, macroflows often should be support with process persistence, model-based change and redeployment, process management and monitoring, and so on. The MACROFLOW ENGINE pattern describes how to support a macroflow using process or workflow technology. An example MACROFLOW ENGINE that could be used in the example above is a BPEL process engine.

For microflows, supporting technology is more seldom used. However, if rapid process change or reuse of existing functionality is needed, MICROFLOW ENGINES can be very useful. We distinguish MICROFLOWS ENGINES for microflows containing human interactions, such as pageflow engines, and MICROFLOWS ENGINES for microflows supporting automatic activities, such as message brokers.

3.1 Pattern: DOMAIN-/TECHNICAL-VIEW

Context
Various stakeholders participate in the development, evolution, and use of a SOA. Typical technical stakeholders are the developers, designers, architects, testers, and system administrators. Typical non-technical stakeholders are the domain experts of the domain for which the SOA is created, the management, and customers.

Problem
How should executable models be designed if both technical and non-technical stakeholders need to participate in model creation and evolution?

Problem Details
Designing one model for a number of distinct stakeholders is challenging because the different stakeholders require different information for their work with the model, as well as different levels of detail and abstraction. A typical – often problematic – case in this context is that a model depicts a concern from the domain for which the SOA is created. So the model is, on the one hand, important for the communication with

and among the domain experts. But, on the other hand, in a SOA often such models should be automatically processed and executed.

"Executable model" means that a model is interpreted by an execution engine, or the model representation is compiled and then executed on an execution engine. Here are some examples of executable models:

- A BPEL business process model that is executed on a BPEL engine.
- A role-based access control model that is interpreted by an access control enforcement component.
- A UML or EMF model that is transformed by the generator of a model-driven development (MDD) solution into executable code (see [Stahl and Völter 2006]). In this case the model is interpreted at design time of the SOA, but at runtime of the generator. An alternative is using an executable model, such as Executable UML [Mellor and Balcer 2002] or the UML virtual machine [Riehle et al. 2001].

In order to be executable, a model must contain all technical information needed for execution. The original intent of modeling is often different, however: to serve as a means of communication among stakeholders and for system understanding. The information needed for execution is usually targeted only at one type of stakeholders: the technical developers. This, in turn, makes the models hard to understand for the domain experts and, in general, hard to use for tasks that require getting an overview of the design. The reason is the executable models are simply overloaded with too many technical details.

Just consider business processes as one example of SOA models. Domain experts usually design with tools that use diagrams such as or similar to diagrams in BPMN, EPC, Adonis process flows, UML activity diagrams, and so on. The diagrams usually contain only the information relevant for the business. Often such models are hard to automate because they miss important technical information, such as how data is passed or transformed, or where a service to be invoked is located and with which interface it is accessed. Technical process modeling languages such as BPEL, jPDL, Windows Workflow Foundation models, or XPDL, in contrast, contain all this information. This makes them useful for technical execution, but also complex and hard to understand for domain-oriented tasks.

Solution
Provide each model that it is required both for domain-oriented tasks, such as getting an overview of the design, and technical tasks, such as execution of the model, in two views: a domain view and a technical view. All elements from the domain view are either imported or mapped into the technical view. The technical view contains additional elements that enrich the domain model elements with the technical details necessary for execution and other technical tasks.

Solution Details
Figure 5 illustrates the solution of the DOMAIN-/TECHNICAL-VIEW pattern.

To realize the DOMAIN-/TECHNICAL-VIEW pattern, the elements from the domain view must be imported or mapped into the technical view. This can be done in various ways. Basically, the differences between these variants of the pattern are the mechanisms used for the import and the mapping, and the degree of automation.

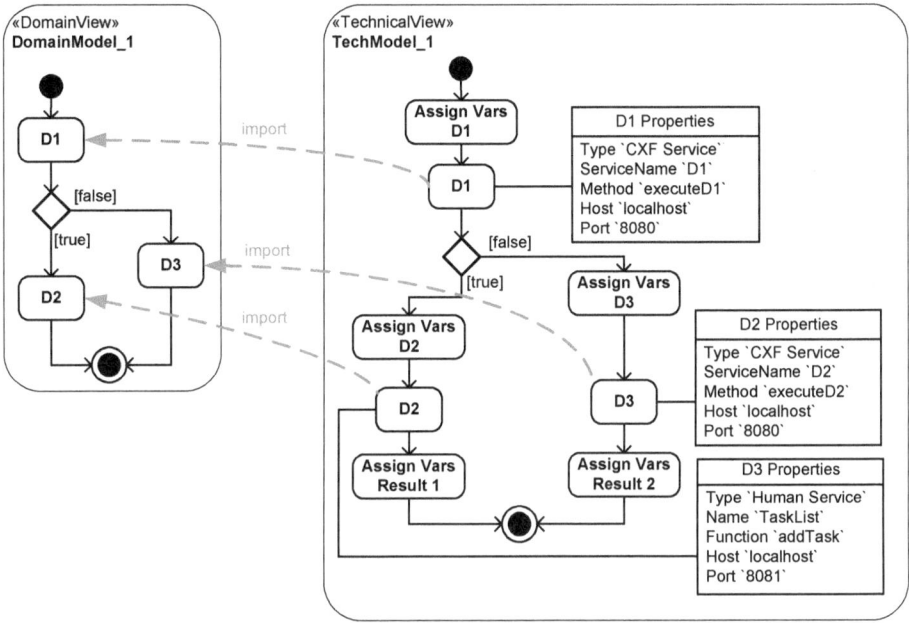

Fig. 5. Illustration of DOMAIN-/TECHNICAL-VIEW

- The simplest variant of the pattern is to perform a manual translation to map the domain model elements into the technical view. First of all, for each domain model element, the most appropriate modeling construct for representing the domain model element in the technical view is chosen, and then the translation is performed. Next, the technical model is enriched with all information needed for technical tasks such as execution and deployment. This variant of the pattern has the benefit of flexibility: Any modeling languages can be mapped in any suitable way. As a creative design step is needed for the mapping, no formal link or mapping between the modeling languages is required, but the translation can happen on a case by case basis. This variant incurs the drawback that – for each change – manual effort is required for performing the translation, and consistency between the models must be ensured manually.
- Sometimes translation tools between a modeling language for domain models and a modeling language for technical models exist, such as a BPMN to BPEL mapping tool. In the mapping process, somehow the additional technical information must be added. For instance, it can be given to the translation tool using an additional configuration file. Using this additional information and the domain view model, the translation tool generates a technical view corresponding to the domain view. This variant of the pattern can potentially reduce the manual mapping effort and ensure consistency automatically. It can be realized for two distinct modeling languages. However, not always an automatic mapping provides the best mapping. Especially for two languages with highly different semantics, the automatic

mapping can cause problems. For instance, technical models can get hard to understand and debug, if they are automatically generated from a domain model with different semantics.

- If both models, technical view and domain view, are described based on a common meta-model, ordinary model extension mechanisms, such as package import, can be used. Extensions in the technical view are then simply added using ordinary extension mechanisms for model elements, such as inheritance or delegation. This variant makes it easy to maintain consistency between the view models. Modeling tools can for instance allow designers to start modeling in the domain view and enrich it with technical details in property views. As an alternative, you can generate the domain view from the technical view model. That is, you just strip the technical information provided in the technical view.

If the domain view is not generated from the technical view, for all the imported domain model elements, all changes should be performed in the domain view. They should then be propagated to the technical view. This means for the three variants of the pattern:

- If manual translation is used, translating the changes made to the domain models is required. Change propagation is a main drawback of this variant: If changes are made to one model and they are forgotten to be propagated or incorrectly propagated, the models are getting inconsistent.
- If an automatic translation tool is used, the tool must be re-run, and it regenerates the domain elements in the technical view. An alternative is a round-trip translation: Changes to the technical view can be translated back into the domain view. Round-trip translation is often not advisable, as tools tend to generate hard to read source code and creating a well-working round-trip tool set is a substantial amount of work.
- If integration based on a common meta-model and package imports are used, changes to the domain model are reflect automatically in the technical view. Hence, no efforts for change propagation are required in most cases. Only if changes cause incompatibilities in dependent models, the models must be adapted accordingly.

Example: Manual BPMN to BPEL translation
We have seen a simple example of a manual BPMN to BPEL translation in the introduction of Section 3.

Example and Known Use: View-based Modeling Framework
The View-based Modeling Framework (VbMF) [Tran et al. 2007] is a model-driven infrastructure for process-driven SOAs. It uses the model-driven approach to compose business processes, services, and other models that are relevant in a SOA. VbMF abstracts each concern in its own view model. Each VbMF view model is a (semi)-formalized representation of a particular SOA concern. The view model specifies the entities and relationships that can appear in a view.

In particular, there is a Core view model from which each other view model is derived. The main task of the Core view model is to provide integration points for the various view models defined as part of VbMF, as well as extension points for enabling the extension with views for other concerns.

The view models derived from Core are *domain views*. Example domain views are: Collaboration, Information, Control-Flow, Long-Running Transactions, Data, and Compliance Metadata. In addition, to these central concerns, many other concerns can be defined. Each of these view models is either extending the core model or one of the other view models. These view models contain no technology-specific information, but information understandable to the domain expert.

In addition, VbMF defines also a second level of extensional view models, derived from these domain views models – the *technical views*. For specific technologies realizing the domain views, such as BPEL, WSDL, BPEL4People, WS-HumanTask, Hibernate, Java services, HTML, or PDF, VbMF provides technical view models, which add details to the general view models that are required to depict the specifics of these technologies.

Figure 6 provides an overview of the VbMF view models and their relationships.

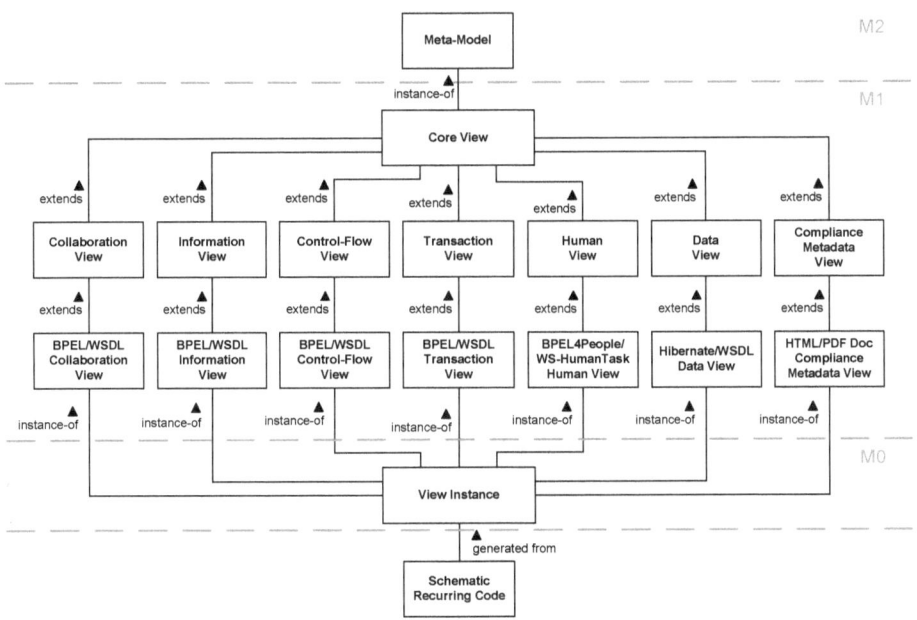

Fig. 6. VbMF view models

The integration of view elements is done using modeling abstractions, such as inheritance and associations, as well as matching algorithms, such as name-based matching. Integration is performed in the transformation templates of the code generator.

The separation of view abstraction levels helps in enhancing the adaptability of the process-driven SOA models to business changes. For instance, the business experts analyze and modify the domain views to deal with change requirements at the level of the business. The technical experts work with technical views to define necessary configurations so that the generated code can be deployed into the corresponding runtime (i.e., the process engines and Web service frameworks). This view-based separation into two view layers, domain views and technical views, also helps to better support the various stakeholders of the SOA: Each stakeholder views only the information necessary for their work. Hence, the view-based approach supports involving domain experts in the design of SOAs.

Known Uses

- The BPMN2BPEL tool [BPMN2BPEL 2008] is an Ecplise plugin for transforming BPMN processes, modeled in Eclipse, to BPEL. Like many other such tools, the tool can only translate the information that is present in BPMN, which might mean that technical details are not considered and semantic differences between BPEL and BPMN are not translated in the best way.
- In [Dikmans 2008] it is discussed how to transform a BPMN model from the Oracle Business Process Analysis Suite to an executable BPEL process. The article also discusses the semantic differences between BPMN and BPEL. If processes are not translatable using the tool, the article advises to change the BPMN process by removing arbitrary cycles that are valid in BPMN, but not in BPEL.
- Sculptor [Fornax 2008] is a cartridge for openArchitectureWare, a model-driven software development infrastructure. Sculptor enables developers to focus on the business domain view, which is designed in a textual, domain-specific language using concepts from Eric Evans' book Domain-Driven Design [Evans 2004], such as Service, Module, Entity, Value Object, Repository, and so on. The code generator is used to generate Java code for well-known frameworks, such as Spring Framework, Spring Web Flow, JSF, Hibernate and Java EE. The technical view is added using configurations and manually written code.

3.2   Pattern: MACRO-/MICROFLOW

Context
If your system is or should be described using process models, it makes sense to think about automating the processes using process technology. Usually, if an organization decides to use business processes to depict their business, high-level and mostly business-oriented models are created.

Problem
How can conceptual or business-oriented process models be implemented or realized?

Problem Details
One important aspect to consider when implementing or realizing business processes is the nature of the processes to be executed. For instance, many typical business processes are long running flows, involving human tasks. Such a business process can run for many hours, days, or even weeks before it is finished. In such cases, the process technology must support persisting the process instances, as the process states

should not get lost if a machines crashes. The process instance should not occupy memory and other system resources, when it is not active. It should be possible to monitor and manage the process instance at runtime. Also, the processes should be interruptible via a process management interface. Such functionalities are supported by process or workflow engines. Process engines usually express processes in a process execution language, such as BPEL, jPDL, Windows Workflow Foundation models, or XPDL.

In contrast to the long-running kind of flows, also short-running flows need to be considered. These often have a more technical nature and rather transactional or session-based semantics. One example is a process in which a number of steps are needed to perform a booking on a set of backend systems. Another example is guiding a human user through a pageflow of a few Web pages. In these examples, process instance persistence is not really needed and typical process execution languages make it rather awkward to express these flows. Hence, it makes sense to realize them using special-purpose modeling languages and technology. For instance, a message flow model and message broker technology or a pageflow model and pageflow engine technology could be used to realize the two examples.

Please note that the named technologies are just examples: The distinction of short-running and long-running flows is in first place a conceptual distinction. Any suitable technology can be chosen. For instance, it is also possible to implement both short-running and long-running flows using ordinary programming language code (e.g., Java source code or code written in a scripting language) – maybe provided as a service. However, as in both cases some features, such as process persistence, wait states, concurrency handling, and so on, are needed over and over again, reusing existing technologies often makes sense.

Finally, in some cases, it turns out that automating the process is not useful or feasible. Then an entirely manual process fulfilled by people with no automation whatsoever can be chosen as a realization of a process as well. Another example is high-level processes, such as strategic business processes of an organization, which would need concretization before they could be implemented.

Unfortunately, in practice often long-running and short-running flows, as well as technical and non-technical concerns, are intermixed. Often concerns with different semantics are modeled in one model. This practice often causes confusion as business analysts do not understand the level of technical detail, and technical modelers do not have the expertise to understand the business issues fully. Thus, these models tend to fail their primary purpose – to communicate and understand the processes and the overall system design.

In addition, models are sometimes mapped to the wrong technology. For instance, a short-running transactional flow should not be realized using a process engine for long-running flows, and vice versa, as the different technologies exhibit significantly different technical characteristics.

Solution
Structure a process model into two kinds of processes, macroflow and microflow. Strictly separate the macroflow from the microflow, and use the microflow only for refinements of the macroflow activities. The macroflows represent the long-running, interruptible process flows which depict the business-oriented process perspective.

The microflows represent the short-running, transactional flows which depict the IT-oriented process perspective.

Solution Details
Figure 7 illustrates the solution of the MACRO-/MICROFLOW pattern.

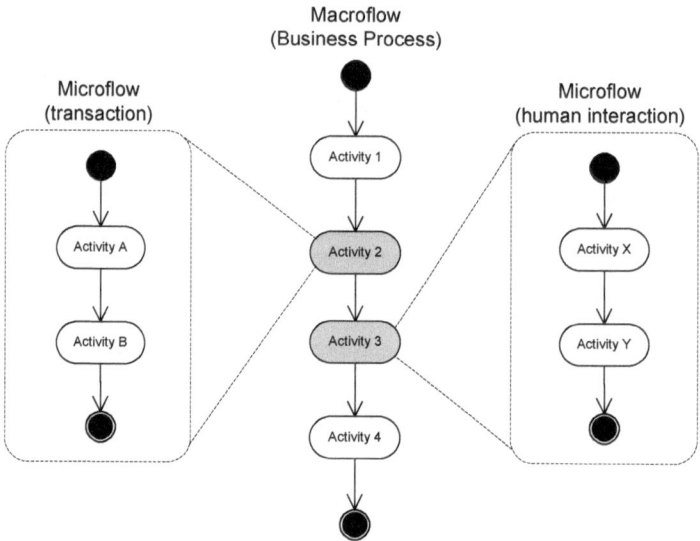

Fig. 7. Illustration of MACRO-/MICROFLOW

The MACRO-/MICROFLOW pattern provides a conceptual solution in which two kinds of flows are distinguished:

- *Macroflows* represent the business-oriented, long-running processes.
- *Microflows* represent the IT-oriented, short-running processes.

The MACRO-/MICROFLOW pattern interprets a microflow as a refinement of a macroflow activity. That is, a microflow represents a sub-process that runs within a macroflow activity. This separation of macroflow and microflow has the benefit that modeling can be performed in several steps of refinement. First the higher level macroflow business process can be designed, considering already that business process activities will further be refined by microflows. Vice versa, if certain microflows already exist, the business process can be modeled accordingly, so that these IT processes fit in as business process activities at the macroflow level. However, this also incurs the drawback that the conceptual separation of the MACRO-/MICROFLOW pattern must be understood and followed by modelers, which requires additional discipline.

The refinement concepts of the MACRO-/MICROFLOW often require adjusting IT processes and business processes according to the concerns of both domains – business and IT – in order to bring them together. The modeling effort is higher than in usual business modeling, as more aspects need to be taken into consideration and, at all refinement levels, activities must be designed at the right level of granularity.

A microflow model can be linked to one or many macroflow activities. The consequence is that the types of relationships between macroflow and microflow are well-defined. Microflows and macroflows both have a defined input and output, i.e., a well-defined functional interface. However, the functional interfaces between IT processes and business processes must be understood and considered by all stakeholder manipulating process models.

Multiple levels of both macroflows and microflows can be modeled. That is, high-level macroflows can be refined by lower-level macroflows. The same is possible for microflows. The refinement is strictly hierarchical: Always an activity in the high-level process is refined by a low-level sub-process, realizing the activity. Never a microflow is refined by a macroflow. Figure 8 illustrates two levels of macroflow refinement and two levels of microflow refinement.

The microflow can be directly invoked as a sub-process that runs automatically, or it can represent an activity flow that includes human interaction. As a result, two types of links between a macroflow activity and a microflow exist:

- *Link to a microflow for an automatic activity (transaction):* A short-running, transactional IT process defines a detailed process model of an automatic activity in a higher-level business process. It represents an executed business function or transaction at the business process level.
- *Link to a microflow for human interaction*: In case an activity of a business process is associated to a user interface, the IT process is a definition of the coherent process flow that depicts the human interaction. This process flow is initiated if a human user executes the business process activity.

The microflow level and the macroflow level distinguish conceptual process levels. Ideally, both levels should be supported by suitable technology. An example for a macroflow technology is a process execution engine, such as a BPEL engine. An exemplary microflow technology for automatic activities is a message broker which provides a message flow modeling language. For short-running human interactions technologies such as pageflow engines can be used.

Both types of microflows are often hard-coded using ordinary code written in a programming language. Sometimes an embedded scripting language is used to support flexible microflow definition in another language such as Java or C#. If this implementation option is chosen, a best practice is to provide the microflows as

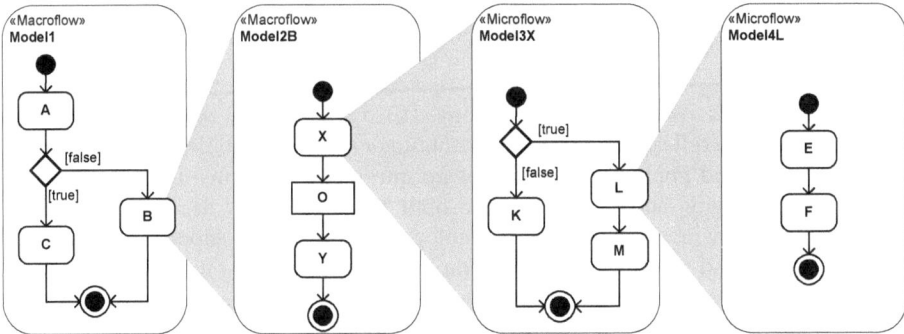

Fig. 8. Illustration of MACRO-/MICROFLOW

independent deployment units, e.g., one service per microflow, so that they can be flexibly changed and redeployed. Microflow implementations should be architecturally grouped together, e.g., in a SERVICE ABSTRACTION LAYER [Vogel 2001], and not scattered across the code of one or more components, which also realize other tasks.

In the ideal case, the modeling languages, techniques, and tools should support the conceptual separation of macroflows and microflows, as well as the definition of links between macroflow activities and microflows using the two types of links described above.

This pattern is strongly related to the DOMAIN-/TECHNICAL-VIEW pattern because typically, at the point where the macroflows are mapped to technologies, we need both views. That is, the macroflows require in any case a domain view (e.g., modeled in BPMN, EPC, or Abstract BPEL), as macroflows need to be discussed with domain experts from the business. At the point where macroflows are mapped to technologies, we also need a technical view of the macroflow (e.g., modeled in BPEL, jPDL, Windows Workflow Foundation models, or XPDL). The same duality can be observed for microflows. Here, in any case, a technical view is needed, as all microflows are executable. Sometimes, an additional domain view is needed, for instance, if microflow models should be designed together with domain experts. Just consider a pageflow model: a domain view would just graphically show the pageflow, and a technical model adds the technology-dependent details.

The most common solution for combining MACRO-/MICROFLOW and DOMAIN-/TECHNICAL-VIEW is:

1. High-level macroflows that depict strategic business processes and that are not implemented are designed only using a domain view (this step is optional).
2. The high-level macroflows are refined by lower-level macroflows that get implemented and offer a domain view as well as a technical view.
3. The macroflows invoke microflows which only have a technical view.

Example: Structural model of macroflow and microflow
Figure 9 shows an exemplary model for explicitly supporting the MACRO-/MICROFLOW pattern. The model shows different kinds of macroflows and microflows, and the relationships between them. The MACRO-/MICROFLOW pattern generally provides a conceptual basis for the development of such models, which could for instance serve as a foundation for model-driven software development.

Known Uses
- In IBM's WebSphere technology [IBM 2008] the MACRO-/MICROFLOW pattern is reflected by different technologies and methodologies being used to design and implement process-aware information systems. Different kinds of technologies and techniques for both types of flows are offered. On the macroflow level, workflow technologies are used that support integration of people and automated functions on the business process level. An example is IBM's WebSphere Process Choreographer, which is a workflow modeling component. The microflow level is rather represented by transactional message flow technologies that are often used in service-oriented approaches.

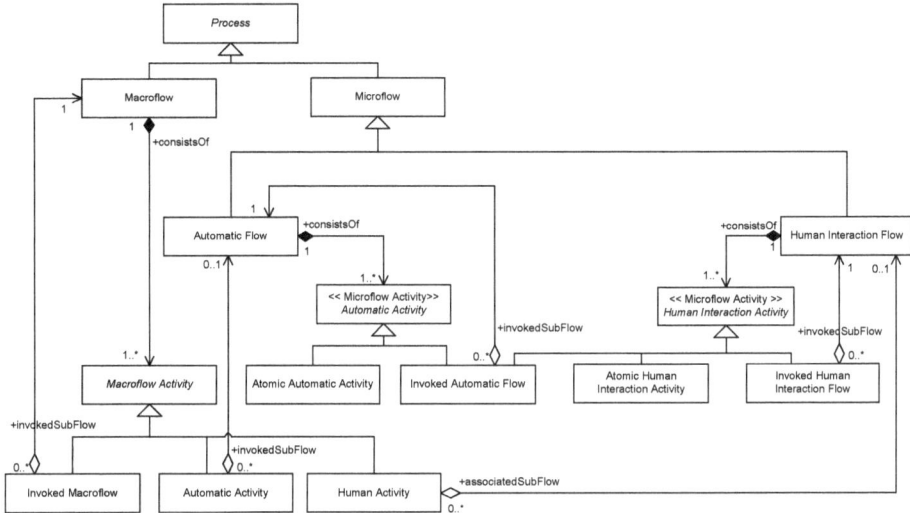

Fig. 9. Structural model of macroflow and microflow

Examples are the WebSphere Business Integration Message Broker and the WebSphere InterChange Server. At the macroflow level, a service is invoked that is designed and implemented in detail by a microflow that performs data transformation and routing to a backend application. Moreover, aggregated services are often implemented at the microflow level using these kinds of message flow technologies.

- GFT's BPM Suite GFT Inspire [GFT 2007] provides a modeler component that uses UML activity diagrams as a notation for modeling the macroflow. Microflows can be modeled in various ways. First, there are so-called step activities, which allow the technical modeler to model a number of sequential step actions that refine the business activity. In the step actions, the details of the connection to other systems can be specified in a special purpose dialog. This concept is especially used to invoke other GFT products, such as the document archive system or a form-based input. Alternatively, the microflow can be implemented in Java snippets, which can be deployed to the server – together with the business process. Finally, services can be invoked that can integrate external microflow technologies, such as message brokers.

- JBoss' jBPM engine [JBoss 2007] follows a slightly different model, as the core component is a Java library and hence can be used in any Java environment. The jBPM library can also be packaged and exposed as a stateless session EJB. JBoss offers a graph-based designer for the macroflow process languages, and works with its own proprietary language, jPDL. A BPEL extension is also offered. The microflow is implemented through actions that are associated with events of the nodes and transitions in the process graph. The actions are hidden from the graphical representation, so that macroflow designers do not have to deal with them. The actions invoke

Java code, which implements the microflow. The microflows need not be defined directly in Java, but can also be executed on external microflow technology, such as a message broker or a pageflow engine.

- Novell's exteNd Director [Novell 2008] is a framework for rapid Web site development. It provides a page flow engine implementing microflows for human interaction. A workflow engine realizes long-running macroflows. A pageflow activity in the workflows is used to trigger pageflows. This design follows the MACRO-/MICROFLOW pattern.

3.3 Pattern: Macroflow Engine

Context
You have decided to model parts of your system using macroflows to represent long-running business processes, for instance following the MACRO-/MICROFLOW pattern. The simplest way to implement and execute your macroflow process models is to manually translate them into programming language code. But, as many tasks and issues in a macroflow implementation are recurring, it would be useful to have some more support for macroflows.

Problem
How can macroflow execution be supported by technology?

Problem Details
One of the main reasons to model macroflows is to enable coping with business change. The reasoning behind this idea is that if you model your processes explicitly, you understand the implementation of your business better and can more quickly react to changes in the business. Changes to business are reflected by changes in the corresponding macroflows. Today a lot of IT systems support business processes, and the required changes often involve significant changes in IT systems with high costs and long development times. In a dynamic business environment, these costs and long development times are often not acceptable, as conditions might have already changed when old requirements are implemented.

One of the major reasons for this problem is that business process logic is hard-coded in the program code. The required changes thus imply to change program code in various systems. The result is a fragmentation (or structural gap) of business processes and IT systems that support them.

Often a lot of different skills are required to achieve this, as the systems are implemented on varying platforms with different technology, programming paradigms, and languages. The heterogeneity of systems and concepts lead also problems for end-users, who have to roughly understand the adaptations of the changed systems. Often the desired business process, as it was originally designed, cannot be realized due to limitations of existing systems or because of the high efforts required to implement the changes.

The complexity generated by this heterogeneity and the interdependencies between the systems let projects fail even before they have started, as the involved risks and the costs may be higher than the estimated benefit of the business process change. Thus incremental evolution cannot be achieved. As a result, IT has gained the reputation of just being a cost driver but not a business enabler. In many cases, this problem causes a situation in which no significant and innovative changes are made, and solving prevalent problems is postponed as long as possible.

Hard-coding business processes also means that recurring functionality required for executing macroflows, such as process persistence, wait states, process management, or concurrency handling, need to be manually coded, too. That is, effort is required to develop and maintain these functionalities.

Solution
Use a dedicated MACROFLOW ENGINE that supports executing long-running business processes (macroflows) described in a business process modeling language. Integrate business functions as services (or modules) that are invoked by the macroflow activities. Changes of macroflows are supported by changing the macroflow models and deploying the new versions to the engine at runtime.

Solution Details
Figure 10 illustrates the solution of the MACROFLOW ENGINE pattern.

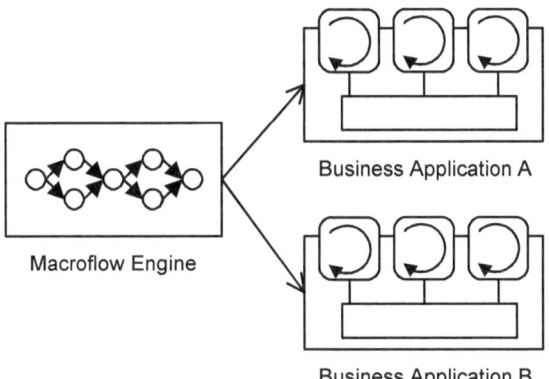

Macroflow Engine

Business Application A

Business Application B

Fig. 10. Illustration of MACROFLOW ENGINE

The MACROFLOW ENGINE pattern's main participant is the engine component that allows developers to describe the business process logic by changing the business process definitions. Using a MACROFLOW ENGINE in an architecture means to decouple the business process logic from the IT systems. However, effort is needed to introduce a MACROFLOW ENGINE based architecture. The pattern has best effects if applied as a long term approach to architecture design and application development. Short term goals may not justify the efforts involved.

Macroflow definitions are defined using a process modeling language. The engine executes the models, written in that modeling language. Changes occur by modifying the macroflow models and deploying the changed versions on the engine. Using this architecture, business process definitions can be flexibly changed, and the corresponding processes in IT systems can be adapted more easily than in hard-coded macroflow implementations in programming language code.

The models executed by a MACROFLOW ENGINE represent a technical view of a macroflow, as described in the DOMAIN-/TECHNICAL-VIEW pattern, and are usually expressed in business process execution languages, such as BPEL, XPDL, Windows Workflow Foundation models, or jPDL. In many cases, a domain view of the models is defined as well, for instance in high-level process modeling languages, such as BPMN or EPC.

Applications are understood as modules that offer business functions, e.g., as services. If the MACRO-/MICROFLOW pattern is applied, of course, a service can internally realize a microflow implementation. The MACROFLOW ENGINE does not see these internal details, however, but only the service-based interface. The business functions are orchestrated by the business process logic described in the MACROFLOW ENGINE'S modeling language. Business functions are either completely automatic or semi-automatic, representing a human interacting with a system.

Business functions are represented in the macroflow as macroflow activities. They are one of a number of different activity types, supported by the engine. Other example activity types are control flow logic activities, data transformation activities, and exception handling activities. The MACROFLOW ENGINE concentrates on orchestration issues of macroflow activities but not on the implementation of these activities. The actual implementation of macroflow activities is delegated to functionality of other systems that the engine communicates with.

The MACROFLOW ENGINE offers an API to access the functionality of the engine, i.e., processing of automatic and semi-automatic tasks. It further offers functions for long-running macroflow execution, such as process persistence, wait states, and concurrency handling. It also offers an interface for managing and monitoring the processes and process instances at runtime.

Various concepts exist for orchestration of macroflow activities in a MACROFLOW ENGINE. Two common examples are:

- Strictly structured process flow, e.g., in terms of directed graphs with conditional paths (this is most common variant in commercially used products and tools)
- Flexibly structured flow of activities, e.g., by defined pre- and post-conditions of macroflow activities

If business processes have already been hard-coded, developers must first extract the implemented business process logic from the systems and model them in the MACROFLOW ENGINE'S modeling language. Hence, in such cases, introducing the MACROFLOW ENGINE pattern has the drawback that efforts must be invested to extract the business process logic out of existing systems implementations and to modify the architecture.

Example: Structural model of a MACROFLOW ENGINE
Figure 11 shows a simple example model of a MACROFLOW ENGINE design that could be used as a starting point if one would realize a MACROFLOW ENGINE from scratch. The Macroflow Engine supports a simple management interface for Macroflows. These have a number of Macroflow Activities. A Macroflow Activity is assigned to a Resource, where a Resource can be some virtual actor like an IT system acting in a certain role, or a human actor who

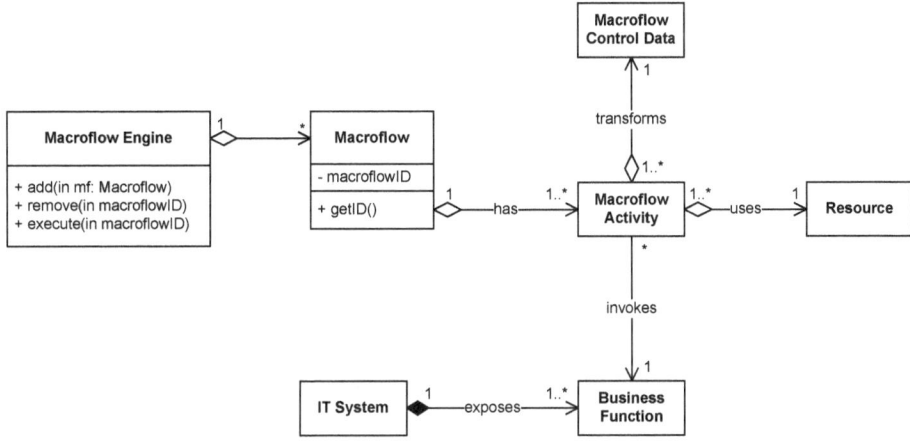

Fig. 11. Structural model of a MACROFLOW ENGINE

interacts with an IT system. As far as a human actor is concerned, constraints may be applied to make the macroflow activity only accessible to a defined set of users, e.g., by roles and rights that a user must have in order to be able to process a macroflow activity. The `Macroflow Activities` always invoke a `Business Function`, whether the `Business Function` is executed with support of a human being or whether it is completely automatic. Control data, such as process variables, is transformed during the execution of `Macroflow Activities`.

Known Uses

- IBM's WebSphere Process Choreographer [IBM 2008] is the workflow modeling component of WebSphere Studio Application Developer Studio, Integration Edition, which provides a MACROFLOW ENGINE. The workflow model is specified in BPEL.
- In the latest WebSphere product suite edition [IBM 2008], the two products WebSphere Process Choreographer and WebSphere InterChange Server have been integrated into one product which is called WebSphere Process Server. Consequently, this new version offers both, a MACROFLOW ENGINE and a MICROFLOW ENGINE.
- GFT's BPM Suite Inspire [GFT 2007] provides a designer for macroflows that is based on UML activity diagrams. The business processes can be deployed to an application server that implements the MACROFLOW ENGINE for running the business processes. The engine also offers an administrator interface for monitoring and management of the processes.
- JBoss' jBPM [JBoss 2007] is an open-source MACROFLOW ENGINE for graph-based business process models that can be expressed either in jPDL or BPEL as modeling languages. jBPM offers a Web-based monitoring and management tool.
- ActiveBPEL [Active Endpoints 2007] is an open-source BPEL engine that acts as a MACROFLOW ENGINE for business processes modeled in BPEL.

- Novell's exteNd Director [Novell 2008] is a framework for rapid Web site development. It provides a workflow engine realizing long-running macroflow.

3.4 Pattern: Microflow Engine

Context

You have realized that the business functions (services) that are orchestrated by macroflows in your system can be understood as short-running, technical processes. Following the MACRO-/MICROFLOW pattern, you introduce microflow models for representing these processes. In many cases, the "conceptual" notion of microflows is useful and sufficient, and microflows are implemented without supporting technology, for instance, using ordinary programming language code or scripts written in a scripting language.

You can further support microflows in hard-coded solutions: A best practice for realizing hard-coded microflows is to place them in their own coding units that can be independently deployed, e.g., each microflow is implemented as its own service in a distinct microflow SERVICE ABSTRACTION LAYER [Vogel 2001]. Support of embedded scripting or dynamic languages for defining microflows can even more support the flexibility of microflow definition and deployment. For many cases, this solution is absolutely good enough. In some cases, however, you would like to get more support for microflow execution.

Problem

How can microflow execution be supported by technology to avoid hard-coded microflow solutions and offer benefits for microflows akin to workflow technologies?

Problem Details

It takes considerable time and effort to realize and change processes, if the technical microflow details are hard-coded in programming language code. Consider you implement a microflow for human interaction. If you realize a hard-coded implementation using a UI technology, you could write a thin client Web UI or a fat client GUI, hard-code certain microflows for human interactions in a layer on top of the UI, and provide a service-based interface to that microflow layer, so that the hard-coded microflow implementations can be accessed from macroflows. Consider you want to perform simple changes to such a design, such as adding or deleting an activity in the microflow. Every change requires programming efforts. In a dynamic environment, where process changes are regular practice, this might not be acceptable.

The design described in this example incurs another drawback: It requires discipline from the developers. Developers must place every microflow in the SERVICE ABSTRACTION LAYER for microflows. If developers do not strictly follow such as design guidelines, the consequence is that microflow code is scattered through one or many components, and hence changes are even more difficult and costly to implement.

For these reasons, in highly dynamic business environments, a similar level of support for changing and redeploying microflows as provided for the macroflow models in a MACROFLOW ENGINE might be needed.

Even though rapid changes and avoiding scattered microflow implementation are the main reasons for requiring a better support for microflows, some other requirements for technology support exist, such as:

- In integrated tool suites, to provide a uniform user experience, tool vendors would like to provide a tooling that is similar to the macroflow tooling, including a modeling language for microflows.
- Even though microflows are short running processes, in some cases it might be necessary to monitor and manage the microflows. To provide monitoring and management for hard-coded microflows usually requires a substantial amount of work.
- Microflows also require recurring functionalities, such as realizing transaction semantics, accessing databases, or handling page flows. Hence, to reuse existing components providing these functionalities is useful.

Solution
Apply the business process paradigm directly to microflow design and implementation by using a MICROFLOW ENGINE that is able to execute the microflow models. The MICROFLOW ENGINE provides recurring tasks of the microflows as elements of the microflow modeling language. It supports change through changing of microflow models and redeployment to the engine. All microflows of a kind are handled by the same microflow engine.

Solution Details
Figure 12 illustrates the solution of the MICROFLOW ENGINE pattern.

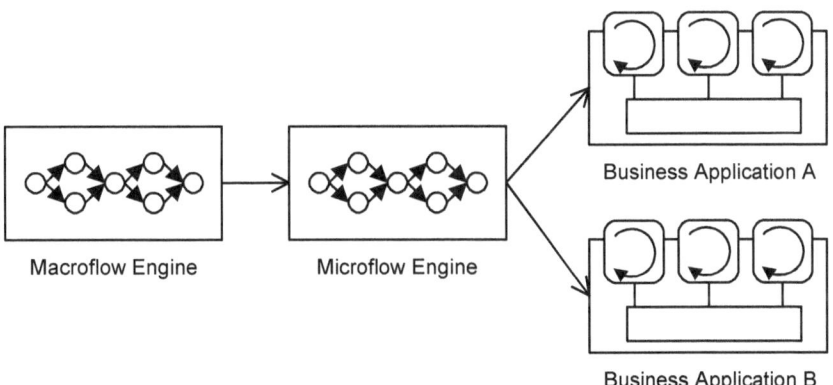

Fig. 12. Illustration of MICROFLOW ENGINE

If a MICROFLOW ENGINE is used, the microflow processes are defined in a microflow modeling language. Processes can be flexibly changed through microflow deployment. The microflow logic is architecturally decoupled from the business applications and centrally handled in one place. The MICROFLOW ENGINE concentrates on orchestration issues of microflow activities but not on implementation of these activities. The actual implementation of microflow activities is delegated to functionality of integrated systems the engine communicates with or to human users.

There are two main kinds of MICROFLOW ENGINES corresponding to the two kinds of microflows:

- MICROFLOW ENGINE for automatic activities: These engines support full-automatic and transaction-safe integration processes. Hence, they offer functions for short-running transactional microflow execution. As integration processes usually must access other technologies or applications, many MICROFLOW ENGINES for automatic activities also support technology and application adapters, such as ODBC, JDBC, XML, Web service, SAP, or Siebel.
- MICROFLOW ENGINE for human interactions: These engines support pageflow handling functionalities. A pageflow defines the control flow for a set of UI pages. The pages usually display information, and contain controls for user interaction. Many pageflow engines focus on form-based input.

The microflow modeling language is a technical modeling language. In many cases, only a technical view of these models is exposed, but some tools also expose a high-level view of the integration processes. If this is the case, the DOMAIN-/TECHNICAL-VIEW pattern is realized by the microflow models. The goal could for instance be to enable designers and architects to gain a quick overview of the microflows. That is, here the domain view depicts a technical domain: either the integration behavior of the systems or the human interactions. Hence, the domain experts are software designers and architects.

Defining executable microflow models using a modeling language does not mean a MICROFLOW ENGINE must be used. An alternative is for instance to generate microflow execution code in a programming language using a model-driven code generator. Using a MICROFLOW ENGINE should be carefully considered, as it has some disadvantages as well. Usually, it is not possible to define a custom microflow modeling language for existing engines, and many existing languages are much more complex than needed for very simple microflow orchestrations. This means additional effort, as developers, designers, and architects must learn the microflow modeling language. The MICROFLOW ENGINE is an additional technology which must be maintained. The additional engine component adds complexity to the system architecture.

The MICROFLOW ENGINE has the advantage that the models are accessible at runtime, e.g., for reflection on the models, and can be manipulated by redeployment. Management and monitoring of running processes is possible – either through an API or a management and monitoring tool. A tool suite similar to the macroflow tools can be provided. Recurring functionalities can be supported by the MICROFLOW ENGINE and reused for all microflows.

Example: Structural model of a MICROFLOW ENGINE
Figure 13 shows a simple example model of a MICROFLOW ENGINE design that could be used as a starting point if one would realize a MICROFLOW ENGINE from scratch. The basic feature of this MICROFLOW ENGINE design is execution of defined microflow integration process logic by orchestrating `Microflow Activities`.

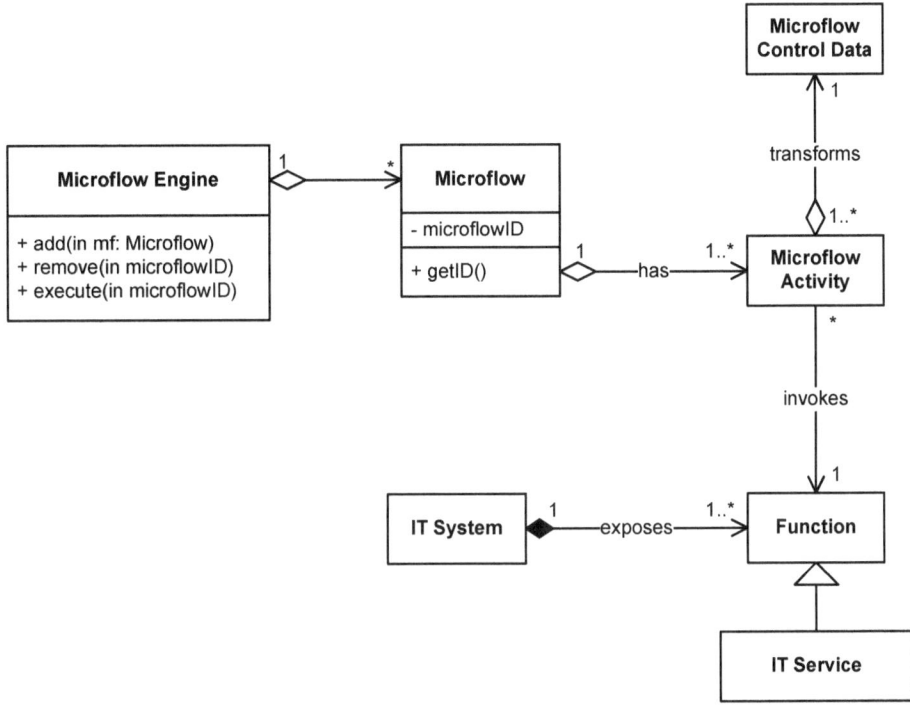

Fig. 13. Structural model of a MICROFLOW ENGINE

Analogous to the similar MACROFLOW ENGINE example presented before, each activity transforms `Control Data` that is used to control the orchestrations of microflow activities and invokes a `Function` of an `IT System`. The main difference to the previous example is: Here the functions are services exposed by IT Systems, not business-related functions (see the BUSINESS-DRIVEN SERVICE pattern for guidelines how to design the IT services). The invocations are performed automatically and in a transaction-safe way.

Example: Java Page Flow Architecture
The previous example mainly illustrates a schematic design of a MICROFLOW ENGINE for automatic activities. A similar design could also be used as a core for a MICROFLOW ENGINE for human interactions. But additionally, we must define how to integrate the MICROFLOW ENGINE component into the UI architecture. Many UIs follow the MODEL-VIEW-CONTROLLER pattern (MVC) [Buschmann et al. 1996].

We want to illustrate one example design for the Java Page Flow Architecture which provides an implementation of a MICROFLOW ENGINE for human interactions. A Java Page Flow consists of two main components: controllers and forms. Controllers mainly contain a control flow, defined by so-called actions and forwards. The forms associated to the actions and forwards are mainly JSP pages.

In Figure 14, you see an example from [Mittal and Kanchanavally 2008], which shows a mapping of the Java Page Flow Architecture to MVC, as implemented in the

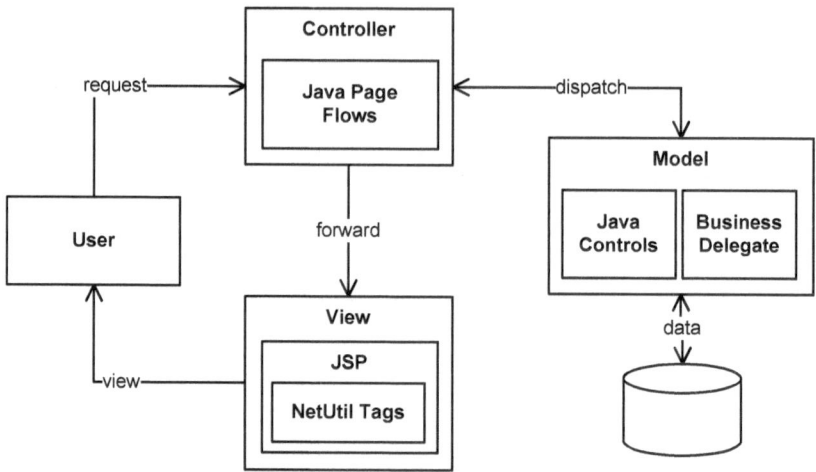

Fig. 14. Java Page Flow Architecture and MVC [Mittal and Kanchanavally 2008]

Apache Beehive project. The main engine component, executing the microflows, is used as the MVC controller. JSP and the NetUI tag libraries are used to display the information in the view. Any model layer can be used, it is not determined by the pageflow engine. In this example architecture, the Controls technology from the Apache Beehive project is used as a model layer technology.

Known Uses
- The WebSphere Business Integration Message Broker and the WebSphere InterChange Server [IBM 2008] are both realizing MICROFLOW ENGINES. Both middleware products can also be used in conjunction. The WebSphere Business Integration Message Broker is used for simpler functions, such as adapter-based integration or dispatching. The product offers support for off-the-shelf adapters, message routing, and transformation. WebSphere InterChange Server offers transaction safe integration process execution. Process definition is done via a GUI, and the product also offers a very large set of INTEGRATION ADAPTERS for most common technologies and applications.
- webMethods' Integration Server (now integrated in the Fabric BPM suite) [webMethods 2007] provides a MICROFLOW ENGINE that supports various data transfer and Web services standards, including JSP, XML, XSLT, SOAP, and WSDL. Its offers a graphical modeler for microflows that models the microflow in a number of sequential steps (including loop steps and branching), as well as a data mapping modeler.
- iWay's Universal Adapter Suite [iWay 2007a] provides an Adapter Manager [iWay 2007b] for its intelligent, plug-and-play adapters. The Adapter Manager is a component that runs either stand-alone or in an EJB container and executes adapter flows. The basic adapter flow is: It transforms an application-specific request of a client into iWay's proprietary XML format, invokes an agent that might invoke an adapter or perform other tasks, and

transforms the XML-based response into the application specific response format. The Adapter Manager provides a graphical modeling tool for assembling the adapters, the Adapter Designer. It allows developers to specify special-purpose microflows for a number of adapter-specific tasks, such as various transformations, routing through so-called agents, encryption/decryption, decisions, etc. Multiple agents, transformations, and decisions can be combined in one flow. The Adapter Manager hence provides a special-purpose MICROFLOW ENGINE focusing on adapter assembly.

- The Java Page Flow Architecture, explained before, is a technology defining MICROFLOW ENGINES for human interactions. Apache Beehive is a project that implements the Java Page Flow Architecture using Java metadata annotations. The implementation is based on Struts, a widely-used MVC framework. BEA WebLogic Workshop is another implementation of the Java Page Flow Architecture, which is provides a declarative pageflow language.

- Novell's exteNd Director [Novell 2008] is a framework for rapid Web site development. It provides a page flow engine that orchestrates pageflows consisting of XForm pages.

4 Integration and Adaptation in Process-Driven SOAs

In the previous section we mainly discussed how to realize various types of executable process flow, macroflows and microflows, and how to connect them to services that realize functions in the processes. In a real-world SOA, usually not all services are implemented by the SOA developers, but in most cases a number of existing (legacy) systems, such as custom business applications, databases, and off-the-shelf business applications (such as SAP or Siebel), must be integrated.

Consider a typical starting point: Your organization uses two primary business applications. The first step to build a SOA orchestrating functions provided by those legacy applications is to provide them with a service-oriented interface. This is usually an incremental and non-trivial task. But let's assume we are able to find suitable business services to access these applications. In order to support orchestration through executable business processes, we will design high-level macroflows representing the business processes of the organization – from the business perspective. Following the MACRO-/MICROFLOW and DOMAIN-/TECHNICAL-VIEW patterns, the high-level macroflows are step-by-step refined into executable macroflows. Next, we realize the executable macroflows in a macroflow engine and use the macroflow activities to invoke the services exposed by the business applications. The result is an architecture as shown in the sketch below in Figure 15.

Unfortunately, often the interfaces provided by the legacy business applications are not identical to what is expected in the business processes. The business application services expose the – often rather technical – interfaces of the legacy business applications. The macroflow processes, in contrast, require interfaces that correspond to the business activities in the processes. Changing the macroflows to use the technical interfaces does not make sense because we want to keep the macroflows

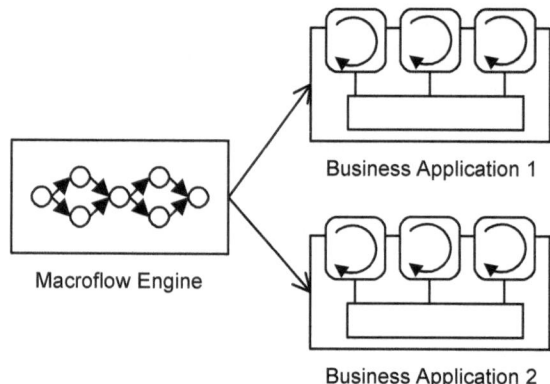

Fig. 15. Macroflow Engine and Business Applications

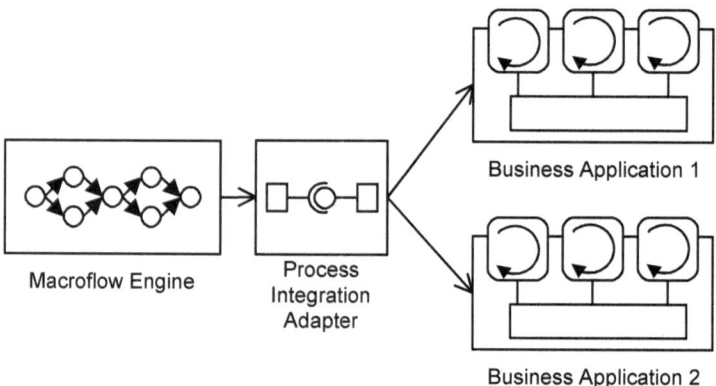

Fig. 16. Introducing a PROCESS INTEGRATION ADAPTER

understandable for business stakeholders. In addition, hard-wiring process activities to the volatile interfaces of backends is not useful, because for each change in the backend the process designs would have to be changed.

For these reasons, it makes sense to introduce INTEGRATION ADAPTERS for process integration, exposing the interfaces that the macroflows require (as shown in Figure 16). The INTEGRATION ADAPTER pattern translates between the interfaces of two systems connected using asynchronous (or if needed synchronous) connectors. The pattern also enables maintenance of both the connected target system and the adapter, by being suspendable and stoppable. Macroflow engine technology often provides such INTEGRATION ADAPTERS for connecting the processes to backend services. These adapters perform interface adaptations and data transformations, as well as data mapping tools to design the transformations.

In many cases, the abstraction of business application services through an adapter is not enough. Still, the macroflows contain technical issues that go beyond simple adaptations and data transformations, but rather deal with orchestration tasks. As explained in the MACRO-/MICROFLOW pattern, these technical flows should not be

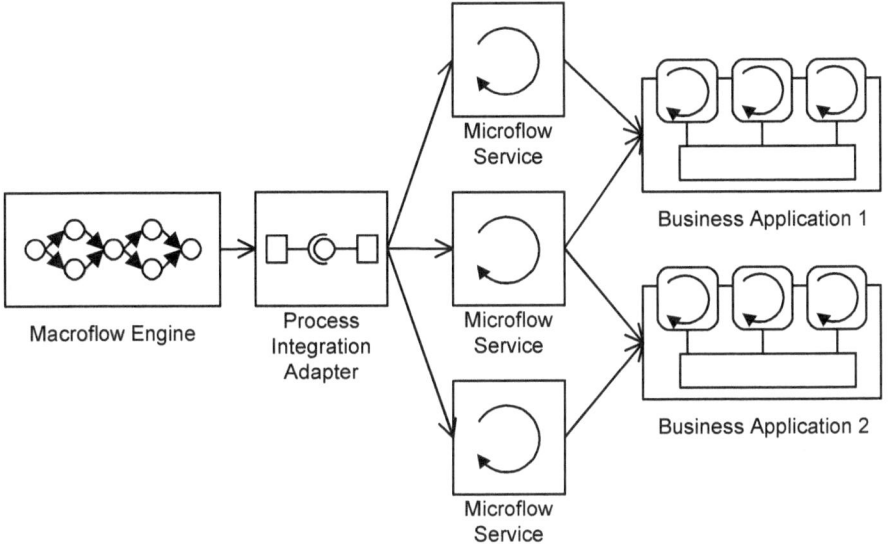

Fig. 17. Introducing a Microflows as Services

realized in a MACROFLOW ENGINE, but strictly distinguished from the macroflows – and realized as microflows. For such a small-scale architecture, it is usually enough to provide a few hard-coded services in a distinct microflow tier, as shown in Figure 17.

In this architecture, the business applications are hard-wired in the service implementations. That means, if the applications need to be stopped for maintenance, the whole SOA must be stopped. If the application service interfaces need to be changed, all dependent services must be changed, too. This is ok for small SOAs with limited maintenance and availability requirements. But consider we require the SOA

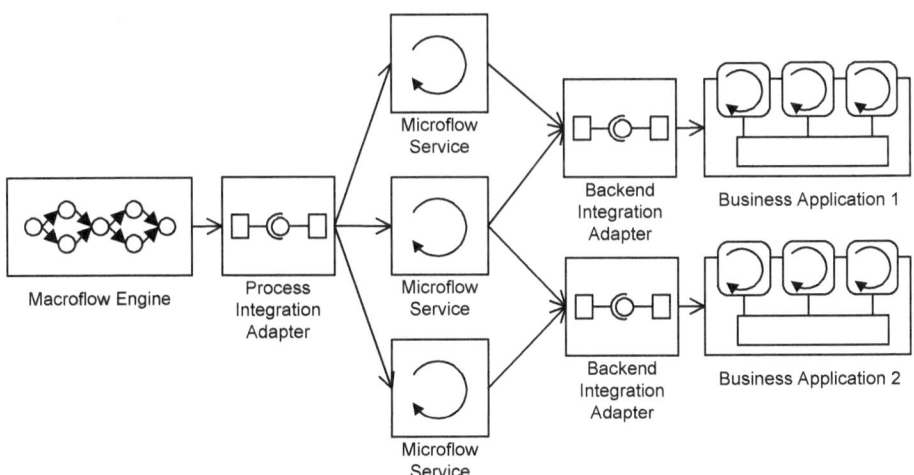

Fig. 18. Introducing Backend Integration Adapters

to continue to run, while new versions of the business applications are deployed. This can be resolved by applying the INTEGRATION ADAPTER pattern again: We provide INTEGRATION ADAPTERS for the business applications as illustrated in Figure 18.

Now consider we run this SOA for a while and our organization merges with another organization. That means the information system of that other organization needs to access our SOA. If the other organization uses explicit business processes as well, it is likely that it runs its own MACROFLOW ENGINE. We can perform the integration of the two systems by providing that other MACROFLOW ENGINE with a process integration adapter that integrates the microflow services of our SOA with the business activity interfaces required by the other organization's macroflows. The resulting architecture is sketched in Figure 19.

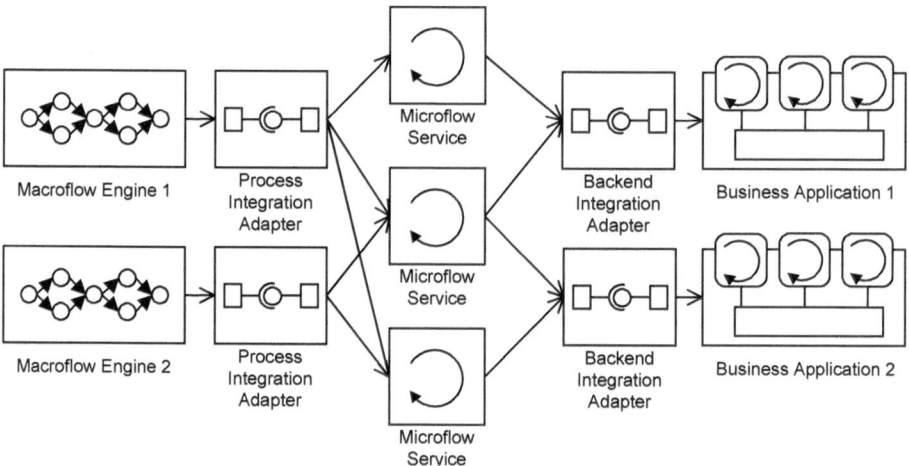

Fig. 19. Introducing multiple Macroflow Engines

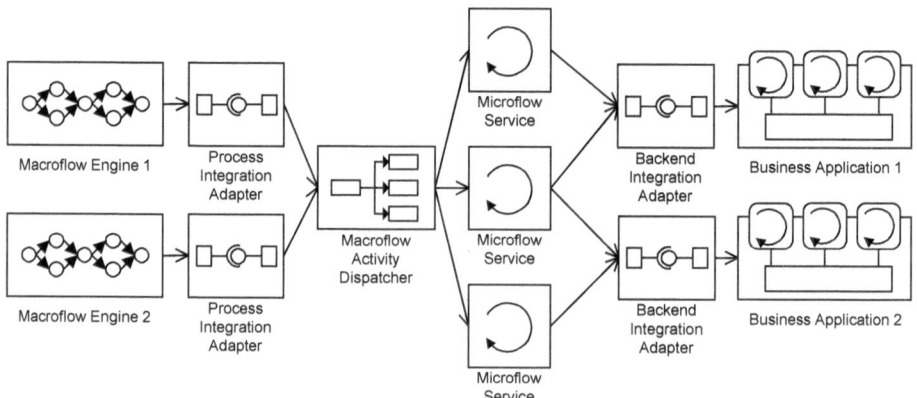

Fig. 20. Introducing a Macroflow Activity Dispatcher

The macroflow tier is currently hard-wired to the technical tiers. If dynamic content-based routing to microflows and backends is needed or load balancing to multiple servers hosting the services should be provided, the introduction of a CONFIGURABLE DISPATCHER (as shown in Figure 20) between macroflows tier and technical tiers can be beneficial to provide more configurability and flexibility. The CONFIGURABLE DISPATCHER pattern connects client and target systems using a configurable dispatch algorithm. Hence, it enables us to postpone dispatch decisions till runtime. It uses configurable dispatching rules that can be updated at runtime.

Over time, we might realize that more and more microflows are needed and more and more recurring tasks are performed in the microflows. In addition, it might make sense to make the microflow orchestrations more configurable. Hence, as a last step, we replace the microflow service tier by two MICROFLOW ENGINES: a page flow engine to realize the human interaction microflows and a message broker to realize the automated microflows. This is illustrated in Figure 21.

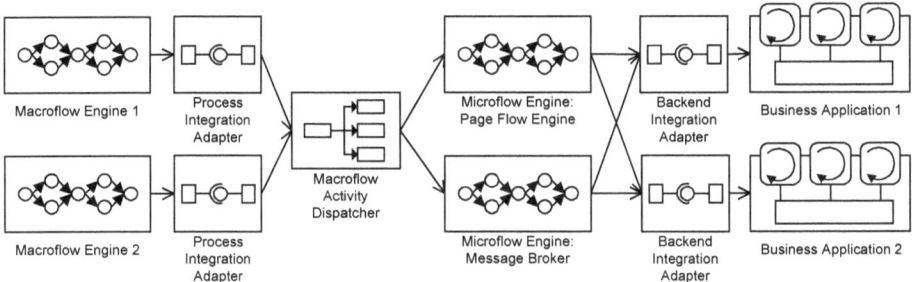

Fig. 21. Introducing Microflow Engines

In our SOA, we have applied multiple INTEGRATION ADAPTERS that must be maintained and managed. Consider further the organization develops other SOAs for other business units that use similar technologies and must operate on similar backends. Then it makes sense to introduce an INTEGRATION ADAPTER REPOSITORY for the backend adapters. The INTEGRATION ADAPTER REPOSITORY pattern provides a central repository and maintenance interface for INTEGRATION ADAPTERS that supports management, querying, and deployment of adapters. It hence facilitates reuse of adapters.

The sketched, incrementally built architecture in this example follows the PROCESS INTEGRATION ARCHITECTURE pattern. This pattern is an architectural pattern that defines a specific configuration using a number of other patterns. It explains a specific architectural configuration of how the other patterns can be assembled to a flexible and scalable SOA.

One of the primary advantages of following the PROCESS INTEGRATION ARCHITECTURE pattern is that is enable architects to build up a SOA incrementally – just as in this example walkthrough. A process-driven SOA initiative is usually a large-scale project in which multiple new technologies must be learned and integrated. Hence, step-by-step introduction of extensions, following an approach that is known to scale well to larger SOAs, is highly useful.

4.1 Pattern: Integration Adapter

Context
In a SOA, various systems need to be connected to other systems. For instance, in a process-driven SOA, among others, the MACROFLOW ENGINES, MICROFLOW ENGINES, business services, and backend systems must be connected. The systems in a process-driven SOA are heterogeneous systems, consisting of diverse technologies running on different platforms and communicating over various protocols. When different systems are interconnected and the individual systems evolve over time, the system internals and sometimes even the public interfaces of these systems change.

Problem
How can heterogeneous systems in a SOA be connected and the impacts of system and system interface changes kept in acceptable limits?

Problem Details
Connecting two systems in a SOA means that a client system must be aligned with a target system that captures the requests, takes over the task of execution, and generates a response. For instance, if a MACROFLOW ENGINE or MICROFLOW ENGINE is the client, it acts as a coordinator of activities. Some of these activities are tasks that need to be executed by some other system. But, in many cases, the target systems are different to what is expected in the process engine. For instance, different technology, different synchronization mechanisms, or different protocols are used. In addition, in case of asynchronous communication, we must provide a way to connect heterogeneous technologies in such a way that the client can correlate the response to the original request.

One important consideration, when connecting systems in a SOA, is the change impact. Changes should not affect the client of a system, if possible. For instance, changes to integrated systems should not have effects on the processes that run in process engines.

In many change scenarios, downtimes of the whole SOA for maintenance are not tolerable. That is, changing a system should not mean that the other systems of the SOA must be stopped, but they should be able to continue to work, as if the changed system would still be functioning. Apart from this issue, internal system changes can be tolerated in a SOA as long as the public interfaces exposed as services do not change.

However, many changes include interface change. Often the public interface of a system changes with each new release of the system. In this context of ongoing change and maintenance, the costs and efforts of changes should be kept at a minimum level. The impact of changes and the related testing efforts must also be kept within acceptable limits.

If your organization is in control of the system that must be changed, sometimes it is possible to circumvent these problems by avoiding changes that influence other systems. However, in a SOA usually many systems by external vendors or open source projects are used. Examples are backend systems, such as databases, SAP, or Siebel, as well as SOA components, such as MACROFLOW ENGINES and MICROFLOW ENGINES. Changes cannot be avoided for these systems. Migration to a new release is often forced as old releases are not supported anymore, or the new functionality is simply required by the business.

Apart from migration to a new version, the problem also occurs if a system shall be replaced by a completely different system. In such cases, the technology and functional interfaces of the new system are often highly different, causing a significant change impact.

Solution

If two systems must be connected in a SOA and keeping the change impacts in acceptable limits is a goal for this connection, provide an INTEGRATION ADAPTER for the system interconnection. The adapter contains two connectors: One for the client system's import interface and one for the target system's export interface. Use the adapter to translate between the connected systems, such as interfaces, protocols, technologies, and synchronization mechanisms, and use CORRELATION IDENTIFIERS to relate asynchronous requests and responses. Make the adapter configurable, by using asynchronous communication protocols and following the COMPONENT CONFIGURATOR pattern [Schmidt et al. 2000], so that the adapter can be modified at runtime without impacting the systems sending requests to the adapter.

Solution Details

Figure 22 illustrates the solution of the INTEGRATION ADAPTER pattern.

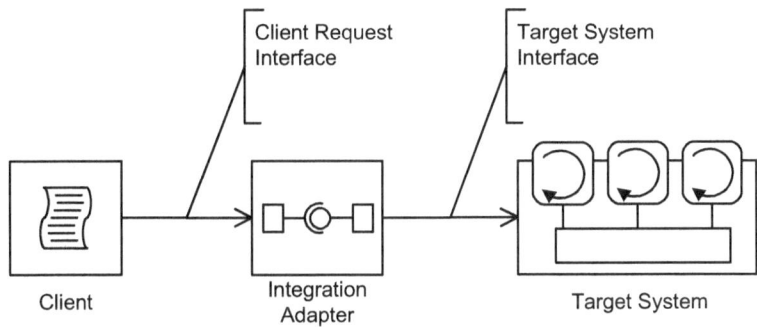

Fig. 22. Illustration of INTEGRATION ADAPTER

The core of the solution of the INTEGRATION ADAPTER pattern is the same as in the classical, object-oriented ADAPTER pattern [Gamma et al. 1994]: An adapter connects the interfaces of a client and a target, and translates between the two interfaces. For instance, if the client is a process engine, it acts as a sender in terms of sending out requests for activity execution, which are received by the adapter and transformed into a request understood by the target system. The INTEGRATION ADAPTER pattern adds to the solution of the ADAPTER pattern by supporting integration at the architectural level of connecting distributed and heterogeneous systems.

In the ADAPTER pattern, invocations are mainly synchronous, object-oriented message calls in the local scope. An INTEGRATION ADAPTER must consider in first place distributed requests and responses, which can be send either synchronously or asynchronously. Receiving a request or response can work via push or pull mechanisms. The request contains an identifier for the function to be executed and input parameters. The INTEGRATION ADAPTER transforms the request into a format that can be understood by the target system's interface and technology. The request will be forwarded to the target system after the transformation is performed. After the adapter has received a response of the target system, the response is transformed back into the format and technology used by the interface of the client.

To make the INTEGRATION ADAPTER maintainable at runtime, the COMPONENT CONFIGURATOR pattern [Schmidt et al. 2000] should be applied. That is, the adapter offers a configuration interface, which supports stopping and suspending the adapter. The adapter is stopped, when new versions of the adapter must be deployed. The adapter is suspended, when new versions of the target system are deployed or the adapter is configured at runtime. Later on, after maintenance activities are finished, the adapter can resume its work and process all requests that have arrived in the meantime. The INTEGRATION ADAPTER can also offer a finalization function such that it finishes all ongoing activities properly and then terminates itself.

To realize an adapter with a COMPONENT CONFIGURATOR interface, the adapter must be loosely coupled to other systems, which is achieved by using connectors to client and target systems, as well as asynchronous communication protocols. As requests must be accepted at any time, no matter whether an adapter is at work or temporally suspended, an asynchronous connector should be used to receive the requests and to send the responses. That is, the connector must be decoupled from the adapter to still accept requests in case the adapter is not active.

Basically, asynchronous communication is only required on client side, i.e., for systems that access the adapter. The target system does not necessarily need to be connected asynchronously. For instance, a connected system might only offer a synchronous interface, or the system is a database which is connected via synchronous SQL. That also means, the connector may accept requests and queue them until they are processed by the adapter.

In case of asynchronous communication, requests and responses are related by applying the CORRELATION IDENTIFIER pattern [Hohpe et al. 2003]. That is, the client sends a CORRELATION IDENTIFIER with the request. The adapter is responsible for putting the same CORRELATION IDENTIFIER into the respective response, so that the client can relate the response to its original request. For instance, if the client is a process engine, the CORRELATION IDENTIFIER identifies the activity instance that has sent the request.

If supported by the target system, the CORRELATION IDENTIFIER will also be used on the target system's side to relate the response of the target system back to the original request. Consequently, the target system will have to send the CORRELATION IDENTIFIER back in its own response so that the adapter can re-capture it. The response will also contain the result of the execution. If CORRELATION IDENTIFIERS cannot be used with the target system, for instance, because it is a legacy system that we cannot change, the INTEGRATION ADAPTER must implement its own mechanism to align requests and results.

The transformations performed by the adapter are often hard-coded in the adapter implementation. In some cases, they need to be configurable. To achieve this, the adapter can implement transformation rules for mapping a request including all its data to the interface and request format of the target system. Transformation rules can also be used for the response transformations. Data mapping tools can be provided to model such transformation rules.

An INTEGRATION ADAPTER is very useful for flexible integration of business applications from external vendors. It also gets more popular to provide interconnectivity by supporting generic adapters for common standards, such as XML and Web Services. That is the reason why many vendors deliver such adapters off-the-shelf and provide open access to their APIs. As standard adapters can be provided for most common standards or products, solutions following the INTEGRATION ADAPTER pattern are usually reusable.

One drawback of INTEGRATION ADAPTERS is that potentially many adapters need to be managed, if many systems exist where adapters for different purposes, systems, or technologies are required. Hence, maintenance and deployment of adapters might become problematic and must be done in a controlled way. The INTEGRATION ADAPTER REPOSITORY offers a way to manage adapters in a centralized and controlled way.

If an adapter is suspended for a long time or if the amount of requests sent to a suspended adapter is very high, then the request queue may contain large amounts of requests that take a long time to be processed or the requests may even have timed out. The workload of requests and the amount of requests that an adapter can process must be in balance. Middleware is required to queue the requests.

Example: Simple example structure of an INTEGRATION ADAPTER
Figure 23 shows an exemplary model for the internal design of INTEGRATION ADAPTER. This adapter receives asynchronous requests from a client system and translates them into synchronous requests for a target system. While waiting for the response, the adapter stores the CORRELATION IDENTIFIER sent by the client and adds it to the respective response message that is sent back to the client. The INTEGRATION ADAPTER offers an API for adapter configuration:

- The adapter can be initialized with `init`.
- The adapter can be stopped with `finalize`.

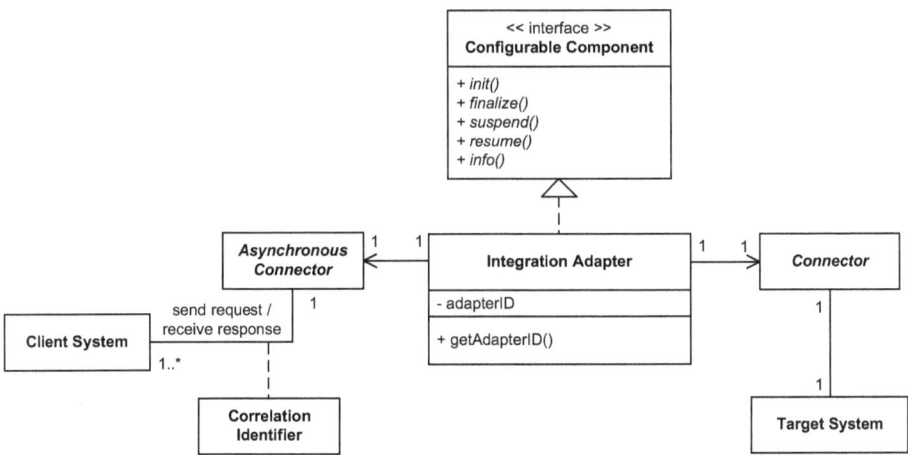

Fig. 23. Example structure of an INTEGRATION ADAPTER

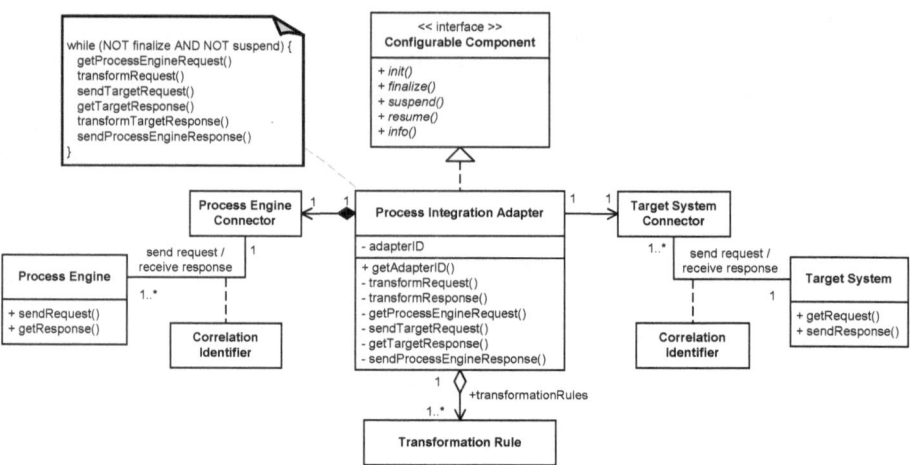

Fig. 24. Example structure of a PROCESS INTEGRATION ADAPTER

- The connected target system can be maintained. Then the adapter must be suspended using the `suspend` operation, and after the maintenance it can `resume`.
- The adaptation status can be queried with `info`.

Example: Process Integration Adapter

Let us consider now a slightly more complex example of an INTEGRATION ADAPTER: An adapter that connects a process engine (i.e., a MACROFLOW ENGINE or MICROFLOW ENGINE) to a target system. Using INTEGRATION ADAPTERS for process integration has the benefit of a clear model for the communication between a process engine and the connected target systems.

In this example, both connectors are asynchronous. The adapter must translate between the two CORRELATION IDENTIFIERS. The adapter uses the same interface for configuration, as in the previous example. It follows a predefined protocol of a few operations to perform the adaptation.

Both request and response message are transformed using transformation rules. Many process engines offer data mapping tools for graphical design of the transformation rules. Figure 24 illustrates the structure of the process integration adapter.

The process integration adapter has a straightforward adaptation behavior, as shown in the following sequence diagram in Figure 25.

Known Uses

- WebSphere InterChange Server [IBM 2008] offers a very large set of INTEGRATION ADAPTERS for most common technologies and applications. Users can extend the set of adapters with self-defined adapters.
- The transport providers of the Mule ESB [Mule 2007] provide INTEGRATION ADAPTERS for transport protocols, repositories, messaging, services, and other technologies in form of their connectors. A connector provides the implementation for connecting to an external system. The connector sends

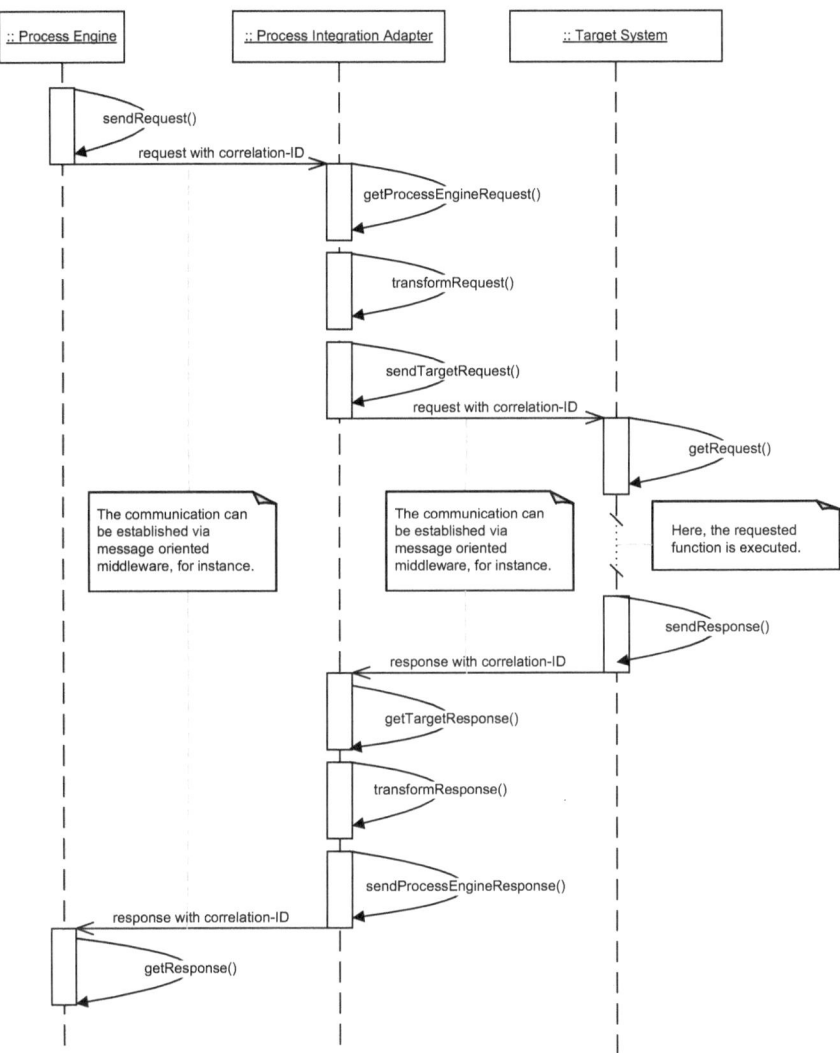

Fig. 25. Behavior of a PROCESS INTEGRATION ADAPTER

requests to an external receiver and manages listeners to receive responses from the external system. There are pre-defined connectors for HTTP, POP3/SMTP, IMAP, Apache Axis Web Services, JDBC, JMS, RMI, and many other technologies. Components can implement a common component lifecycle with the following lifecycle interfaces: Initialisable, Startable, Callable, Stoppable, and Disposable. The pre-defined connectors implement only the Disposable and Initialisable interfaces.

- iWay's Universal Adapter Suite [iWay 2007a] provides so-called intelligent, plug-and-play adapters for over 250 information sources and broad connectivity to multiple computing platforms and transport protocols. It provides a repository of adapters, a special-purpose MICROFLOW ENGINE for assembling adapters called the Adapter Manager, a graphical modeling tool for adapter assembly, and integration with the MACROFLOW ENGINE and EAI frameworks of most big vendors.

- WebSphere MQ Workflow [IBM 2008] offers a technical concept called a User-Defined Program Execution Server (UPES), which implements this pattern for process integration. The UPES concept is a mechanism for invoking services via XML-based message adapters. Basis of the UPES concept is the MQ Workflow XML messaging interface. The UPES concept is all about communicating with external services via asynchronous XML messages. Consequently, the UPES mechanism invokes a service that a process activity requires, receives the result after the service execution has been completed, and further relates the asynchronously incoming result back to the process activity instance that originally requested execution of the service (as there may be hundreds or thousands of instances of the same process activity).

- CSC offers within their e4 reference meta-architecture the concept of INTEGRATION ADAPTERS for process integration. For an insurance customer in the UK the e4 adapter concept has been used to integrate FileNet P8 Business Process Manager with an enterprise service bus based on WebSphere Business Integration Message broker.

- Within the Service Component Architecture (SCA) concept of IBM's WebSphere Integration Developer various INTEGRATION ADAPTERS are offered off-the-shelf, e.g., for WebSphere MQ, Web services, or JMS.

4.2 Pattern: Integration Adapter Repository

Context
Various systems shall be connected via INTEGRATION ADAPTERS. That means, a large number of adapters is used or can potentially be used in a SOA.

Problem
How can a large number of INTEGRATION ADAPTERS be maintained and managed?

Problem Details
INTEGRATION ADAPTERS are important to connect systems that have incompatible interfaces and to minimize the change impact, when multiple systems are integrated. But with each system integrated into a SOA, the number of adapters to be maintained grows. In addition, when the adapters evolve, new adapter versions need to be supported as well, meaning that actually multiple versions of each adapter need to be maintained and managed.

Not always the organization running the SOA also provides the adapters. Especially for standard software, vendors offer INTEGRATION ADAPTERS. The result is often a large set of reusable standard adapters. Reusable adapter sets can also be built inside an organization, for instance, if the organization builds multiple SOAs and wants to reuse the adapters from previous projects. To facilitate reuse of adapters, it should be possible to search and query for an adapter or an adapter version in such a larger adapter set.

Managing multiple INTEGRATION ADAPTERS also introduces a deployment issue: Usually connected systems should not be stopped for deploying a new adapter or adapter versions. Instead it should get "seamlessly" deployed at runtime. That means, tools should support seamless deployment.

The problem of INTEGRATION ADAPTER maintenance and management especially occurs in larger architectural contexts, where different systems have to communicate and larger sets of adapters exist. The problem does not have such a great impact within the boundaries of one closed component or application, as the whole component or application needs to be redeployed if changes are made.

Solution
Use a central repository to manage the INTEGRATION ADAPTERS as components. The INTEGRATION ADAPTER REPOSITORY provides functions for storing, retrieving, and querying of adapters, as well as adapter versioning. It also provides functions for automatic deployment or supports automatic deployment tools. The automatic deployment functions use the COMPONENT CONFIGURATOR interface of the INTEGRATION ADAPTERS to suspend or stop adapters for maintenance. The functions of the repository are offered via a central administration interface.

Solution Details
Figure 26 illustrates the solution of the INTEGRATION ADAPTER REPOSITORY pattern.

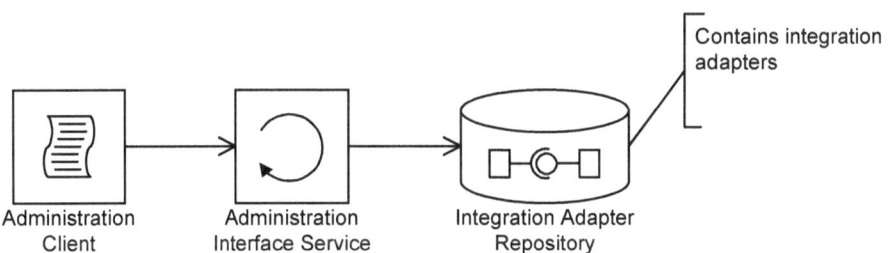

Contains integration adapters

Administration Client   Administration Interface Service   Integration Adapter Repository

Fig. 26. Illustration of INTEGRATION ADAPTER repository

The INTEGRATION ADAPTERS are stored in a central repository that offers operations to add, retrieve, and remove adapters in multiple versions. Optionally, the repository can provide functions to search for adapters and adapter versions by given attributes.

In the simple case, the INTEGRATION ADAPTER REPOSITORY just identifies the adapter by adapter ID (name) and version. More sophisticated variants support metadata about the adapters as well.

The INTEGRATION ADAPTER REPOSITORY can be used to support adapter deployment. In the simplest form it fulfills tasks for external deployment tools, such as delivering the right adapter in the right version. But it can also provide the deployment functions itself.

The automatic deployment functions use the COMPONENT CONFIGURATOR interface of the INTEGRATION ADAPTERS. That is, maintenance or deployment tasks are supported because each single adapter can be stopped and restarted, new adapters or adapter versions can be deployed, and old adapters can be removed via a centralized administration interface.

It is important that requests sent to adapters are processed asynchronously (see INTEGRATION ADAPTER pattern) to bridge maintenance times when the adapters are modified. The requests are queued while the adapter is suspended. The pending requests can be processed when the adapter restarts work after maintenance, or after an adapter is replaced by a new adapter. The deployment functions must trigger this behavior of the adapters.

The INTEGRATION ADAPTER REPOSITORY can pattern addresses the flexible management of adapters at runtime. Following the pattern, changes to adapters can be deployed rather quickly and easily.

However, the pattern requires changing the adapters because a configuration interface is necessary for maintaining the adapters. As all adapters must implement the interface needed by the repository, putting third-party adapters with a different interface into the repository is not trivial. In some cases, it is impossible to add the required configuration functions to the third-party adapter; in other cases, writing a wrapper for the third-party adapter's interface is required.

Example: Simple integration adapter repository design

Figure 27 shows the simplest INTEGRATION ADAPTER REPOSITORY design. In this design the INTEGRATION ADAPTERS are just managed and retrieved using the adapter ID.

This design can easily be extend with more sophisticated search and query options. For instance, we could add metadata about the adapters. Using simple versioning we could further improve this repository design.

At the moment the provided administration interface only supports deployment by delivering the adapter using get. More sophisticated deployment functionality could be added that can stop a running adapter, deploy a new adapter, and initialize that adapter then.

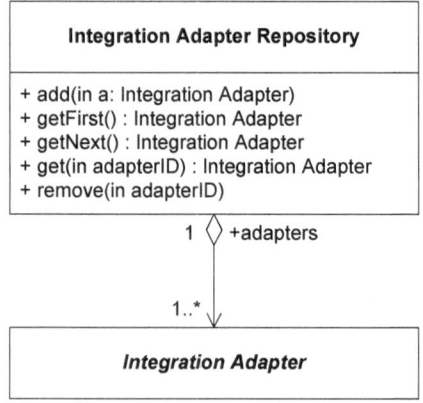

Fig. 27. Illustration of INTEGRATION ADAPTER REPOSITORY

Known Uses

- WebSphere InterChange Server [IBM 2008] offers an INTEGRATION ADAPTER REPOSITORY in which a pre-defined large set of INTEGRATION ADAPTERS is provided. Self-defined adapters can also be added.
- The connectors of transport providers of the Mule ESB [Mule 2007] are, like all other components in Mule, managed either by the Mule container or an external container like Pico or Spring. The container manages the lifecycle of the connectors using the component lifecycle interfaces, which the components can optionally implement. Thus the container acts as an INTEGRATION ADAPTER REPOSITORY for the connectors.
- iWay's Universal Adapter Suite [iWay 2007a] provides a repository of adapters in the Adapter Manager [iWay 2007b]. The graphical modeler of iWay, the Adapter Designer, is used to define document flows for adapters. The Adapter Designer can be used to maintain and publish flows stored in any Adapter Manager repository. The adapters in the repository can be deployed to the Adapter Manager, which is the MICROFLOW ENGINE used for executing the Adapter flows.

4.3   Pattern: Configurable Dispatcher

Context
In a SOA, multiple systems need to be integrated. Not always you can decide at design time or deployment time, which service or system must execute a request.

Problem
How to decide at runtime which service or system has to execute a request?

Problem Details
There are numerous issues that require a decision about request execution at runtime. Some examples are:

- As system architectures usually change over time, it is necessary to add, replace, or change systems in the backend for executing process activities. In many process-driven systems, this must be possible at runtime. That is, it must be dynamically decided at runtime which component has to execute a request, e.g., sent by a macroflow activity. If the architecture does not consider these dynamics, then modifications to the backend structures will be difficult to implement at runtime.
- Scalability can be achieved through load balancing, meaning that multiple services on different machines are provided for serving the same type of requests. Depending on the load, it must be dynamically decided using a load balancing scheme or algorithm which service is invoked.
- Sometimes for the same functionality, multiple systems are present in an organization. For instance, if two or more organizations have merged and the information systems have not yet been integrated, then it is necessary to decide based on the content of a request to which system the request must be

routed. For instance, if multiple order handling systems are present, orders can be routed based on the product IDs/categories.

- If some functionality is replicated, for instance to support a hot stand-by server, requests must be sent to all replicas.

All these issues actually point to well known issues in distributed architectures and can be conceptually classified as dimensions of transparency [Emmerich 2000]: access transparency, location transparency, migration transparency, replication transparency, concurrency transparency, scalability transparency, performance transparency, and failure transparency. The core problem is thus how to consider those dimensions of transparency appropriately.

One important aspect of handling dynamic request execution decisions properly is that the rules for these decisions can also change at runtime. For instance, consider we change the system architecture, add more servers for load balancing, require different content-based routing rules, or add additional replicas. In all these cases, the rules for routing the requests change.

Solution

Use a CONFIGURABLE DISPATCHER that picks up the incoming requests and dynamically decides on basis of configurable dispatching rules, where and when the request should be executed. After making the decision, the CONFIGURABLE DISPATCHER forwards the requests to the corresponding target system that handles the request execution. New or updated dispatching rules can be deployed at runtime.

Solution Details.

Figure 28 illustrates the solution of the CONFIGURABLE DISPATCHER pattern.

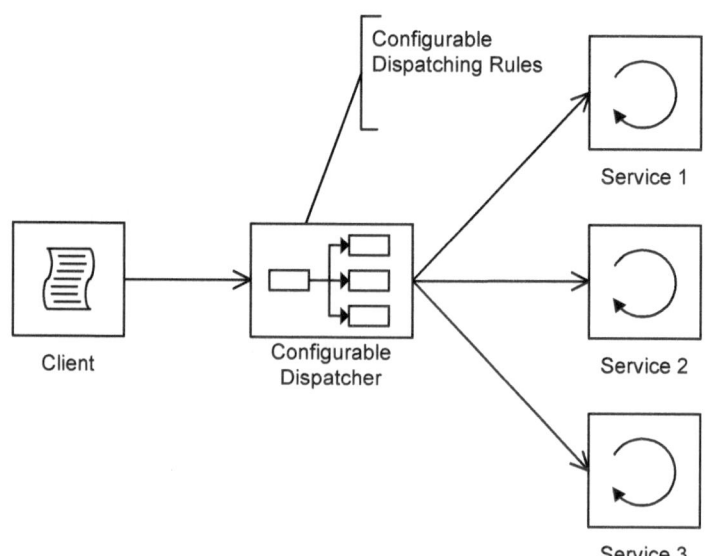

Fig. 28. Illustration of CONFIGURABLE DISPATCHER

The dispatcher decides based on dispatching rules. The term "rule" is not very strictly defined, however. Any directive that can decide – based on an incoming request – how to handle the request can be used. For instance, the rules can be implemented as event-condition-action rules and a rule engine can be used to interpret the rules. Another implementation variant is to embed a scripting language interpreter and execute scripts that perform the decision.

In any case, the rules must be triggered upon dispatching events (mainly incoming requests). They must be able to evaluate conditions. That is, the rule engine or interpreter must be able to access the relevant information needed for evaluating the conditions. For instance, if content-based routing should be supported, the content of the request must be accessible in the rule implementation. If a round-robin load balancing should be implemented, the accessible target systems as well as a state of the round-robin protocol need to be accessed. Finally, functionality to realize the decision is needed, such as a command that tells the dispatcher to which target system it should dispatch the request.

The CONFIGURABLE DISPATCHER pattern supports the flexible dispatch of requests based on configurable rules. These dispatching rules can be changed at runtime. Dynamic scripting languages or rule engines enable developers to update dispatching rules on the fly. If this is not possible, the dispatcher can apply the COMPONENT CONFIGURATOR pattern [Schmidt et al. 2000] to suspend dispatching, while the rules are updated. In any case, the dispatcher should provide a dynamic rule maintenance interface.

The dispatcher also has the task to pick up the request result from the component and send it back to the adapter. It is optionally possible to apply dispatching rules for the results as well. If asynchronous communication is used, a CORRELATION IDENTIFIER [Hohpe et al. 2003] is used to correlate the requests and responses.

The CONFIGURABLE DISPATCHER pattern can be used to make the workload in a SOA manageable by scaling the architecture in terms of adding instances of

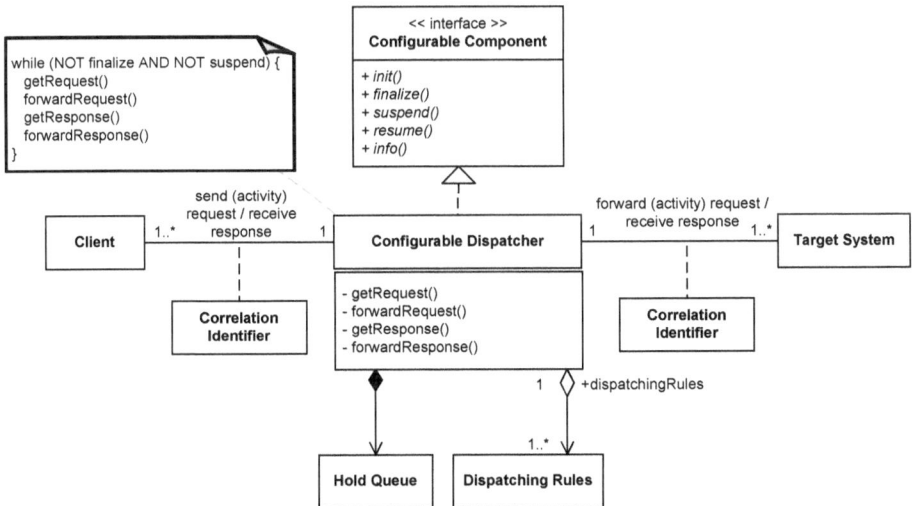

Fig. 29. Simple asynchronous CONFIGURABLE DISPATCHER

services/systems to execute the requests. However, a central component like a CONFIGURABLE DISPATCHER is a single-point-of-failure. It might be a bottleneck and hence have a negative influence on the performance of the whole system.

Example: Simple asynchronous CONFIGURABLE DISPATCHER
Figure 29 shows an exemplary model for an asynchronous CONFIGURABLE DISPATCHER. The dispatching rules are simply stored in aggregated objects. The dispatcher design uses a CONFIGURABLE COMPONENT interface to suspend the dispatcher while the dispatch rules are updated. The dispatcher follows a simple linear algorithm to forward requests and responses (of course, this algorithm can also be parallelized). The CORRELATION IDENTIFIER pattern is used to correlate asynchronous requests and responses.

Known Uses
- Using IBM's WebSphere Business Integration Message Broker [IBM 2008] a CONFIGURABLE DISPATCHER can be implemented with a message flow definition that represents the dispatching logic. The dispatching rules are stored in a database and are accessed via a database access node in the flow.
- The Service Container of the Mule Enterprise Service Bus [Mule 2007] offers support for content-based and rule-based routing. Inbound and outbound message events, as well as responses, can be routed according to declarative rules that can be dynamically specified. A number of predefined routers are available (based on the patterns in [Hohpe et al. 2003]). Pre-defined (or user-defined) filters, like a payload type filter or an XPath filter, can be used to express the rules that control how routers behave.
- Apache ServiceMix [ServiceMix 2007] is an open source Enterprise Service Bus (ESB) and SOA toolkit. It uses the rule-language Drools to provide rule-based routing inside the ESB. The architecture is rather simple: A Drools component is exposed at some service, interface, or operation endpoint in ServiceMix and it will be fired, when the endpoint is invoked. The rule base is then in complete control over message dispatching.

4.4 Pattern: Process Integration Architecture

Context
Process technology is used and the basic design follows the MACRO-/MICROFLOW pattern. Process technology is used at the macroflow level, and backend systems need to be integrated in the process flow. The connection between the macroflow level and the backend systems needs to be flexible so that different process technologies can (re-)use the connection to the backend systems. The architecture must be able to cope with increased workload conditions, i.e., it must be scalable. Finally, the architecture must be changeable and maintainable to be able to cope with both changes in the processes and changes in the backends. All those challenges cannot be mastered without a clear concept for the whole SOA.

Problem
How to assemble a process-driven SOA in way that is flexible, scalable, changeable, and maintainable?

Problem Details

To properly consider the qualities attributes flexibility, scalability, changeability, and maintainability a number of issues must be addressed. First, there are technology specifics of the process technology being used at the macroflow level. In principle, implementations of macroflow activities represent reusable functions that are not restricted to one specific process technology but which can rather be used with different types and implementations of process engines. If the process technology is tightly coupled to implementations of activities, changes in the process technology may potentially have larger impact on the corresponding activity implementations which means a loss of flexibility.

Activities at the macroflow level are usually refined as microflows following the MACRO-/MICROFLOW pattern. Thus, one has to consider where and how these microflows are executed. Aspects of scalability must be considered to cope with increasing workload. As requests for activity execution are permanently initiated and business will usually go on day and night, we additionally have to deal with the question: What further mechanisms are necessary to maintain the whole architecture at runtime?

Changes to the microflow and macroflow should be easy and of low effort. Actual backend system functionality will be invoked at the microflow level, and it is obviously an issue how this can be achieved, as those backend systems are in principle independent and are subject to individual changes themselves. The impact of these changes must be kept within acceptable limits, in a way that those changes can be managed.

Solution

Provide a multi-tier PROCESS INTEGRATION ARCHITECTURE to connect macroflows and the backend systems that need to be used in those macroflows. The macroflows run in dedicated macroflow engines that are connected to the SOA via INTEGRATION ADAPTERS for the connected services. Microflows are realized in a distinct microflow tier, and they either run in dedicated MICROFLOW ENGINES or are implemented as microflow services. The backend systems are connected to the SOA using INTEGRATION ADAPTERS, too. To cope with multiple backends, multiple microflow engines, as well as for replication and load balancing, CONFIGURABLE DISPATCHERS are used.

Solution Details

Figure 30 illustrates the solution of the PROCESS INTEGRATION ARCHITECTURE pattern.

The PROCESS INTEGRATION ARCHITECTURE pattern assumes service-based communication. That is, the systems connected in PROCESS INTEGRATION ARCHITECTURE are exposed using service-oriented interfaces and use services provided by other systems in the PROCESS INTEGRATION ARCHITECTURE to fulfill their tasks. In many cases, asynchronous communication is used, to facilitate loosely coupling. Then usually CORRELATION IDENTIFIERS are used to correlate the requests and results. Sometimes it makes sense to use synchronous communication, too, for instance because blocking on a results is actually required or a backend in batch mode can only work with synchronous invocations.

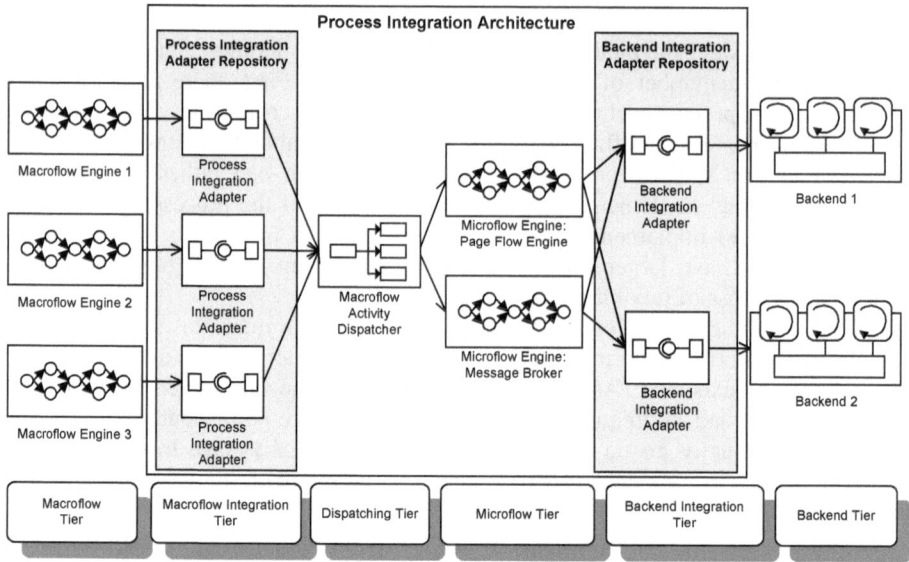

Fig. 30. Illustration of PROCESS INTEGRATION ARCHITECTURE

The PROCESS INTEGRATION ARCHITECTURE provides a flexible and scalable approach to service-oriented and process-driven architectural design. The main architectural task of a PROCESS INTEGRATION ARCHITECTURE is to connect the macroflows, representing the executable business processes, to the backend systems and services providing the functions needed to implement these processes. In a naïve approach to architectural design, we would simply invoke the services (of the backend systems) from the macroflow activities running in the MACROFLOW ENGINE. But this only works well for small examples and very small-scale architectures. The benefit of the PROCESS INTEGRATION ARCHITECTURE is that we can start from this very simple architecture and step-by-step enhance it, as new requirements emerge. The enhancements are described by the other patterns of this pattern language.

The process integration architecture introduces multiple tiers:

- The *Macroflow Tier* hosts the implementations of the executable macroflows. Usually MACROFLOW ENGINES are used to execute the macroflows.
- The *Macroflow Integration Tier* is a common extension to the Macroflow Tier. It introduces one INTEGRATION ADAPTER for the processes per MACROFLOW ENGINE. This adapter integrates the process activities with the technical functions provided by the SOA. That is, it connects the business-oriented perspective of the business activities in the macroflows to the technical perspective of the services and microflows.
- The *Dispatching Tier* is an optional tier that can be added to the PROCESS INTEGRATION ARCHITECTURE if content-based routing, load balancing, or other dispatching tasks are needed for connecting the macroflow requests to the microflow or service execution.

- The *Microflow Tier* is a common tier, if the PROCESS INTEGRATION ARCHITECTURE design follows the MACRO-/MICROFLOW pattern. This makes sense, if short-running, technical orchestrations of services are needed. In the simplest version, a number of hard-coded services can be provided for microflow execution. A more sophisticated realization introduces MICROFLOW ENGINES.
- The *Backend Integration Tier* is an optional tier which is used to provide backends with an interface that is needed by the SOA. As this tier uses INTEGRATION ADAPTERS it to enable independent maintenance of backend systems, it is highly recommended for SOAs that need to continue operating when connected systems are maintained.
- The *Backend Tier* contains the systems that are connected to the SOA and perform the functions required to execute the business processes. Typical backend systems are custom or off-the-shelf business applications (such as SAP or Siebel), custom business applications, databases, services, and so on. The backend systems are usually connected to the SOA via service-based interfaces that expose the API of the backend system without great modifications. For providing a specific interface to the SOA, INTEGRATION ADAPTERS in the Backend Integration Tier should be used.

The PROCESS INTEGRATION ARCHITECTURE pattern provides a systematic way to scale up a process-driven SOA. It can be applied for a single macroflow engine, and multiple engines can be added later one. Similarly, only one a few services or business applications can be initially provided, and later on more services or business applications can be added. In both cases, the INTEGRATION ADAPTER pattern provides a clear guideline how to perform the connection in a maintainable fashion. The INTEGRATION ADAPTER REPOSITORY pattern should be used, if a larger number of adapters must be maintained.

The various systems connected in the PROCESS INTEGRATION ARCHITECTURE are treated as exchangeable black-boxes. The business applications, macroflows, and microflows can be maintained as independent systems as long as the service interfaces do not change. Load balancing and prioritized or rule-based processing of requests can be supported, for instance via the CONFIGURABLE DISPATCHER. Many existing off-the-shelf engines can be used in a PROCESS INTEGRATION ARCHITECTURE, which might reduce the necessary in-house development effort.

The pattern has the drawback that greater design effort might be necessary compared to simpler alternatives, because of the multi-tier model with corresponding loosely coupled interfaces. To buy (and customize) different off-the-shelf engines or system can be costly, just like inhouse-development of these engines or systems. Hence, for small, simple process-driven SOAs, it should be considered to start-off with a single process engine and follow the MACRO-/MICROFLOW pattern only conceptually. A more sophisticated PROCESS INTEGRATION ARCHITECTURE can then still be introduced later in time, when requirements for higher flexibility, scalability, changeability, and maintainability arise.

Even though the PROCESS INTEGRATION ARCHITECTURE pattern concerns the design of the services used as backends, it does not solve problems of service design.

In various parts of the PROCESS INTEGRATION ARCHITECTURE pattern business objects (or business data) must be accessed. The business objects relevant to microflows and macroflows essentially form a CANONICAL DATA MODEL [Hohpe et al. 2003] for storing process relevant business data. The BUSINESS OBJECT REFERENCE [Hentrich 2004] pattern is used to keep the references to the business objects in the process flows (macroflows and microflows) and services.

Example: Step-by-step design of a PROCESS INTEGRATION ARCHITECTURE
A schematic example for a step-by-step design of a PROCESS INTEGRATION ARCHITECTURE has been given in the introduction of this chapter.

Known Uses
- In a supply chain management solution for a big automotive customer in Germany this architectural pattern has been applied. WebSphere MQ Workflow has been used as the MACROFLOW ENGINE. The integration adapters, the dispatching layer, and the microflow execution level have been implemented in Java. The application services are implemented using MQ messaging technology. In this realization of the pattern, a Java architecture has been implemented to represent the CONFIGURABLE DISPATCHER, a MICROFLOW ENGINE, and the application adapters. No off-the-shelf middleware has been used.
- For a telecommunications customer in Germany, the pattern has been used in a larger scale variant. The MICROFLOW ENGINE has been implemented by an enterprise service bus based on WebSphere Business Integration Message Broker. WebSphere MQ Workflow has been used as the process engine at the macroflow layer. The off-the-shelf MQ Workflow adapters provided by the message broker served as the process integration adapters. The architecture has been laid out initially as to support different instances of MQ Workflow engines to cope with growing workload using a dispatcher represented as a routing flow that routes the messages received by the adapter to another message broker instance. New message broker instances have been created according to the growing workload.
- A simple variant of the pattern is implemented in IBM's WebSphere Integration Developer [IBM 2008], which includes WebSphere Process Server, a process engine that represents both the micro- and macroflow levels. It further offers an architectural concept called Service Component Architecture (SCA) to wire up services, including the corresponding adapters.

5 Literature Review and Overview of Related Patterns

A lot of related work taking process perspectives in conjunction with patterns can be found in the workflow and process domains. Many languages have been proposed for the design and specification of workflow processes. Similarly, languages and tools have been proposed for business process modeling (e.g., the extended EPCs in ARIS and the various stereotypes in UML). Also in other domains such as ERP, CRM, PDM, and Web Services, languages have been proposed to model processes and other perspectives such as the organization and data perspective. Some of these languages are based on well-known modeling techniques such as Petri Nets and UML. Other languages are system specific.

To the best of our knowledge the work on workflow patterns conducted by van der Aalst et al. was the first attempt to collect a structured set of patterns at the level of process-aware information systems (summarized in [Workflow Patterns 2008, van der Aalst et al. 2003]). Several authors have used these workflow patterns to evaluate existing workflow management systems or newly designed workflow languages. The work has also been augment with other pattern collections, such as service interaction patterns [Barros at al. 2005]. These works on patterns strongly focuses on the workflow perspective and does not take an overall architectural perspective. The workflow patterns rather address finer grained structural elements of workflows than software patterns in their actual sense of emergent design solutions.

Other authors have coined the term workflow patterns but addressed different issues. In [Weigand et al. 2000] a set of workflow patterns inspired by Language/Action theory and specifically aiming at virtual communities is introduced. Patterns at the level of workflow architectures rather than control-flow are given in [Meszaros and Brown 1997]. Collaboration patterns involving the use of data and resources are described in [Lonchamp 1998].

Patterns for exception handling in process execution languages are introduced in [Russel et al. 2006b]. [Schümmer and Lukosch 2007] provide patterns for human-computer interaction, and some of them include process or service perspectives. [Buschmann et al. 2007] describe a summary of the most successful emerging software architecture patterns and integrate patterns from different sources in a consistent manner, as to provide a comprehensive summary on architecture patterns. However, these architecture patterns do not address SOAs specifically.

The POSA 1 book introduces a number of general architectural patterns [Buschmann et al. 1996]. These are implicitly used in our pattern language. For instance, it is assumed in a SOA that a BROKER architecture is used. The CONFIGURABLE DISPATCHER pattern resembles the general solution of CLIENT/DISPATCHER/SERVER. The INTEGRATION ADAPTER pattern implicitly resembles the general solution of FORWARDER/RECEIVER.

Enterprise integration patterns [Hohpe et al. 2003] are also related to this work, as they mainly describe asynchronous messaging solutions. This communication paradigm is often used in process driven SOAs.

Specific architectural guidance for SOA construction is given in [Josuttis 2007]. However, this book does neither focus on process-driven SOAs nor patterns in specific, and hence can be seen as complementary to our pattern language.

In his work on micro-workflows [Manolescu 2000, 2002], Manolescu provides a workflow approach that is used to realize mainly workflows for object-oriented compositions. The work is also based on patterns. Please note that the term micro-workflows in Manolsecu's work has a different meaning than microflow in our work. Micro-workflows can be microflows but could also exhibit macroflow characteristics. We chose to use the macroflow/microflow terminology despite the overlap in terminology because this terminology has already been established and proven to be intuitive to pattern language users in our experience.

Evans identified that it is not just design patterns but also many different types of patterns that are influential when developing systems in a certain domain [Evans 2004]. This work does not yet combine aspects of organizational flexibility with a SOA and pattern-based approach.

The typical tooling around process engines has been described in pattern form by Manolescu (see [Manolescu 2004]). These patterns can be used to link our rather architectural patterns on process engines, MACROFLOW ENGINE and MICROFLOW ENGINE to the tooling provided by concrete technologies.

Some patterns are directly related and referenced in the patterns in this work. These patterns and their sources are summarized in Table 1.

Table. 1. Related Patterns Overview

Pattern	Problem	Solution
GENERIC PROCESS CONTROL STRUCTURE [Hentrich 2004]	How can data inconsistencies be avoided in long running process instances in the context of dynamic sub-process instantiation?	Use a generic process control data structure that is only subject to semantic change but not structural change.
BUSINESS OBJECT REFERENCE [Hentrich 2004]	How can the management of business objects be achieved in a business process, as far as concurrent access and changes to these business objects is concerned?	Only store references to business objects in the process control data structure and keep the actual business objects in an external container.
ENTERPRISE SERVICE BUS [Zdun et al. 2006]	How is it possible in a large business architecture to integrate various applications and backends in a comprehensive, flexible, and consistent way?	Unify the access to applications and backends using services and service adapters, and use message-oriented, event-driven communication between these services to enable flexible integration.
CORRELATION IDENTIFIER [Hohpe et al. 2003]	How does a requestor that has received a response know to which original request the response is referring?	Each response message should contain a CORRELATION IDENTIFIER, a unique identifier that indicates which request message this response is for.
CANONICAL DATA MODEL [Hohpe et al. 2003]	How to minimize dependencies when integrating applications that use different data formats?	Design a CANONICAL DATA MODEL that is independent from any specific application. Require each application to produce and consume messages in this common format.
COMPONENT CONFIGURATOR [Schmidt et al. 2000]	How to allow an application to link and unlink its component implementations at runtime without having to modify, recompile, or relink the application statically?	Use COMPONENT CONFIGURATORS as central components for reifying the runtime dependencies of configurable components. These configurable components offer an interface to change their configuration at runtime.
SERVICE ABSTRACTION LAYER [Vogel 2001]	How do you develop a system which can fulfill requests from different clients communicating over different channels without having to modify your business logic each time a new channel has to be supported or a new service is added?	Provide a SERVICE ABSTRACTION LAYER as an extra layer to the business tier containing all the necessary logic to receive and delegate requests. Incoming requests are forwarded to service providers which are able to satisfy requests.

6   Conclusion

In this article we have documented the fundamental patterns needed for an architecture that composes and orchestrates services at the process level. The patterns explain two important kinds of design and architectural decisions in this area:

- Modeling and executing business-driven and technical processes
- Integration and adaptation in process-driven SOAs

The individual patterns can be used on their own to address certain concerns in a process-driven SOA design, but the general architecture following the PROCESS-INTEGRATION ARCHITECTURE pattern – in first place – aims at larger architectures. The pattern language as a whole focuses on separating business concerns cleanly from technical concerns, in macroflows and microflows. All integration concerns are handled via services, and macroflows and microflows are used for flexible composition and orchestration of the services.

Acknowledgements

We like to thank Andy Longshaw, our EuroPLoP 2006 shepherd, for his useful comments. We also like to thank the participants of the EuroPLoP 2006 writers' workshop for their valuable feedback. Finally, we could like to thank the anonymous reviewers of the Transactions on Pattern Languages of Programming journal for their in-depth comments that helped us to improve this article.

References

[van der Aalst et al. 2003] van der Aalst, W.M.P., ter Hofstede, A.H.M., Kiepuszewski, B., Barros, A.P.: Workflow Patterns. Distributed and Parallel Databases 14(1), 5–51 (2003)

[Active Endpoints 2007] Active Endpoints. ActiveBPEL Open Source Engine (2007), http://www.active-endpoints.com/active-bpel-engine-overview.htm

[Barros at al. 2005] Barros, A., Dumas, M., ter Hofstede, A.H.M.: Service interaction patterns. In: van der Aalst, W.M.P., Benatallah, B., Casati, F., Curbera, F. (eds.) BPM 2005. LNCS, vol. 3649, pp. 302–318. Springer, Heidelberg (2005)

[Barry 2003] Barry, D.K.: Web Services and Service-oriented Architectures. Morgan Kaufmann Publishers, San Francisco (2003)

[BPMN2BPEL 2008] bpmn2bpel. A tool for translating BPMN models into BPEL processes (2008), http://code.google.com/p/bpmn2bpel/

[Buschmann et al. 1996] Buschmann, F., Meunier, R., Rohnert, H., Sommerlad, P., Stal, M.: Pattern-Oriented Software Architecture - A System of Patterns. John Wiley and Sons Ltd., Chichester (1996)

[Channabasavaiah 2003 et al.] Channabasavaiah, K., Holley, K., Tuggle, E.M.: Migrating to Service-oriented architecture – part 1, IBM developerWorks (2003), http://www-106.ibm.com/developerworks/webservices/library/ws-migratesoa/

[Dikmans 2008] Dikmans, L.: Transforming BPMN into BPEL: Why and How (2008), http://www.oracle.com/technology/pub/articles/dikmans-bpm.html

[D'Souza and Wills 1999] D'Souza, D., Wills, A.: Objects, Components and Frameworks with UML: The Catalysis Approach. Addison-Wesley, Reading (1999)

[Emmerich 2000] Emmerich, W.: Engineering Distributed Objects. Wiley & Sons, Chichester (2000)

[Enhydra 2008] Enhydra. Enhydra Shark (2008),
http://www.enhydra.org/workflow/shark/index.html

[Evans 2004] Evans, E.: Domain-Driven Design. Addison-Wesley, Reading (2004)

[Fornax 2008] Fornax Project. Sculptor (2008), http://www.fornax-platform.org/cp/display/fornax/Sculptor+CSC

[Gamma et al. 1994] Gamma, E., Helm, R., Johnson, R., Vlissides, J.: Design Patterns: Elements of Reusable Object-Oriented Software. Addison-Wesley, Reading (1994)

[GFT 2007] GFT. GFT Inspire Business Process Management (2007),
http://www.gft.com/gft_international/en/gft_international/Lei
stungen_Produkte/Software/Business_Process_Managementsoftware
.html

[Hentrich 2004] Hentrich, C.: Six patterns for process-driven architectures. In: Proceedings of the 9th Conference on Pattern Languages of Programs, EuroPLoP 2004 (2004)

[Hohpe et al. 2003] Hohpe, G., Woolf, B.: Enterprise Integration Patterns. Addison-Wesley, Reading (2003)

[IBM 2008] IBM, WebSphere Software (2008), http://www-01.ibm.com/software/websphere/

[iWay 2007a] iWay Software. iWay Adapter Technologies (2007), http://www.iwaysoftware.jp/products/integrationsolution/adapter_manager.html

[iWay 2007b] iWay Software. iWay Adapter Manager Technology Brief (2007), http://www.iwaysoftware.jp/products/integrationsolution/adapter_manager.html

[JBoss 2007] JBoss. JBoss jBPM (2007), http://www.jboss.com/products/jbpm

[Josuttis 2007] Josuttis, N.M.: SOA in Practice - The Art of Distributed System Design. O'Reilly, Sebastopol (2007)

[Lonchamp 1998] Lonchamp, J.: Process model patterns for collaborative work. In: Proceedings of the 15th IFIP World Computer Congress. Telecooperation Conference, Telecoop. Vienna, Austria (1998)

[Meszaros and Brown 1997] Meszaros, G., Brown, K.: A pattern language for workflow systems. In: Proceedings of the 4th Pattern Languages of Programming Conference. Washington University Technical Report 97-34, WUCS-97-34 (1997)

[Manolescu 2004] Manolescu, D.A.: Patterns for Orchestration Environments. In: The 11th Conference on Pattern Languages of Programs (PLoP2004), Allterton Park, Monticello, Illinois, September 8 - 12 (2004)

[Manolescu 2002] Manolescu, D.A.: Workflow enactment with continuation and future objects. ACM SIGPLAN Notices 37(11) (November 2002)

[Manolescu 2000] Manolescu, D.A.: Micro-Workflow: A Workflow Architecture Supporting Compositional Object-Oriented Software Development. Ph.D. Thesis and Computer Science Technical Report UIUCDCS-R-2000-2186, University of Illinois at Urbana-Champaign, October 2000, Urbana, Illinois (2000)

[Mellor and Balcer 2002] Mellor, S.J., Balcer, M.J.: Executable UML: A Foundation for Model Driven Architecture. Addison-Wesley, Reading (2002)

[Mittal and Kanchanavally 2008] Mittal, K., Kanchanavally, S.: Introducing Java Page Flow Architecture (2008),
http://www.developer.com/open/article.php/10930_3531246_1

[Mule 2007] Mule Project. Mule open source ESB (Enterprise Service Bus) and integration platform (2007), http://mule.mulesource.org/

[Novell 2008] Novell. Novell exteNd Director 5.2 (2008), http://www.novell.com/documentation/extend52/Docs/Start_Director_Help.html

[Riehle et al. 2001] Riehle, D., Fraleigh, S., Bucka-Lassen, D., Omorogbe, N.: The Architecture of a UML Virtual Machine. In: Proceedings of the 2001 Conference on Object-Oriented Programming Systems, Languages, and Applications (OOPSLA 2001), pp. 327–341. ACM Press, New York (2001)

[Russel et al. 2006] Russell, N., van der Aalst, W.M.P., ter Hofstede, A.H.M.: Exception handling patterns in process-aware information systems. BPM Center Report BPM-06-04, BPMcenter.org (2006)

[ServiceMix 2007] Apache ServiceMix Project. Apache ServiceMix (2007),
http://www.servicemix.org/

[Schmidt et al. 2000] Schmidt, D.C., Stal, M., Rohnert, H., Buschmann, F.: Patterns for Concurrent and Distributed Objects. In: Pattern-Oriented Software Architecture. J. Wiley and Sons Ltd., Chichester (2000)

[Schümmer and Lukosch 2007] Schümmer, T., Lukosch, S.: Patterns for computer-mediated interaction. Wiley & Sons, Chichester (2007)

[Stahl and Völter 2006] Stahl, T., Völter, M.: Model-Driven Software Development. John Wiley & Sons, Chichester (2006)

[Tran et al. 2007]Tran, H., Zdun, U., Dustdar, S.: View-based and Model-driven Approach for Reducing the Development Complexity in Process-Driven SOA. In: Proceedings of International Conference on Business Processes and Services Computing, Leipzig, Germany (September 2007)

[Vogel 2001] Vogel, O.: Service abstraction layer. In: Proceedings of EuroPlop 2001, Irsee, Germany (July 2001)

[webMethods 2007] webMethods. webMethods Fabric 7 (2007),
http://www.webmethods.com/products/fabric

[Weigand et al. 2000] Weigand, H., de Moor, A., van den Heuvel, W.J.: Supporting the evolution of workflow patterns for virtual communities. Electronic Markets 10(4), 264 (2000)

[Workflow Patterns 2008] Workflow Patterns home page (2008),
http://www.workflowpatterns.com/

[Zdun et al. 2006] Zdun, U., Hentrich, C., van der Aalst, W.M.P.: A Survey of Patterns for Service-Oriented Architectures. International Journal of Internet Protocol Technology 1(3), 132–143 (2006)

A Pattern Story for Combining Crosscutting Concern State Machines

Mark Mahoney[1] and Tzilla Elrad[2]

[1] Carthage College, Kenosha WI
mmahoney@carthage.edu
[2] Illinois Institute of Technology, Chicago IL
elrad@iit.edu

Abstract. This paper describes a solution to a real world problem using a combination of well-known patterns. The problem deals with combining state machines that represent core concerns and crosscutting concerns in a loosely coupled manner. The state based behaviors are modeled with state machines and implemented with the State Pattern[3]. The coordination between the loosely coupled state machines is achieved with the Interceptor Pattern[9][11]. The Abstract Factory Pattern[3] is used to shield the original state machine developers from being aware that their state machines are being combined in new and different ways.

1 Introduction

A pattern story describes the application of patterns to a specific design. This paper tells the story of the design of an application with core and crosscutting concerns. The concerns are state based and the patterns describe how to combine state machines in a manner that maximizes reusability and loose coupling.

Separating a software system into concerns is one way to deal with the increasing complexity of constructing large systems. However, not all concerns can easily be modularized. Some concerns crosscut others. A crosscutting concern is one that is scattered throughout a system and is tangled with other core application concerns. Fault tolerance, for example, is a crosscutting concern that is often tangled with many core application concerns. Aspect-Oriented Software Development (AOSD) [2] provides a means to separate crosscutting concerns so that they can be reasoned about in isolation. It also provides the means to weave the crosscutting concerns into a set of core concerns to form a functioning system.

State machines are an excellent way to model reactive behavior. A state machine fully describes how an object or subsystem behaves in response to stimuli. State machines can easily be transformed into executable code using, for example, the State Pattern [3]. In addition, heavyweight tools such as Telelogic's Tau [13] can be used to build massively state based systems. State machine models typically do not cleanly

J. Noble and R. Johnson (Eds.): TPLOP I, LNCS 5770, pp. 192–206, 2009.

separate the interaction between core and crosscutting concerns. There is a tendency to tangle concerns together in a single state machine. For example, in a banking application there may be state behavior in depositing into an account as well as separate state behavior for authentication and authorization. Traditional state based design techniques tend to mix these concerns together into the same state machine model even though the authentication and authorization behavior may be required in many other places in the system. A superior solution would allow the two independent reactive behaviors to be modeled separately and later be woven together. Each state machine would then be reusable in different contexts.

Once a set of state based core and crosscutting concerns have been separated into disparate state machines a mechanism is required to specify how they will interact. This weaving mechanism is currently not present in the most used state machine modeling languages. Our goal is to use a combination of patterns to create state based components that can easily interact in a loosely coupled manner. The state based behavior is implemented with the State Pattern [3] and the interaction between disparate implementations of the State Pattern is accomplished with the Interceptor Pattern [9][11]. The Abstract Factory Pattern [3] provides loose coupling in the cooperating state machines.

Using this approach will benefit developers who have recognized state based behaviors in the core and the crosscutting concerns. Traditionally, reactive systems are modeled with a set of state machines. Reactive systems tend to be embedded, distributed, or real-time in nature. However, as the size of non-reactive transformational systems get larger it is likely that some state based concerns will appear. Our pattern is targeted toward systems that are not entirely state based, but do have state based core and crosscutting concerns.

The rest of this paper is organized as follows: Section two describes the problem context, section three describes the forces, section four describes the solution, section five describes the forces resolved by our solution, and section six describes related work.

2 Problem Context

Early in his career, the first author worked on wireless accessories for two-way radios that police officers and firefighters carry for communication. This section describes a simplified version of the devices. A two-way radio can be in an Idle state, a Transmit state (Tx), or a Receive State (Rx), see figure 1. Translation from a state machine model to an implementation of the State Pattern [3] is straightforward, see figure 2. An Abstract State class (TwoWayStates) is created from which all Concrete States (Rx, Idle, Tx) inherit. For each event in the state machine a method is placed in the Abstract State class. The derived Concrete State classes override the events that have meaning to them. A Context class (TwoWayRadio) creates and maintains a reference to each of the Concrete States and maintains a reference to the current state. The context object handles all events by sending them to the current state object.

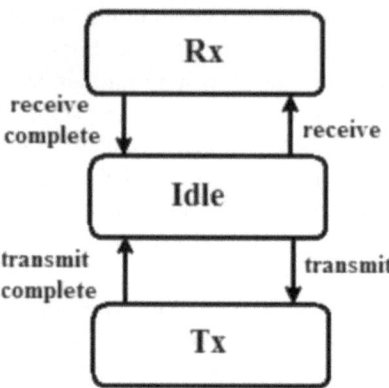

Fig. 1. State Machine of a Two-Way Radio

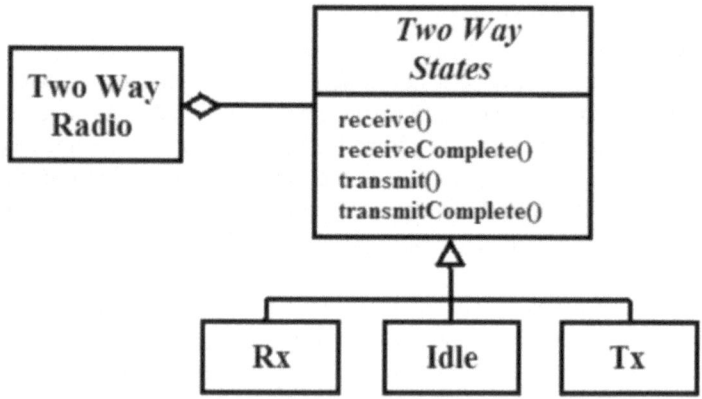

Fig. 2. State Pattern Implementation for a Two-Way Radio

Imagine a state machine for a wireless accessory (perhaps using a technology like Bluetooth) that connects to the two-way radio wirelessly and includes both a speaker and a microphone to transmit and receive audio. The wireless accessory can be in an Idle state, a Connecting state, and an Audio state, see figure 3. The classes for the State Pattern implementation are shown in figure 4.

The control of the wireless accessory is a crosscutting concern because it must interact with the two-way radio in many different ways and in many different contexts. For example, when the two-way radio is in the 'Idle' state and a 'receive' event is received the wireless accessory must enter the 'Audio' State to transmit the two-way radio's audio to the speaker on the accessory. Similarly, when the two-way radio's battery falls below a certain threshold an audio alert is sent to the accessory and

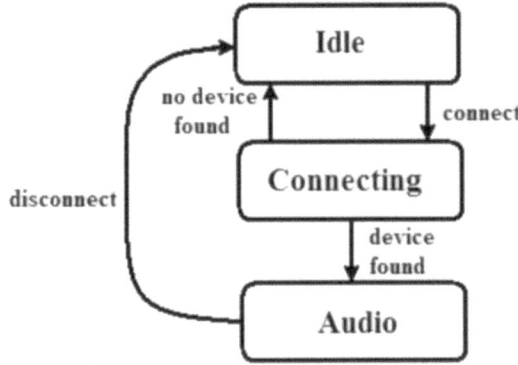

Fig. 3. State Machine for Two-Way Radio Accessory

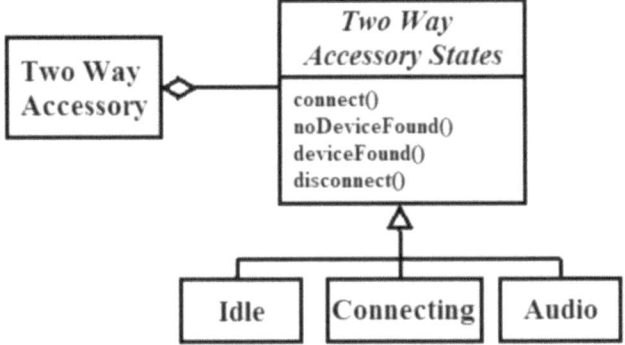

Fig. 4. State Pattern Implementation for a Two-Way Radio Accessory

requires an audio connection. There are many times when the two-way radio's audio needs to be sent to the accessory.

3 Forces

The forces influencing a solution to this problem have to do with the fact that the application is not entirely state based. Many of the requirements can be described as data-transformational in nature. Since the system is not entirely state based it doesn't make sense to use specialized tools [13][14] to create state machines. Using such tools might not even be possible in an embedded application environment. Rather, the solution should use standard Object-Oriented techniques to address the combination of state based concerns.

Ideally the solution will also allow the disparate state machines to be loosely coupled. Each state based concern should be reusable in different contexts. The two way radio, for example, should not be directly tied to the accessory because not every radio will have an accessory. Similarly, the audio accessory might be used with devices other than a two-way radio, like a cell phone. The combined state machines should not directly reference each other, rather, an intermediary should bind the state machines together. Such an approach will be more complex but will allow for greater reuse.

4 Solution

One can think of a state machine as the behavioral interface to a class, feature, or reactive subsystem. It is a metaphor for the subsystem. When the cooperating subsystems are also state based a method is required to compose them together. However, a desirable quality is to reduce coupling between the subsystems' state machines. In our previous work [7][8] we describe using state machines to implement reactive systems with crosscutting concerns. Each of the concerns is modeled with a state machine. The state machines can be used in isolation but they can also be brought together to share broadcast events. The events in the cooperating state machines are bound to each other to affect one another. Figure 5 shows two state machines with bound events.

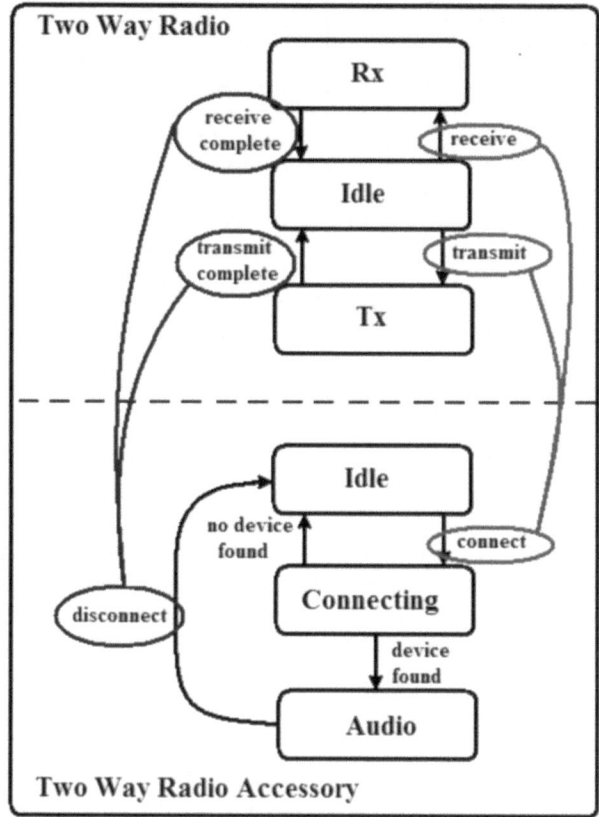

Fig. 5. Combined State Machines with Event Bindings

For incoming audio, the 'receive' event in the two-way radio state machine is bound to the 'connect' event in the accessory state machine. The 'receive complete' event is bound to the 'disconnect' event. A similar approach is taken for outgoing audio. The primary benefit of this approach is that because neither state machine directly refers to the other, each one is reusable in different contexts. Only the weaving developer is aware of the interactions. One can imagine a developer creating complex systems by composing state machines from a library and simply specifying the bindings in a non-invasive manner.

In order to provide a means to combine independent state machine models and generate an executable system from them we propose using the State Pattern [3], the Interceptor Pattern [11] [9], and the Abstract Factory Pattern [3]. The State Pattern is used to create an executable implementation of a state machine while the Interceptor Pattern is used to coordinate the binding of events in different state machines. The Abstract Factory pattern is used to achieve obliviousness in the core state machine models.

The Interceptor Pattern [11] [9] allows one to monitor what an application is doing and add services transparently to a framework. We use Interceptor to monitor a core state machine and inject bound events into other state machines. The description from Bosak [9] varies slightly from pattern described in the POSA2 book [11], the structure of the pattern is shown in figure 6.

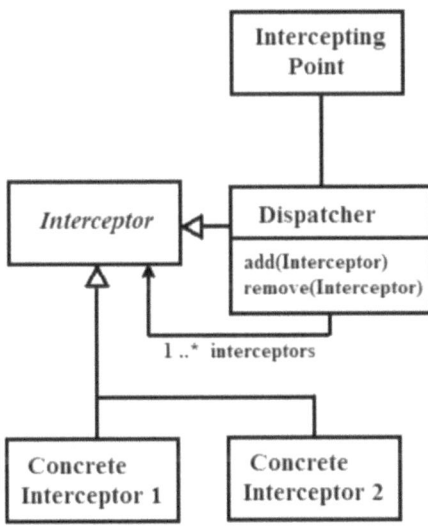

Fig. 6. Interceptor Pattern Structure

In this variation of the pattern an Interceptor interface describes an object where behavior will be added before or after a call. The Interceptor Interface looks like an object that the Intercepting Point interacts within its domain. The core state machine's abstract state class will serve as the Interceptor interface in this example because it is necessary to know when to inject events in a crosscutting state machine. Concrete Interceptors implement the interface to provide additional services. The Concrete Interceptors will be responsible for notifying other state machines when certain events are handled.

The Dispatcher is responsible for coordinating the different calls to the Concrete Interceptors. It can accomplish this based on a priority for Interceptors or using some other intelligent scheme. Since some events are bound before, after, or in place of others the dispatcher provides the granularity needed to inject events at the right time. The Intercepting Point is associated with a Dispatcher and sends all requests to it. The State Pattern's context object will refer to Dispatchers rather than concrete State objects when binding occurs in those states. When a method from the Dispatcher is called the Dispatcher will call the associated methods of all the Concrete Interceptors associated with it.

State [3] and Interceptor [9][11] can be combined to allow independent state machines to interact, see figure 7. In this case the Abstract State from the State Pattern acts as the Interceptor interface. It has all the methods of a Concrete State and will act as a stand in when event binding is required. When combining state machines a weaving developer will inherit from the Abstract State class to create Concrete Interceptors. The State Pattern's Context object maintains a reference to the Dispatcher rather than the Concrete State object. When a bound event occurs the event is handled by the Dispatcher rather than the Concrete State object. The Dispatcher then coordinates the injecting of events in another state machine.

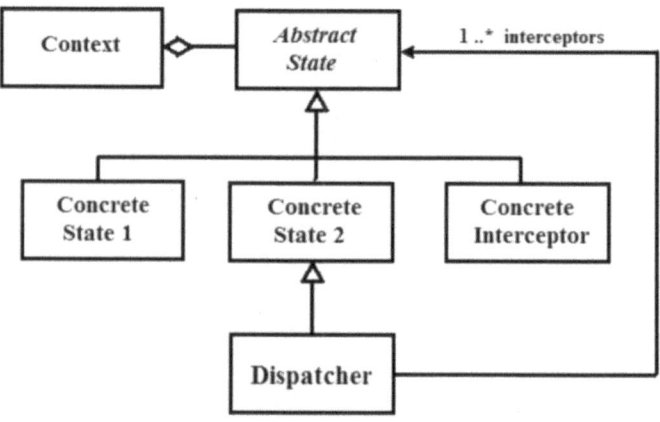

Fig. 7. Combined State and Interceptor Patterns

To relate this approach to the example from above, the Two-Way Radio and Accessory state machines can be combined to bind the 'receive' event in the Two-Way Radio state machine to the 'connect' event in the Wireless Accessory state machine, see figure 8 and Listing 1.

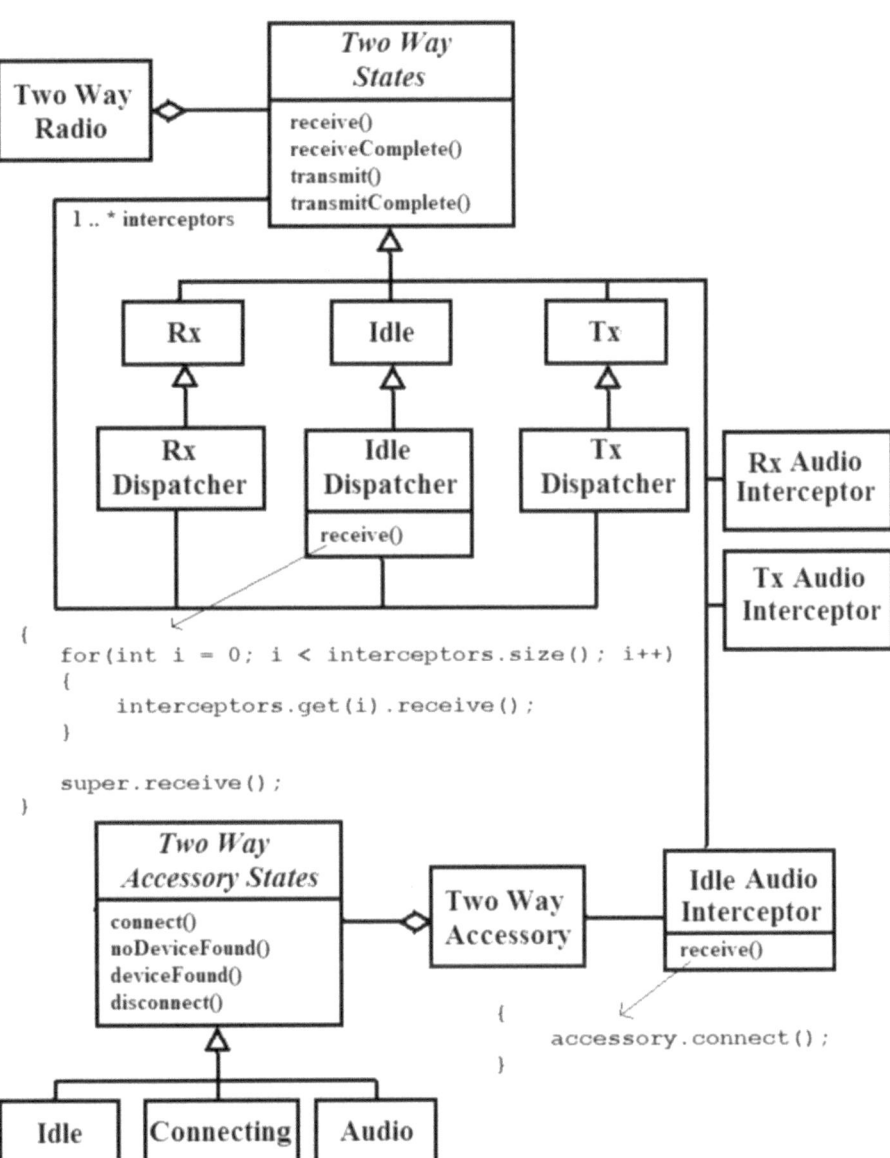

Fig. 8. Combined Two-Way Radio and Wireless Accessory Implementation

```
public class IdleDispatcher extends Idle
{
  private List <TwoWayStates> interceptors;

  //...

  public void receive()
  {
    for(int i = 0;i < interceptors.size();i++)
    {
      interceptors.get(i).receive();
    }

    super.receive();
  }

  //similar for other events
  //...
}
public class IdleAudioInterceptor extends TwoWayStates
{
  private TwoWayAccessory accessory;

  public IdleInterceptor(TwoWayAccessory a)
  {
    super(null);
    accessory = a;
  }

  public void receive()
  {
    accessory.connect();
  }

  public void transmit()
  {
    accessory.connect();
  }
}
```

Listing 1. Idle Dispatcher and Idle Interceptor

The key to making this an oblivious solution is using an Abstract Factory in the State Pattern's Context object to create State objects. The State Pattern's Context object uses a concrete factory to create the Dispatcher and Interceptors rather than a Concrete State class. The weaving developer is responsible for creating an implementation of a Concrete Binding Factory along with the Dispatcher and Concrete Interceptors, see figures 9 and 10 and Listings 2, 3, and 4.

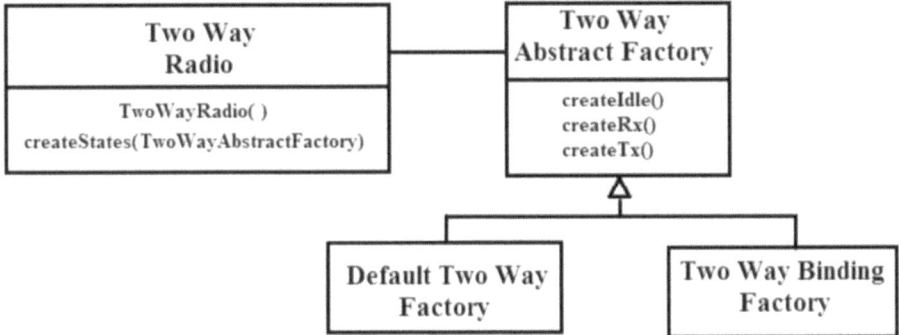

Fig. 9. Abstract Factory Pattern

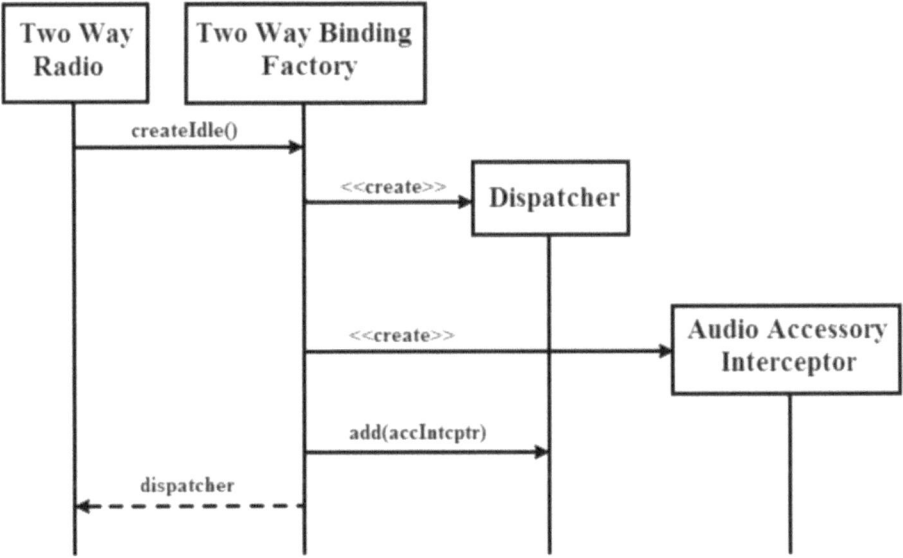

Fig. 10. Sequence Diagrams for State Creation

```
public class TwoWayBindingFactory extends TwoWayAbstract-
Factory
{
  //...
  //...
  public TwoWayStates createIdle()
  {
    //create an idle dispatcher
    IdleDispatcher idleDispatcher = new
                IdleDispatcher(getContext());
```

Listing 2. Factory for Creating States

```
    //add all interceptors
    idleDispatcher.addInterceptor(new
        IdleInterceptor(accessoryStatemachine));

    return idleDispatcher;
  }
  //...
  //...
}
```

Listing 2. (*continued*)

```
public class TwoWayRadio
{
  private TwoWayStates idle; //concrete idle state
  private TwoWayStates rx;   //concrete rx state
  private TwoWayStates tx;   //concrete tx state

  //current state in the state machine
  private TwoWayStates currentState;

  public void createStates(TwoWayAbstractFactory factory)
  {
    //use the factory to create each of the states
    idle = factory.createIdle();
    rx = factory.createRx();
    tx = factory.createTx();
    //...
  }
}
```

Listing 3. Creating States in the Context Object

```
TwoWayRadio radio = new TwoWayRadio();

TwoWayAbstractFactory radioFactory = new
                TwoWayBindingFactory(radio, accessory);

radio.createStates(radioFactory);
```

Listing 4. Creating the Context Object

Here the two state machines are linked by the Dispatcher and a Concrete Interceptor used to bind 'receive' to 'connect'. The Two-Way Radio Binding Factory object creates the Dispatcher and Audio Accessory Interceptor objects instead of the Concrete Idle State using a provided implementation of the Context's Abstract Factory. The Two-Way Radio object treats the reference to the Dispatcher as if it were the Concrete Idle state. When the 'receive' event occurs in the Idle state the Two-Way Radio context object calls the Dispatcher's receive() method, see figure 11. The Dispatcher then marches through all the Concrete Interceptors for this event in this state and calls receive() on those objects. The Idle Interceptor calls the Two-Way Accessory's connect() method to inject the event into the state machine and then relies on the base class to do its normal processing by calling Idle's receive() method (with a call to super.receive()).

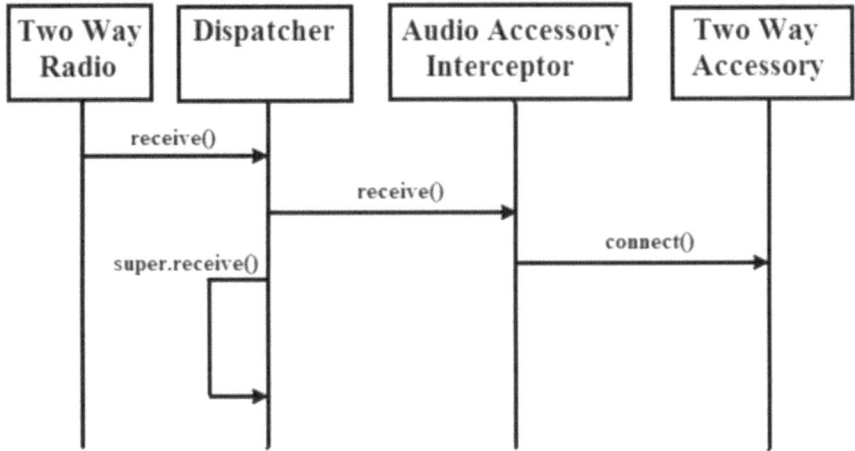

Fig. 11. Sequence Diagram Showing the Two-Way Radio Interact with an Accessory Through an Interceptor

5 Forces Resolved

The Interceptor Pattern [9][11] is ideal for allowing developers to add behavior into an existing system without requiring intimate knowledge of the system and without changing the base system. The Interceptor allows the State Pattern's Concrete States to be extended in such a way that they can inject events into other state machines. When multiple state machines are combined the Dispatcher handles the coordination of injecting events. The Dispatcher may be built with a preference for handling certain interactions above others.

Other patterns related to this one that were considered were Decorator[3], Template Method[3], Chain of Responsibility[3], and Interceptor Filters[15]. Interceptor is very similar to the Decorator Pattern [3] but we were able to take advantage of inheritance of the concrete states to simplify the dispatcher. Interceptor provides more flexibility in the presence of multiple crosscutting state machines. Interceptor has just the right granularity to intelligently coordinate calls to multiple Concrete Interceptors.

Template Method [3] proved to be an inferior solution because it required all binding be done in one place. It is not easy to add and take away crosscutting behaviors without affecting the other state machines. Chain of Responsibility [3] proved to be an inferior solution because the crosscutting concern state machines would need to be aware of each other creating a tight coupling between them. Interceptor Filters [15] proved to be an inferior solution because it is slightly more complex than Interceptor. Interceptor proved to be the simplest solution that worked.

The Abstract Factory Pattern [3] allows the State Pattern's Context object to be oblivious to whether concrete states are being created or Interceptors to inject events in other state machines. The weaving developer is responsible for creating implementations of the Abstract Factory to create the correct objects.

This approach works best for systems that are not predominantly state based. In some telecommunication and avionic systems the predominant decomposition technique is to break the system down entirely into state machines. In a massively state based system the overhead and complexity of the design would warrant using a different approach. This method is designed for systems that encounter state based concerns but are not defined by them. Systems that are defined by massive state machines tend to have special tools and languages to help create them[13][14].

6 Related Work

In our previous work [7][8] we implemented a framework for dealing with state based crosscutting concerns. This framework is called the Aspect-Oriented Statechart Framework (AOSF). There are classes in this framework for states, events, state machine containers, etc. This framework does not make use of any patterns, is somewhat complex, and is language dependent. For these reasons we are proposing a more straightforward solution that still allows a developer to combine state machines in a loosely coupled, reusable fashion.

Volter [12] describes a general method of achieving AOSD using a patterns-based approach. In this work the use of interceptors, proxies, and factories is used to describe how to achieve some of the same goals as AOP. We are extending that work a step further by apply those principles directly to state based AOSD.

In Aldawud et. al. [1] a similar approach for handling state based crosscutting concerns is addressed. In that work, different state machines model different concerns. The state machines are brought together in concurrent, orthogonal regions, however, the broadcast events are explicitly hard coded between disparate state machines making each model tightly coupled with each other and not reusable in different contexts.

In the work of Prehofer [10] feature composition is addressed for state based features. Each feature is modeled with a state machine and combined using one of two different approaches. In the first approach separate state machine models are combined in to a single model containing all the behavior by binding transitions. This leads to tangled state machine models that are hard to reason about. In the other proposed approach a similar method combining concurrent state machines is proposed with explicitly shared broadcasted events. This eliminates the reusability of the state machines in isolation or in different contexts. The author's implementation strategy did not use patterns and relied on a language specific pre-processing tool.

In France et. al. [5] State Machine Pattern Specifications model state machine interactions. The approach involves specifying binding statements that compose state machines together. The abstract state machines are not usable in isolation and the composed state machines are tangled and difficult to reason about.

7 Conclusion

The State Pattern is ideal for creating implementations of state based behavior from a state machine. The problem with the it, however, is there is no easy way to combine state machines while keeping them loosely coupled and reusable. Our contribution is to provide a language/framework independent approach to loosely coupled state machines. Loosely coupled state machines can be reused in different contexts. Further, because no new languages or frameworks are required this approach can be used in legacy systems with no additional tool support.

We have described an approach to state based Aspect-Orientation that involves only the use of well-known patterns. The State Pattern is used for implementing state based behavior. The Interceptor Pattern coordinates event binding between state machines. The Abstract Factory permits core concern developers to be oblivious to additions made to their state machines. A concrete example was given describing use of the combination of patterns.

Acknowledgements

We would like to thank Michael Weiss for helping us through the shepherding process with several iterations of useful and insightful comments. In addition, we would like to thank the 'Fu Dog' group at the writer's workshop at PLOP '07 for providing excellent feedback.

References

1. Aldawud, O., Elrad, T., Bader, A.: Aspect-oriented Modeling- Bridging the Gap Between Design and Implementation. In: Proceedings of the First ACM SIGPLAN/SIGSOFT International Conference on Generative Programming and Component Engineering (GPCE), Pittsburgh, PA, October 6–8, 2002, pp. 189–202 (2002)
2. AOSD web site, http://aosd.net
3. Gamma, H., Johnson, V.: Design Patterns, Elements of Reusable Software Design. Addison-Wesley, Reading (1995)
4. Filman, R.E., Friedman, D.P.: Aspect-Oriented Programming is Quantification and Obliviousness. In: Workshop on Advanced Separation of Concerns, OOPSLA 2000, Minneapolis (October 2000)
5. France, R., Kim, D., Ghosh, S., Song, E.: A UML-Based Pattern Specification Technique. IEEE Transactions on Software Engineering 30, 193–2006 (2004)
6. Kiczales, G., et al.: Aspect-Oriented Programming. In: Aksit, M., Matsuoka, S. (eds.) ECOOP 1997. LNCS, vol. 1241, pp. 220–242. Springer, Heidelberg (1997)
7. Mahoney, M., Elrad, T.: A Pattern Based Approach to Aspect-Orientation for State Based Systems. In: Workshop on Best Practices in Applying Aspect-Oriented Software Development (BPAOSD 2007) at the Sixth International Conference on Aspect-Oriented Software Development (AOSD 2007), Vancouver, BC (March 2007)
8. Mahoney, M., Bader, A., Elrad, T., Aldawud, O.: Using Aspects to Abstract and Modularize Statecharts. In: The 5th Aspect-Oriented Modeling Workshop in Conjunction with UML 2004, Lisbon, Portugal (October 2004)
9. Bosak, R.: Daily Development Blog (April 2007), http://dailydevelopment. blogspot.com/2007/04/interceptor-design-pattern.html

10. Prehofer, C.: Plug-and-Play Composition of Features and Feature Interactions with State-chart Diagrams. In: International Workshop on Feature Interaction in Telecommunications and Software Systems, Ottawa, Canada, June 2003. IOS Press, Amsterdam (2003)
11. Schmidt, D.C., Stal, M., Rohnert, H., Buschmann, F.: Pattern-Oriented Software Architecture - Patterns for Concurrent and Networked Objects, vol. 2. Wiley and Sons Ltd., Chichester (2000)
12. Volter, M.: Patterns for Handling Cross-Cutting Concerns in Model-Driven Software Development. In: 10th European Conference on Pattern Languages of Programs (EuroPlop 2005), Irsee, Germany (July 2005)
13. Telelogic Tau, http://telelogic.com
14. ILogix Rhapsody, http://telelogic.com
15. Core J2EE Patterns - Interceptor Filters, Core J2EE Pattern Catalog, http://java.sun.com/blueprints/corej2eepatterns/Patterns/InterceptingFilter.html

An Example of the Retrospective
Patterns-Based Documentation
of a Software System

James Siddle

jim@jamessiddle.net
http://www.jamessiddle.net

Abstract. An example pattern-based documentation that was created
retrospectively from pattern applications on an industrial project is presented. In addition to the example documentation, the paper examines
the approach taken, divergence of the documentation from the real system, benefits, liabilities, and applicability of the approach. The paper
closes by drawing conclusions from the experience of creating the documentation.

Keywords: Patterns, software patterns, pattern stories, software system, software design, software architecture, retrospective pattern-based
documentation.

1 Introduction

This paper examines the retrospective documentation of a concrete software system through patterns, by presenting an example patterns-based documentation
based on a particular project and drawing conclusions from the experience of
creating the documentation.

The motivation for creating the pattern-based documentation that appears
in this paper is to retrospectively capture and communicate the historical intent behind, and contribution of, pattern applications to software development.
The documentation in this paper serves as both an example, and as the basis
of analysis and conclusions that follow. In practice, such documentation could
be expected to support interested parties such as software maintainers in understanding software.

The documentation approach taken captures the contributions that individual
patterns made to the concrete software system, in a stepwise fashion. Discrete
contributions are captured in individual steps of the documentation, and the
entire collection of these contributions make up the complete documentation.

The remainder of the paper is organised as follows: First, the intended au-
dience and key terms are introduced, then a description of the software development project where patterns were applied or recognised retrospectively is
provided. The documentation in this paper attempts to capture and communicate the contributions of pattern applications on the project described. This

J. Noble and R. Johnson (Eds.): TPLOP I, LNCS 5770, pp. 207–230, 2009.
© Springer-Verlag Berlin Heidelberg 2009

is followed by a description of the documentation approach, an overview of the documentation that follows, and then the complete patterns-based documentation. An analysis examines differences between the documentation and the real system, along with potential benefits, liabilities, and applicability of the approach. The paper closes by drawing a number of conclusions related to creating patterns-based documentation.

1.1 Intended Audience

The ideal reader of this paper is a software practitioner - whether programmer, developer, engineer, or architect with an interest in how software patterns can be employed to capture and communicate the concrete software system that results from their application.

The reader may also be interested in how patterns can be combined, because while applying a pattern in isolation is useful, a complex software system is likely to require the application of more than one pattern. The reader may also be familiar with the idea of architecture patterns and want to know how to fit patterns together into an overall architecture.

1.2 Terminology

To frame the following discussion, it's necessary to introduce the following concepts:

Patterns and Pattern Stories: A pattern describes a recurring solution to a problem that occurs in a particular context by resolving the forces acting in that context. The reader is referred to [8] and [11], arguably the best known patterns works, for an introduction to and examples of patterns.

Another patterns-related concept mentioned in this paper that needs a little introduction is that of a pattern story [9]: A pattern story describes a concrete software system in terms of the patterns used to create it.

Software Architecture: There are many definitions of software architecture in software design literature, Grady Booch's recent definition is particularly suited to understanding the application of software patterns to the creation of software architecture:

> As a noun, design is the named (although sometimes unnameable) structure or behavior of a system whose presence resolves or contributes to the resolution of a force or forces on that system. A design thus represents one point in a potential decision space. A design may be singular (representing a leaf decision) or it may be collective (representing a set of other decisions). [...]
>
> All architecture is design but not all design is architecture. Architecture represents the significant design decisions that shape a system, where significant is measured by cost of change. [3]

Note that cost of change was not necessarily the most significant factor understood by the team developing the software under discussion, who it is thought did not share a common understanding of architecture.

2 Project Context

The software system documented in this paper originated on a project where patterns were applied to create a component middleware software architecture; this project is briefly introduced below. For reasons of confidentiality, the following description has been anonymized.

2.1 Project Introduction

The aim of the project under consideration was to develop the software for an innovative telephony product using C, C++ and Java programming languages, and it was necessary for the software to run on a custom hardware platform that was being developed at the same time. Scrum [17] and XP [4] Agile methodologies were followed on the project.

In addition to functional requirements from the telephony domain, there were also non-functional requirements on the software. In particular, a custom, service-oriented, embedded middleware was required in order to support a product line strategy that was being taken. The key requirements on the middleware were:

- Support for reusable, telephony-domain services
- Dynamic deployment of services
- Platform independence
- Abstraction of service communication
- Location transparent service communication
- Abstracted service execution
- A common approach to management and testing of services
- An extensibility mechanism in the communication path between services

The middleware was also required to support specific services from the telephony domain that had been envisaged as part of the product-line strategy, such as distributed directory lookup services, "presence" propagation services, and journal services to record user actions.

The middleware was developed by a team of eight people over a period of approximately six months, as part of a wider development effort. Early project iterations focussed on elaborating middleware, platform, and application-level architecture. Patterns played an important role in the design and implementation that took place as part of middleware elaboration. The elaboration was driven by requirements (such as those described above) that were drawn from an architecture road map containing a loosely ordered collection of broadly stated architectural concerns.

Figure 1, reproduced from [18], provides an overview of the middleware architecture that was envisaged at the start of the project.

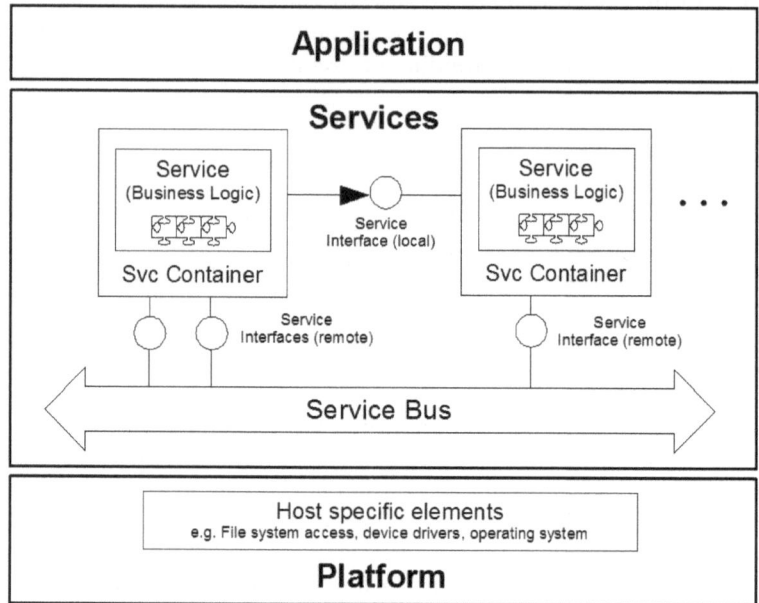

Fig. 1. Envisaged middleware architecture

2.2   Pattern Applications

A broad selection of patterns were applied in creating the middleware. These
were drawn from several sources. Several were drawn from the *Pattern Oriented
Software Architecture* [11] [12] [13] and *Design Patterns* [8] books, while others
were recommended by a knowledgeable source rather than being drawn from a
patterns publication. For a fuller picture of the patterns that were applied on
the project, the reader is referred to [18], which provides a broad overview of the
patterns applied on the project.

3   Documentation Approach

The documentation presented in the following section was created by capturing
the structure and behaviour associated with patterns that were either applied or
retrospectively recognised in the software system. Four aspects of the approach
taken are examined below - purpose, focus, form, and pattern selection.

3.1   Purpose

The patterns-based documentation presented in this paper was created as an
example of how patterns can support the communication of software system
knowledge between software professionals. Each pattern is included in order to

communicate concepts, structure, and behaviour resulting from pattern applications, informing readers of the important elements of a software system and ultimately supporting the creation and maintenance of quality software.

Section 6.2 below provides further examination of the potential benefits of a patterns-based approach to software documentation.

3.2   Documentation Focus

The focus of the documentation is historical, in order to show the evolution of the middleware up to a specific point in it's elaboration. This is to help the reader to understand the early evolution of the software to support their understanding of why the system is the way it is today. The software development that took place following architecture elaboration followed the course that many projects do, where the clean separation and guidelines associated with the elaborated architecture gradually dissolved and were discarded. Thus, the focus of the documentation is on the original intent of the software, which is what is presented here.

The documentation is also focussed on the structure and behaviour of the software system, specifically the classes and interfaces that resulted from pattern application and the roles and responsibilities taken. This focus was chosen because the aim was to enable readers to quickly orientate themselves with the system, both in it's current form (when subsequent changes have not been made), and with the system as originally intended (where changes have been made).

The documentation does not focus on presenting the software architecture, though the documentation may be architecturally relevant because architectural significance was one criteria used to select patterns for inclusion (see below). The emphasis on structure and behaviour is selected because an extended period of time (approximately 2 years) has passed since the the software was developed, and a focus on concrete software elements is likely to be more accurate than a focus on architecture rationale.

Finally the focus is high-level, (i.e. class and interface), rather than low-level (i.e. method, function). The aim being to present an overall view of the software system rather than to dive into details.

3.3   Documentation Form

A simple form was selected to communicate the software system by way of patterns.

A section is included for each pattern in the documentation, the problem encountered and solution selected are described, and then concrete structure and behaviour associated with the pattern is presented.

Note that section 5.7 actually captures the contribution of two patterns. This slight variation of the form allows for a cleaner presentation of the software system because each pattern's contribution was relatively small, and the two patterns are closely related.

Each section contains:

- Title - pattern name and reference
- Problem and Solution
- System Structure and Behaviour
- Class Diagram

The patterns are presented in an order to allow an understanding of the software system to gradually build up in the readers mind. This is partially possible because the order selected is similar to the order in which patterns were applied and implemented during development, on an iteration by iteration basis. This means that certain software elements (e.g. the 'service' layer) are introduced by one pattern, before being referred to by the documentation associated with following patterns.

Additionally, certain later steps describe refinements to earlier steps. Mostly this is because refinements took place as described, however in some places this approach allows for a simpler and clearer presentation of the software system.

3.4   Patterns Selected, Selection Criteria

Patterns were selected for inclusion primarily according to architectural significance, in order to provide an understanding of significant parts of the middleware to the reader. The judgement of the significance of each pattern was made in a subjective manner, according to the understanding of the software system that is held by the author as the architect of the middleware. So while the documentation itself is not architectural in nature, it can be seen as architecturally relevant. This criteria is considered to be valid because the aim of the documentation is to provide an historical introduction to the software rather than to serve as the basis of formal analysis or comprehensive education.

The type of pattern application was another consideration for pattern selection; that is whether a pattern was explicitly applied, implicitly applied, or retrospectively recognised. An examination of selection criteria was performed following the documentation creation, an overview of which can be found the first appendix. This examination suggests that:

- Architectural significance was the main criteria for inclusion.
- Implicitly applied patterns were excluded on the grounds of being obvious to developers (e.g. CACHING).
- Some architecturally significant elements were retrospectively recognised as patterns in order to allow their documentation here (e.g. BROKER).
- One pattern was excluded because the resulting implementation was not effective at solving the problem (ASYNCHRONOUS COMPLETION TOKEN). [1]

The pattern story mentioned in [18] provides a detailed description of the patterns that served as the selection pool for the documentation, and the complete

---

[1] This is thought to be because of a naive understanding of patterns (i.e. the model solution is the pattern), and subsequently a poor selection of context in which to reapply the pattern (i.e. at the service interface rather than middleware level).

selection pool is listed in the appendices. The patterns selected for inclusion in
the documentation can be found in table 1 below.

4   Documentation Overview

To serve as an introduction to the complete documentation that follows, a documentation overview can be found in Table 1. The table summarises the pattern
applications that took place to create the middleware architecture. The three
columns in the table represent:

- *Step* - a discrete numbered step in the documentation. The steps correspond
  to subsections in the documentation.
- *Pattern name* - the name of the pattern (or patterns) that are presented at
  each step
- *Contribution* - a summary of the contribution of the pattern(s) to the software system

Table 1. Documentation overview

Step	Pattern	Contribution
1	LAYERS	Encapsulate major functional areas to enable reuse and independent variation
2	WRAPPER FACADE	Encapsulate low-level, host-specific functions and data structures
3	COMPONENT CONFIGURATOR	Enable dynamic service deployment and runtime life-cycle management of services
4	BROKER	Establish service communication and location transparency
5	EXECUTOR	Abstract service execution, support concurrent service execution
6	EXPLICIT INTERFACE	Add explicitly defined service interfaces
7	ENCAPSULATED CONTEXT OBJECT	Introduce service discovery context object, make available to services
..	DECOUPLED CONTEXT INTERFACE	Decouple services from context implementation by introducing service discovery interface
8	PROXY	Add client-side object implementing explicit service interface, encapsulates remote communication
9	INVOKER	Add server-side object, receives service invocations and invokes explicit service interface; encapsulates service interface invocation
10	LOOKUP	Provide service discovery mechanism
11	INTERCEPTOR	Introduce flexible interception points on communication path between services

5 Pattern-Based Software System Documentation

This section presents the documentation of the software system that was developed, in the form described in section 3.

5.1 Layers [11]

Problem and Solution: There is a requirement to create a product line architecture where major building blocks can be reused, but this won't be possible without clean and careful dependency management between the building blocks.

"Application", "Service", and "Platform" LAYERS are introduced. These layers establish high level groupings for software elements that will be introduced later, and introduce some basic concepts such as "Service" and "Platform".

System Structure and Behaviour: Each layer may only depend on those below it in the stack; in this case the Service layer is non-strict in recognition that Application layer code may need to invoke Platform layer functionality. The Platform layer however is strict in order to enforce platform independence.

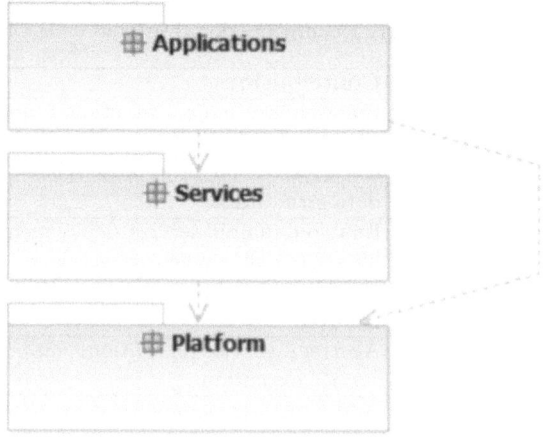

Fig. 2. LAYERS diagram

5.2 Wrapper Facade [12]

Problem and Solution: Service and Application layer code should be platform independent, but how do you achieve this without littering the code with conditional compilation?

WRAPPER FACADE classes are introduced into the Platform layer, to encapsulate low-level host specific functions and data structures. These classes provide a set of abstractions which in conjunction with the strict Platform layer provide platform independence.

System Structure and Behaviour: `FileAccess` provides access to the file system, `LibraryLoader` provides library management and symbol resolution,

`Inter- ProcessCommunication` allows communication between processes and `Threading` supports starting, stopping, and synchronising threads.

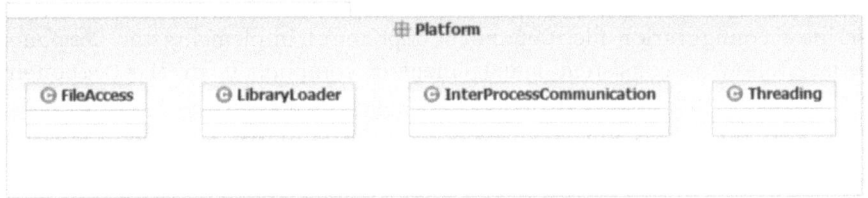

Fig. 3. WRAPPER FACADE diagram

5.3   Component Configurator [12]

Problem and Solution: Dynamic service deployment and life-cycle management is needed, but how can this be achieved in a consistent, common way, and so that services have to perform as little self-management as possible?

COMPONENT CONFIGURATOR is applied so that service deployment and life-cycle are consistently managed via a common interface, along with "creator functions" from each service's library, and a component descriptor file.

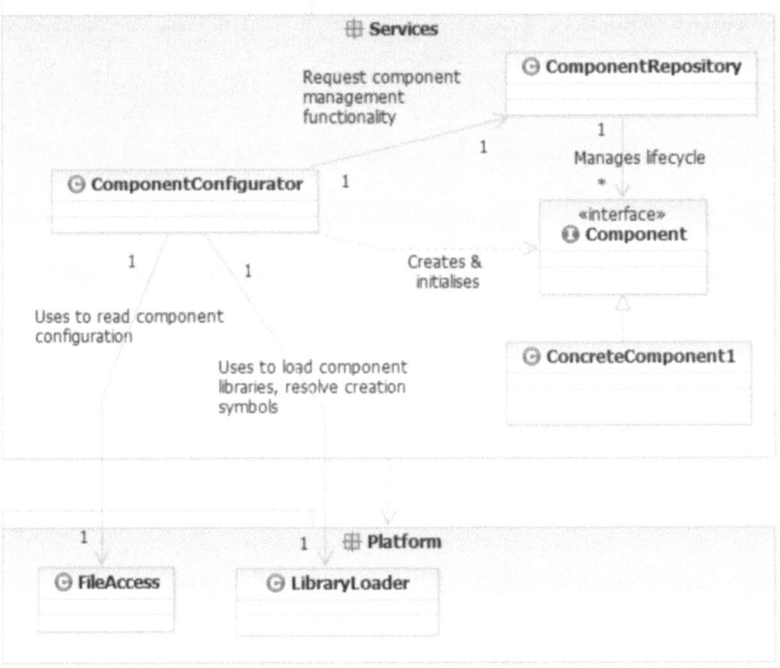

Fig. 4. COMPONENT CONFIGURATOR diagram

System Structure and Behaviour: `ConcreteComponent1` is created and initialised via a "creator function" in the same library as the component. The `Component-Configurator` class loads the library via the `LibraryLoader` class and calls the creator function within it based on information contained in a component descriptor configuration file. `ConcreteComponent1` implements the `Component` interface, allowing consistent management of components by the `Component-Configurator` and `ComponentRepository` classes. `FileAccess` and `Library-Loader` are WRAPPER FACADE classes introduced above; the other classes are introduced by COMPONENT CONFIGURATOR. [2]

5.4 Broker [11]

Problem and Solution: Flexible service deployment is needed, but if services have direct, hard-wired communication paths to other services the system will not be flexible, so how do you achieve location transparent communication between services?

The BROKER pattern is applied so that services communicate indirectly via an instance of a `Broker` class in a well known location.

System Structure and Behaviour: The `ComponentConfigurator` class creates and initialises an instance of the BROKER `CommunicationChannel` class for each `Component`, then passes it to the `Component` during initialisation so that

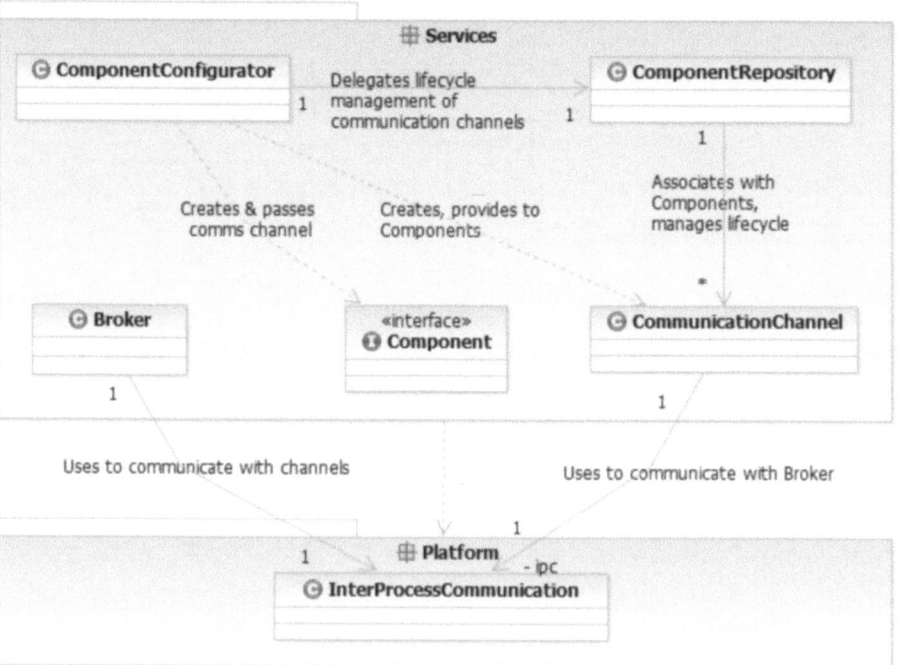

Fig. 5. BROKER diagram

---

[2] From this point on, services are taken to be realised as `Component` objects.

it can send and receive messages. The `CommunicationChannel` is associated with the `Component` in the `ComponentRepository` to ensure that it is cleaned up correctly. `CommunicationChannel` instances communicate with each other in a location transparent way, by sending and receiving all messages via an instance of the `Broker` class in a well-known location. Low level communication takes place between the `Broker` and `CommunicationChannel` classes via the `InterProcessCommunication` WRAPPER FACADE class.

5.5   Executor [6]

Problem and Solution: Services need to be executed when they receive a message, but how can service execution be handled in a consistent way?

EXECUTOR is applied to introduce an `Executor` class which is responsible for handling execution for all services.

System Structure and Behaviour: The `Executor` waits for messages to arrive over a service's `CommunicationChannel` object and for each message that arrives an appropriate thread of execution for message processing is established; the associated `Component` is informed of the message on the resulting thread. The `ComponentConfigurator` class is refined to associate an `Executor` instance with each `Component`, and the `Executor` associated with each `Component` is initialised with the appropriate `CommunicationChannel` object.

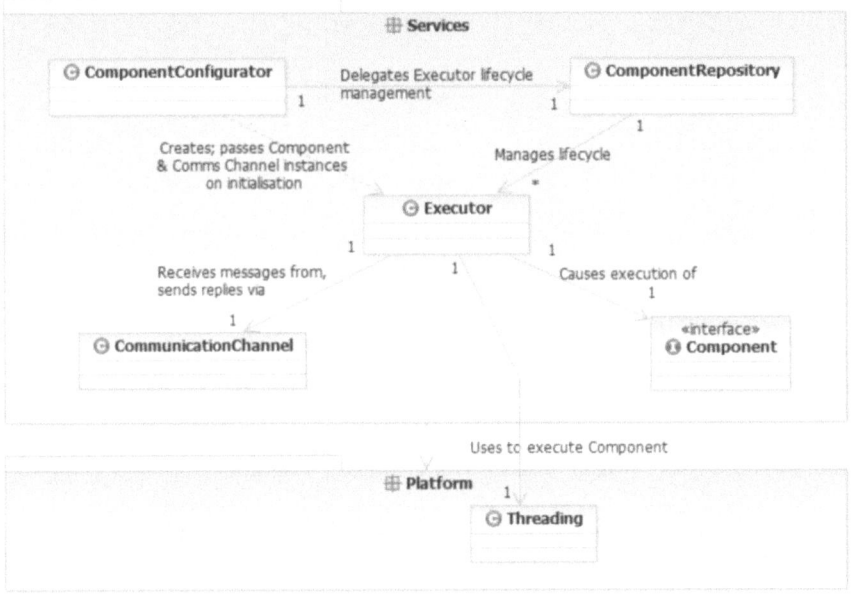

Fig. 6. EXECUTOR diagram

The `Executor` uses it's knowledge of the incoming message and `Component` instance to determine a threading policy such as single or multi-threading, or priority. The thread itself is controlled via a WRAPPER FACADE class.

Because `Executors` are now interacting with `CommunicationChannel` objects on each `Components` behalf, `CommunicationChannel` objects are no longer passed to `Components`.

5.6   Explicit Interface [14]

Problem and Solution: Services can send and receive messages to invoke other services, but this tightly couples service invocation with message formatting and transmission; how do you decouple service invocation from component communication or internals?

EXPLICIT INTERFACE is applied to provide a way of calling services via abstract, implementation agnostic interfaces.

System Structure and Behaviour: The `ExplicitInterface` and `ConcreteExplicitInterface` interfaces together provide the implementation of the pattern. `Components` implement interfaces according to the abstractly defined services that they offer, and call objects that implement the interfaces which define the services they require.

The `ExplicitInterface` class is introduced to allow consistent handling of objects which expose defined services. The explicit interfaces that define services are referred to as 'service interfaces' from this point onwards.

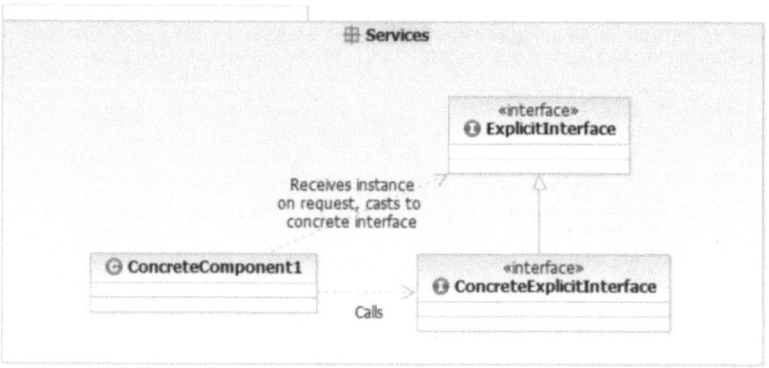

Fig. 7. EXPLICIT INTERFACE diagram

5.7   Encapsulated Context Object, Decoupled Context Interface [9]

Problem and Solution: Services need to discover other services, but how can the services be shielded from potentially complex discovery logic?

An ENCAPSULATED CONTEXT OBJECT with a DECOUPLED CONTEXT INTER-
FACE is introduced to provide a service discovery object that services can call as
necessary.

System Structure and Behaviour: The `ComponentConfigurator` class provides
the implementation of the ENCAPSULATED CONTEXT OBJECT pattern, while
the `ServiceContext` interface is the realisation of the DECOUPLED CONTEXT
INTERFACE pattern.

`Components` call the `ServiceContext` interface (which is provided to them on
initialisation) to request objects that implement particular services; objects that
implement the requested services are returned to the `Component` as instances of
`ExplicitInterface`. `Components` cast returned `ExplicitInterface` instances
to specific service interfaces to be able to request required services.

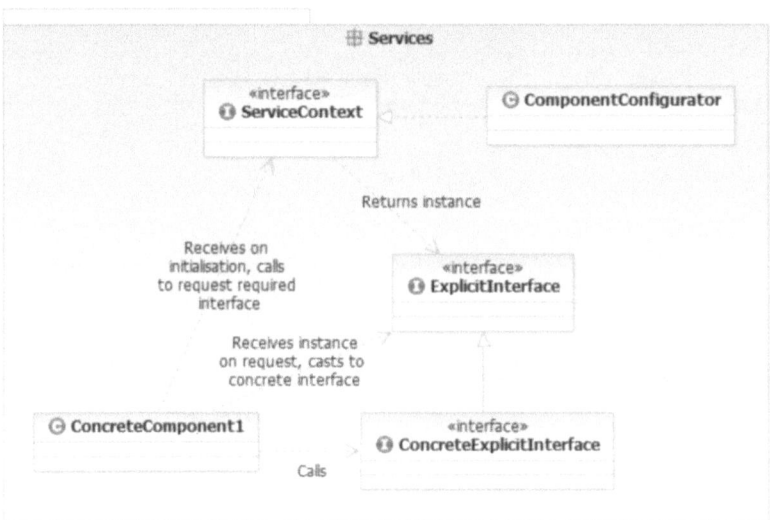

Fig. 8. ENCAPSULATED CONTEXT OBJECT and DECOUPLED CONTEXT INTERFACE diagram

5.8   Proxy [8]

Problem and Solution: Services can request other services and obtain EXPLICIT
INTERFACEs to them, but how are service invocations translated into messages
then sent via the location transparent BROKER?

A PROXY is introduced to encapsulate the remote invocation of service interfaces via the location transparent communication provided by the BROKER
implementation.

System Structure and Behaviour: `Proxy` objects are provided to `Components` by
the `ComponentConfigurator` on service discovery. The `Proxy` is initialised with

the `CommunicationChannel` object of the requesting service, along with address-
ing information of the remote service that the `Proxy` represents. `Proxy` life-cycle
is managed by the `ComponentConfigurator`, in a similar way to `Component` and
`CommunicationChannels`.

`ConcreteProxy` encodes the request (including methods, parameters, and reply
information) in a format suitable for transmission, then uses a `Communication-`
`Channel` to send the request. Replies are received via the same channel, then de-
coded and returned to the calling `Component` by the `Proxy`.

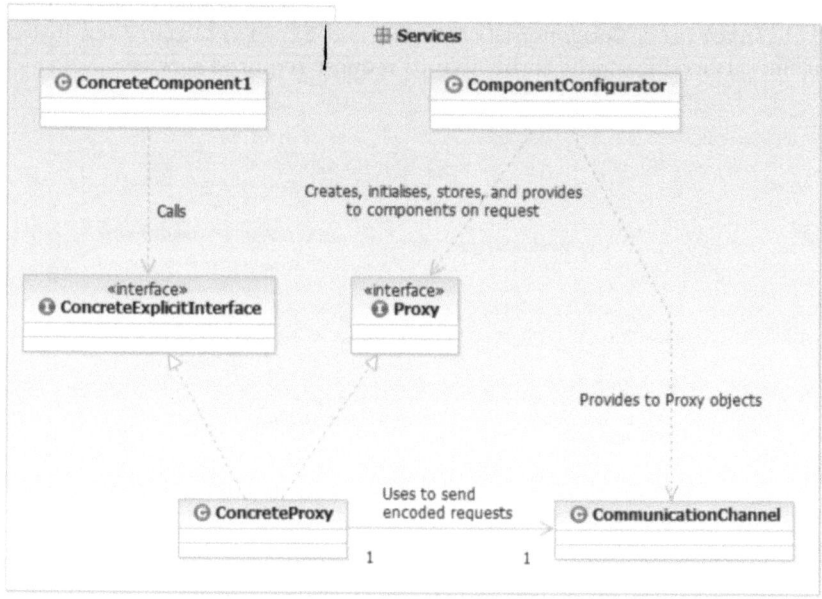

Fig. 9. PROXY diagram

5.9   Invoker [19]

Problem and Solution: Services support explicit service interfaces, but how are
messages received from another service via the BROKER translated into invocations on the service itself?

An INVOKER is introduced to encapsulate the receipt and translation of messages
into an invocation on a particular service interface.

System Structure and Behaviour: We now see how remote service invocations
from `Proxy` objects are handled when they arrive in the locality of the `Component`
that provides the remote implementation.

When an `Executor` receives a message for its `Component` it discovers an appropriate `Invoker`. This discovery will be based on the required service interface

(named in the message) and will be requested via the `FrameworkContext` instance (another ENCAPSULATED CONTEXT OBJECT with a DECOUPLED CONTEXT INTERFACE). The `Executor` will have received the `FrameworkContext` during initialisation.

The `Executor` delegates invocation of its `Component` to the discovered `Invoker`, which decodes the received message to determine the method to invoke and parameters to pass. As with `Proxy` objects, `Invoker` object lifecycle is managed by the `ComponentConfigurator`, in a similar way to `Component` and `Communication-Channels`. After invocation, any return value or parameters are encoded by the `Invoker` into a reply message, which will be sent to the originating communication channel by the `Executor`. To ensure correct routing of replies, the `Proxy` will have associated a unique identifier with the outgoing request message, and requests that it's `CommunicationChannel` passes incoming messages with that identifier to the `Proxy`.

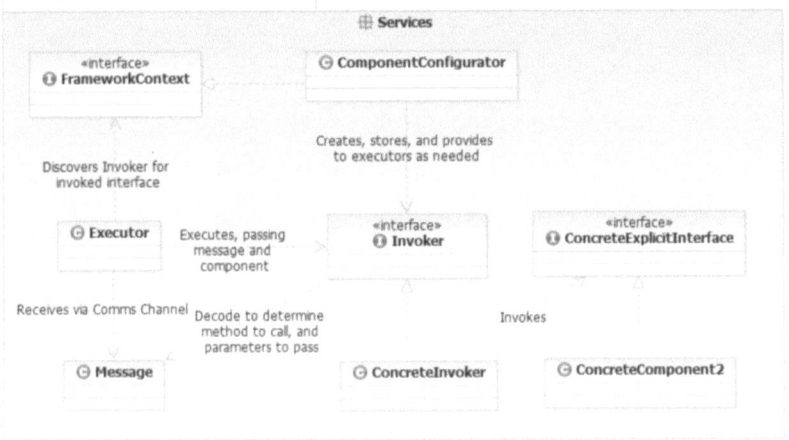

Fig. 10. INVOKER diagram

5.10   Lookup [13]

Problem and Solution: Remote services can now be invoked via explicit service interfaces, but how is service discovery performed?

The introduction of LOOKUP provides resolution of objects that provide required services.

System Structure and Behaviour: A remote `Registry` is introduced that can be consulted to discover the named `CommunicationChannel` location of implementations of particular service interfaces; the `ComponentRepository` is also searched in case required services are provided locally.

A Component requests, via the ServiceContext, an object that provides a required service. The ComponentConfigurator class, in implementing the Service-Context interface, must provide an object back to the requester.

The ComponentConfigurator searches the local ComponentRepository for any local (i.e. in-process) Components that support the interface. If found, the Component is returned directly to the requester. Otherwise, the remote Registry is searched, and if a remote object supporting the interface is found, location information is obtained. The location information is used to initialise a Proxy which is then returned to the requester.

The remote Registry is initialised with remote object interface and location information by ComponentConfigurator instances during Component initialisation.

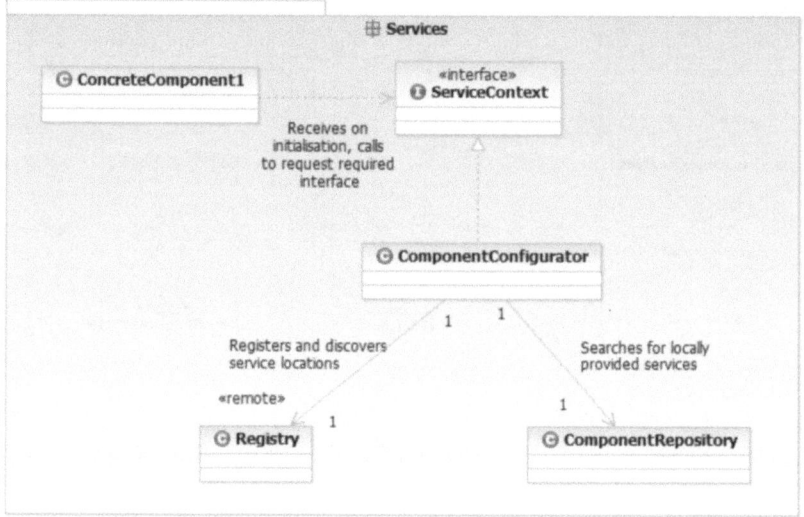

Fig. 11. LOOKUP diagram

5.11   Interceptor [12]

Problem and Solution: An interception point is needed on the communication path between services, but how can this be provided dynamically, without requiring code changes to the communication path?

The INTERCEPTOR pattern provides a flexible, dynamic interception point with the minimum disruption to code. The following text along with the class diagram in figure 12 describe an interception point immediately prior to service execution, when a message is received.

System Structure and Behaviour: When an Executor object receives a message for its service, it creates an instance of the ExecutionInterceptionContext class and initialises it with the received message. The `Executor` informs an instance of the `ExecutionInterceptionDispatcher` class of the event, passing it the interception context object as a parameter. The dispatcher object is responsible for maintaining a list of interested interceptors, each of which implements the `ExecutionInterceptor` interface. The dispatcher informs the interceptors of the event, passing on the context object it received. The interceptors can examine the message via the context object. The can also interact with the context object to perform any interception activities they wish to, such as redirecting or blocking the message, or performing security checks of statistic gathering.

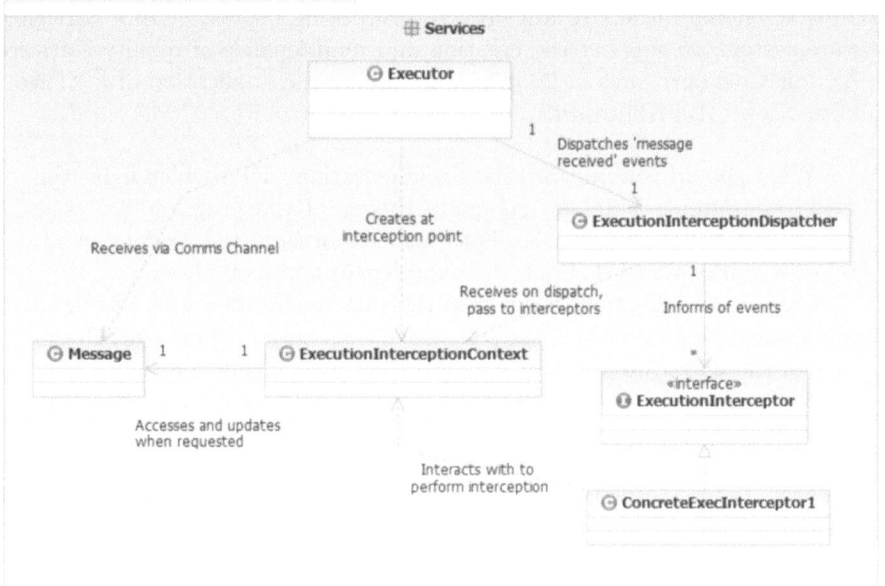

Fig. 12. INTERCEPTOR diagram

6   Analysis

Below, an analysis of the patterns-based documentation is described by examining how the documentation differs from the actual software system, what the benefits and liabilities of the approach are, and where the approach may be applied.

6.1   Differences between Documentation and Software System

The software system as presented in the previous section differs from the actual software system that was developed in two ways.

Firstly, the documentation presents an historical view of the system at a point when the project was transitioning from architecture elaboration to full-scale production, and differs from the final software that was produced, tested, fixed, and ultimately entered maintenance.

Secondly, the system described differs from the actual system in order to more clearly communicate the intent of the original design to the reader. The documentation also presents simplifications and implementation reorderings to educate readers on significant aspects of the design which may be confused by the complexities of the real system.

The differences between the real system and the system as presented are described in the first appendix, and are also discussed in the conclusions section below.

6.2   Benefits and Liabilities

Benefits. The main benefit of using patterns as the basis of software documentation is to enable readers to quickly gain a working knowledge of a particular software system, to support the creation and maintenance of quality software. As Alistair Cockburn says in [5], when discussing the application of a "Theory Building View" [10] [16] to software documentation:

> What should you put into the documentation? That which helps the next programmer build an adequate theory of the program. [...] The purpose of the documentation is to jog memories in the reader, set up relevant pathways of thought and experiences and metaphors. [...]
>
> Experienced designers often start their documentation with just: The metaphors; Text describing the purpose of each major component; Drawings of the major interactions between the major components.
>
> These three items alone take the next team a long way to constructing a useful theory of the design.

In this case, the patterns provide the metaphors, and for each pattern there is a description and a diagram describing purposes and interactions of software elements. It is considered that this approach provides just enough documentation to enable the reader to quickly establish the "theory of the design", based on an understanding of patterns. For readers knowledgeable about patterns, a documentation overview similar to that presented in table 1 may be enough to gain a useful understanding of the software system.

It is also thought that the software system can be better understood by describing many small steps that are similar to the actual evolution of the software system. Each step describes a problem encountered, the pattern used to solve the problem, and the resulting implementation and effect on the evolving software system. This is similar to the tea garden example in [2], where the application of many patterns contribute to an understanding of the architecture as a whole.

The documentation also gradually introduces important entities and concepts from the problem domain, and gives a grounding in the UBIQUITOUS LANGUAGE [7] of the project as understood by the writer. Understanding an existing software system via pattern based documentation can help readers to understand the project's underlying problem domain and associated language.

Another important benefit is that the documentation presented is significantly shorter than would normally be found, the consequences of this being that it will be more easily understood and also that it is more likely to be written in the first place.

By including patterns which are considered to be architecturally significant, the documentation can also serve as a kind of architecture introduction, drawing the reader's attention to elements of the software system which are of greater significance than others. Additionally, the patterns not only explain the architecture that was chosen, but also the rationale behind that architecture to some degree.

Additionally, the historical focus of the documentation may provide insight into why a system is the way it is. Due to evolution and maintenance, class names or relationships that no longer make sense may be explained to the reader, however simplifications or intentional differences from the real system may undermine this.

Finally the documentation can provide examples of pattern applications in the context in which they were made, which may be useful for patterns education or research. However the usefulness of the examples will depend on their accuracy - in this paper the documentation does not describe the created system exactly, so the examples should not be taken literally.

Liabilities. The main liability of the approach is that the documentation is not an exact representation of the software system. The benefit of being able to quickly build a mental model of the historical evolution of a software system may outweigh this liability. However it is important to present an honest view and to include the differences from the real system in some form, and to explain the purpose for the variations, as shown in the second appendix.

Secondly, this approach may not be applicable for design decisions made that are not motivated by a pattern. This may be the case where the design is so unique that no pattern exists.

The documentation may also be hard to understand for readers who have not been exposed to the patterns, and who may find the documentation confusing. However the provision of references for each pattern may alleviate this, and well-named patterns may help the reader to grasp the purpose of the pattern without further reference.

The fact that low level details of the patterns and the software system are not included may be problematic to readers who wish to understand more about them. By increasing the level of detail, more useful information can be included, but at the cost of a succinct presentation.

Finally, the reader may have a different understanding of the patterns used, resulting in misinterpretation. This may be exacerbated by the fact that multiple, occasionally conflicting versions of patterns can sometimes be found. A description of how the pattern contributed to the software system should help to bridge the gap in the reader's understanding, though this does require the reader to be open to the interpretation of the patterns used.

6.3   Applicability

The documentation approach outlined in this paper may prove applicable when creating software using ad-hoc pattern application, i.e. where patterns are applied as the opportunity arises. This approach was taken on the project under discussion, so naturally should be considered as a candidate for applying the documentation approach.

An Agile approach was taken on the originating project, where patterns were selected and applied in an iterative way. As such the documentation partially reflects the evolution of the software, showing intermediate steps in it's growth. The documentation approach may therefore prove useful where patterns are applied during architecture evolution.

The approach may prove useful when a pattern language based approach to pattern application is taken, where the transition from one pattern to the next is guided by the context resulting from each particular pattern application. The closer match between the initial and resulting context of patterns applied from a pattern language may lead to documentation that is easier to understand if the approach outlined in this paper is taken.

Patterns-based documentation of a software system may also be useful to teaching patterns. In a similar way to pattern stories, the concrete focus and practicality of the documentation may support students in applying patterns by showing them the real-world consequences of pattern applications. Exposing students to several examples of patterns-based documentation with variations of a particular pattern may also help them to understand how patterns provide design guidance, rather than rubber-stamp solutions.

7   Conclusions

The following conclusions relate to the process of creating pattern-based documentation, and were drawn by reflecting on the experience of creating the documentation presented.

The main conclusion that can be drawn is that it is important to avoid varying the documentation from the real system if possible. If variations are needed for example to simplify the presentation or to communicate historical intent, then such variations should be called out when they are made along with an indication of why they are being made.

Variations from patterns should also be documented to ensure the reader does not assume the design as described is synonymous with the documented pattern. A potential improvement on the approach would be reorient the documentation primarily around problems faced in design, then to document how each pattern contributed to the design.

Each pattern application should ideally be documented in an ongoing way during design and development. A template document with fields for pattern-based elements such as context, problem, pattern selected, solution implemented, contribution of pattern, variation from actual system etc. may prove useful in such a scenario.

The documentation should also include an indication of whether a pattern was explicitly applied, implicitly applied, or retrospectively recognised to avoid confusion around design intent.

Finally care should be taken during documentation to ensure problem related fields really do describe problems rather than requirements for solutions. The latter are useful, but should be motivated with the problem that resulted in the requirement in the first place.

Acknowledgements

Thanks to Kevlin Henney for suggesting that I write this paper and for feedback and support during it's development, to James Coplien for providing helpful comments and feedback on an early draft of the paper, to James Noble for shepherding the paper for EuroPLoP 2007 and offering many useful comments. Thanks also to workshop group 'Gray' at EuroPLoP 2007, and to the patient reviewers for "Transactions on Pattern Languages of Programming" for providing extensive and in-depth feedback which has improved this paper substantially. Finally, thank you to David Illsley from IBM for helpful review comments, and to IBM generally for supporting the publication of this paper.

References

1. Alexander, C., Ishikawa, S., Silverstein, M., et al.: A Pattern Language. Oxford University Press, Oxford (1997)
2. Alexander, C.: The Nature of Order Book 2: The Process of Creating Life. The Center for Environmental Structure (2002)
3. Booch, G.: Handbook of Software Architecture Blog. On Design (March 2, 2006), `http://booch.com/architecture/blog.jsp?archive=2006-03.html`
4. Beck, K.: Extreme Programming Explained: Embrace Change. Addison-Wesley Professional, Reading (1999)
5. Cockburn, A.: Agile Software Development: The Cooperative Game, 2nd edn. Pearson Education / Addison Wesley (1997)
6. Crahen, E.: Executor. Decoupling tasks from execution. VikingPLoP (2002)
7. Evans, E.: Domain-Driven Design: Tackling Complexity in the Heart of Software. Addison-Wesley Professional, Reading (2003)
8. Gamma, E., Helm, R., Johnson, R., Vlissides, J.: Design Patterns - Elements of Reusable Object-Oriented Software. Addison-Wesley, Reading (1995)
9. Henney, K.: Context Encapsulation. Three Stories, a Language, and Some Sequences. In: EuroPLoP 2005 (2005), `http://www.two-sdg.demon.co.uk/curbralan/papers.html`
10. Naur, P.: Programming as Theory Building. In: Computing: A Human Activity, pp. 37–48. ACM Press, New York (1992)
11. Buschmann, F., Meunier, R., Rohnert, H., Sommerlad, P., Stal, M.: Pattern-Oriented Software Architecture - A System of Patterns, vol. 1. John Wiley and Sons, Chichester (1996)
12. Schmidt, D.C., Stal, M., Rohnert, H., Buschmann, F.: Pattern-Oriented Software Architecture - Patterns for Concurrent and Distributed Objects, vol. 2. John Wiley and Sons, Chichester (2000)
13. Kircher, M., Jain, P.: Pattern-Oriented Software Architecture - Patterns for Resource Management, vol. 3. John Wiley and Sons, Chichester (2004)

14. Buschmann, F., Henney, K., Schmidt, D.C.: Pattern-Oriented Software Architecture: A Pattern Language for Distributed Computing, vol. 4. John Wiley and Sons, Chichester (2007)
15. Buschmann, F., Henney, K., Schmidt, D.C.: Pattern-Oriented Software Architecture: On Patterns and Pattern Languages, vol. 5. John Wiley and Sons, Chichester (2007)
16. Ryle, G.: The Concept of Mind. Harmondsworth, England (1963) (First published 1949)
17. Schwaber, K., Beedle, M.: Agile Software Development with SCRUM. Prentice Hall, Upper Saddle River (2001)
18. Siddle, J.: Using Patterns to Create a Service-Oriented Component Middleware, VikingPLoP 2006 (2006),
    http://jms-home.mysite.orange.co.uk/docs/patternspaper.pdf
19. Voelter, M., Kircher, M., Zdun, U.: Remoting Patterns: Foundations of Enterprise, Internet and Realtime Distributed Object Middleware. John Wiley and Sons, Chichester (2005)

Appendix A: Pattern Selection Pool

Table 2 presents the patterns that were considered for inclusion in the documentation, along with selection criteria analysis performed after documentation creation.

Table 2. Patterns and selection criteria

Pattern	Sig.	Exp.	Imp.	Retr.
LAYERS	1	X		
WRAPPER FACADE	1	X		
COMPONENT CONFIGURATOR	1	X		
BROKER	1			X
EXECUTOR	1	X		
EXPLICIT INTERFACE	1	X		
ENCAPSULATED CONTEXT OBJECT	1	X		
DECOUPLED CONTEXT INTERFACE	1	X		
PROXY	1	X		
INVOKER	1	X		
LOOKUP	1			X
CLIENT-SERVER	1		X	
INTERCEPTOR	2	X		
LAZY AQUIZITION	2		X	
POOLING	2		X	
CACHING	2		X	
ASYNCHRONOUS COMPLETION TOKEN	2	X		
OBSERVER	3	X		
TEMPLATE METHOD	3	X		
SINGLETON	3	X		

The patterns in the selection pool were categorized by:

- *Architectural Significance* (Sig.) - a mark from one to three, indicating the relative contribution the pattern was considered to have made to the architecture.
- *Explicitly applied* (Exp.) - patterns that were consciously chosen for application during development.
- *Implicitly Applied* (Imp.) - pattern that were not consciously applied, but were thought to have been applied by developers because the design captured by the pattern is well known; for example caching.
- *Retrospectively Recognised* (Retr.) - indicates that the pattern was not consciously applied, but was recognised in the software system in retrospect.

Appendix B: Documentation Differences

The differences between the real system and the system as presented are described below.

Implementation Differences

The WRAPPER FACADE classes shown at step 2 represent the intended rather achieved level of platform independence. Classes emerged over the course of the project, requiring (but not always receiving) rework to ensure architecture conformance. The Thread implementation was more complex than shown, and included classes that were closely coupled with service execution infrastructure rather than being general purpose WRAPPER FACADEs.

The collaboration between BROKER and COMPONENT CONFIGURATOR classes at step 4 was not taken explicitly on the project; services actually created their own channels for communication until EXECUTOR was applied. This is shown as a separate step because it is useful for understanding the software system, i.e. that each service is associated with a communication channel.

The initial implementation of EXECUTOR was simpler than that described at step 5. The threading policy was actually introduced later when it was needed.

PROXY objects in the real system were actually associated with their own unique communication channel and shared between services because of concerns over excessive numbers of PROXY objects being created. In hindsight, it was considered better that all messages associated with a particular service should flow over one communication channel, and that the risk of excessive memory consumption from large numbers of proxies was low. As such, the system design was revised in the documentation to associate PROXY objects with service communication channels.

The inheritance hierarchy around Components, Proxy, and ExplicitInterface classes has been simplified. Certain areas of the real software system had a complex and difficult to understand class hierarchy, with some unnecessary relationships which caused implementation challenges.

The INTERCEPTOR shown has been simplified from the actual implementation; on the originating project, the interception point was actually within the misplaced threading wrapper mentioned above.

Some name changes were made - for example ExplicitInterface was retrospectively renamed from Service in the real system.

Ordering Differences

COMPONENT CONFIGURATOR and BROKER were applied concurrently and independently, they are presented in order because the extra step introduced by separating the patterns allows for a cleaner presentation.

Additionally, the ordering of steps 6-10 of the documentation has been introduced retrospectively - the patterns shown at these steps were applied in a much more disorderly way compared to the rest of the patterns, which were applied in the order presented (except for the two patterns mentioned in the previous point which were applied simultaneously).

Author Index